JULY 30 1966
Football's
Longest
Day
Norman Giller

NGB

A Norman Giller Books publication
First published 2016
Swallowfields, Test Valley, Hampshire

Website: www.normangillerbooks.com

A CIP catalogue record is available for this book from the British Library.

ISBN 9780956771162

Typesetting and origination by NMG Enterprises
Printed in Great Britain

Printed and bound in the United Kingdom
by CPI/Antony Rowe Ltd
Bumper's Farm, Chippenham, Wiltshire SN14 6LH

Distribution: CPI Melksham, Wiltshire

In fond memory
of Sir Alf Ramsey
Bobby Moore
Alan Ball
John Connelly
Gerry Byrne
Ron Springett
Harold Shepherdson
Les Cocker
and all
those heroes
of 1966
who did not
make it
to the
50th
anniversary
of England
football's
longest
(and most
glorious)
day

ACKNOWLEDGEMENTS

Author/publisher Norman Giller thanks **Ian Allen** for his diligent copy editing and Gill Allen for letting me borrow him. I greatly appreciated the early guidance of CPI negotiator Mark Radley, the friendly help and advice of all his colleagues and in particular Mark Bowler and Dave 'The Hammer' Biggs, Jan King and her efficient distribution team at Melksham, the enthusiasm and efficiency of Gardners Books quartet Karolina Radtkie, Sharon Hughes, Gail Harbour and Flying Dutchman Willem Harlaar.

And thanks to my omniscient son and right hand man Michael Giller for always being there as a constant inspiration, and daughter Lisa for her encouragement. Thank you, too, to my partner Jackie Wright, for managing to support me while being plastered (again) with a broken leg. She waited on me hand and foot.

The majority of photographs published in this book are from my private collection, and 50-year-old *Daily Express* scrapbooks lovingly kept for me by sports desk secretary, the incredibly efficient Cora Weston. A special nod in the direction of my old Fleet Street snapper pals, the late and great Monte Fresco, Norman 'Speedy' Quicke and Bob Stiggins, all master photographers who were there with me at Wembley on July 30 1966, capturing the great day in graphic pictures while I had to make do with mere words.

I appreciate the enthusiastic support of Dave Berry, Editor and driving force behind the premier football nostalgia magazine, *BackPass*, also the encouragement from *Spurs Odyssey* webmaster Paul Smith and his many enthusiastic members who take part in my Spurs Odyssey Quiz League.

The two major websites I visited most in my quest for accurate and enlightening information were www.englandfootballonline.com (the dedicated work of Alan Brook in Middlesbrough, Josh Benn in London, and Peter Young in the USA), and the all-embracing www.myfootballfacts.com, conscientiously compiled by London-born, Israel-based Paul Yarden.

Special thanks to my friends at the premier photo agency Press Association Images for their help with research.

And, of course, thanks to Sir Alf and his Boys of '66, and particularly to Jimmy Greaves (and his gorgeous wife Irene) for still being there.

JULY 30 1966
Football's
Longest Day
Contents

JULY 30 1966

FOOTBALL'S LONGEST DAY

Opening Shots

THIS is the story of a day. Not any old day, but unquestionably the greatest day in the history of English football. Saturday July 30 1966. And here's a sentence no author or football journalist has been able to improve on for 50 years: It was the day England became champions of the world, winners of the Jules Rimet trophy.

There will be scores of books, newspaper and magazine feature articles, TV and radio programmes turning a searchlight on the golden anniversary of England's victory, but few will be produced by people who were actually right at the heart of the action. Much of what you read will be second-hand cut and paste views. I promise this book is as intimate and informative as you can get.

For any England football lover, it is the ultimate 'I Was There' story. You must be at least in your mid-70s to have had a substantial part in the recording and reporting of the historic day, and you will need to have been one of the accredited media eyewitnesses. My press card can be seen on the back of the book jacket – yes, that handsome young man who was at Wembley representing the *Daily Express* in the days when it sold 4.2 million copies a day.

There were three of us in the Wembley press box for the London edition of the *Express*. Colourful columnist Desmond Hackett, chief football reporter Clive Toye, and me as the eyes and ears, briefed to look for the off-beat stories. I was what is known in the reporting trade as on 'quotes' duty, and that was like trying to get secrets from the Kremlin at a time when Wembley security was neurotically tight for three reasons: 1) they did not want the World Cup stolen again, as had happened shortly before the finals; 2) the Argentine players had tried to kick down the England dressing-room door after the venomous quarter-final battle; 3) Her Majesty the Queen was in the house.

I was in the privileged position of spending the entire day with the England team, from breakfast to supper time and beyond, watching them making last preparations for the final against West Germany, suffering through the dramatic match that was an ordeal in itself, and then going off into the night with them to enjoy the wild celebrations that were described by a spokesman for the Automobile Association as being like VE Day, New Year's Eve and Election Night rolled into one.

Now I invite you to join me for an action replay of the day, and hopefully I will give you the sense that you are right there as I interview all the main characters in the drama.

I was the only reporter to get into the England dressing-room after the match, and as you will read it was a short-lived visit. For manager Alf Ramsey, even at the Everest of euphoria, he considered the dressing-room as private as a woman's boudoir, and for this always suspicious and sometimes supercilious man, prying pressmen were nothing but a pest. He did not have a clue how to handle the media, and his public image suffered as a result. And you know what? He did not give a monkey's.

Ramsey had the biggest last laugh in English football history, although as I reveal in this book he made dangerous enemies at the Football Association during his finest hour, and eventually they got their revenge. And it was Alf's blood that was on the carpet.

To make sure I cover all moments of the great day, I invited people to send their personal memories of the match. I was swamped by emails and steam-age letters, and present a cross section of eyewitness reports from spectators who were there or observers who have personal stories and tales of the unexpected to tell about 1966 and all that. As an added bonus I have collated a facts-and-stats section so that this, my 101st book, brings you a summary of every game, every goal and the name of every player who took part in the greatest football show on earth.

On top of that I report on a memorable night we had on May 12 2016, when the surviving veteran football writers who have come through life's storms and challenges were reunited half a century after capturing that magical World Cup victory in newsprint back in the pre-digital black-and-white hot metal days.

Please join me as I travel back 50 years to what could be another planet. They played the game differently there.

First of all, let's meet the cast ...

Come back with me to July 30 1966 to meet the 22 players in Alf Ramsey's squad as they prepared for the biggest match of their lives and in England football history. I introduce them in shirt number order, and all the statistics are up to but not including the final ...

1. GORDON BANKS
Born: Sheffield, Yorkshire, 30 December 1937
Club: Leicester City. 6ft 1in, 13st

Beaten just once on the way to the final by a Eusebio penalty in a classic semi-final against Portugal, Gordon was coming into his 33rd game for England. He had started his career with Chesterfield while bagging coal, and was now Leicester City goalkeeper, holding off the challenge of a young understudy called Peter Shilton. His wife, Ursula, was German. *Style of play*: A master of positioning, and with lightning reflexes. He could literally pull saves out of the air, and was considered to have the safest hands in football. Along with Bobby Charlton and Bobby Moore, he was one of three players Alf Ramsey always referred to as world class.

2. GEORGE COHEN
Born: Kensington, London, 22 October 1939
Club: Fulham. 5ft 10in, 12st 7lb

George had taken over from former skipper Jimmy Armfield as first choice right-back and was about to win his 30th England cap. He was trusted with the No 2 shirt that Alf Ramsey had worn with distinction in 32 internationals until a nightmare farewell in the 1953 6-3 defeat by Hungary at Wembley, a match that gave him ideas about deep-lying centre-forwards. *Style of play*: George played with a crouching stance, like a boxer preparing to throw hooks. He had perfected overlapping play and could gallop down the wing at sprint speed, but was not always accurate with his crosses. Impressively energetic and solid and reliable in the tackle. A true team player.

3. RAY WILSON

Born: Shirebrook, Derbyshire, 17 December 1934

Club: Everton. 5ft 8in, 11st 13lb

Winning his 51st cap, Ray was England's most experienced defender and had collected an FA Cup winners' medal with Everton against Sheffield Wednesday two months earlier. He worked as a railwayman while starting his career with Huddersfield and was noted for his cool temperament and vision. *Style of play*: A thoroughbred of a defender, he always performed with precision even when upending wingers trying to take him on in one-on-one duels. Ray was out of the old school who considered that his main priority was to stop attackers, but he gradually adopted the overlapping technique that was a speciality of his more physical partner George Cohen.

4. NOBBY STILES

Born: Collyhurst, Manchester, 10 May 1942

Club: Manchester United. 5ft 6in, 10st 5lb

A hugely competitive midfield ball-winner, Nobby had come into the final under a cloud of controversy because of his uncompromising tackles in an era when the game had the emphasis on physical contact. Alf Ramsey refused to bend to pressure to drop the famously toothless Manchester United warrior, and he was about to collect his 20th England cap. *Style of play*: Nobby never tried to pretend he was something that he was not. He left the fancy-Dan tricks to others and got on with his no-nonsense job of stopping more skilful players playing, and winning the ball before passing it to more gifted team-mates. He often put what seemed badly timed tackles down to short-sightedness and having to wear contact lenses.

5. JACK CHARLTON

Born: Ashington, Northumberland, 8 May 1935

Club: Leeds United. 6ft 2in, 12st 9lb

Two years older than brother Bobby, Jack had come late into the Ramsey fold after Tottenham's Maurice Norman broke a leg, Peter Swan was banned in the 1960s bribery scandal, and Everton's Brian Labone chose to go on his honeymoon rather than stay with the squad for eight weeks. Nicknamed the Giraffe because of his long neck, Jack was the tallest player in the team and dominated the centre of the defence. Like Stiles, he was winning his 20th cap. *Style of play*: Jack was the opposite of brother Bobby in physique and presentation. While Bobby was all smoothness and skill, big Jack was gawky and extremely physical. He would have kicked his granny to win the ball, and often belted it out of defence rather than deliver it in the elegant Bobby Charlton manner. The sort of man's man you would want alongside you in the trenches.

6. BOBBY MOORE
Born: Barking, Essex, 12 April 1941
Club: West Ham United. 6ft. 12st 3lb

Bobby was out of contract with West Ham coming into the World Cup and had to sign a rushed agreement with the Hammers to become eligible to play in the finals. He would be winning his 47th cap in the final after skippering West Ham to FA Cup and European Cup Winners' Cup victories at Wembley in the previous two years. He knew the way to the Royal Box. *Style of play*: Notoriously, Bobby could not/would not head the ball or run faster than snail's pace, yet there was nobody in his league for reading situations and he was always in the right place at the right time. His distribution from the back was immaculate, and he refused to be rushed into hurried clearances. He always coolly made time and space for himself. Simply, The Master.

7. ALAN BALL
Born: Farnworth, Lancashire, 12 May 1945
Club: Blackpool. 5ft 6in, 10st

The 'baby' of the team, 21-year-old Alan had threatened to walk out on the squad when he was dropped after the goalless opening World Cup draw with Uruguay. But recalled by Alf Ramsey for the quarter-final against Argentina, he was ready to run himself into the ground for the team as he prepared to collect his tenth England cap. He was hugely influenced by the coaching of his father, Alan Ball Senior. *Style of play:* Alan mixed atomic energy with well-polished, close ball control, and would run all day for the team. He passed with imagination, and would never ever concede defeat until the final whistle. Ballie had a tinderbox temperament to go with his flame-red hair, and he sometimes allowed his temper to tow him into trouble with the referees.

8. JIMMY GREAVES
Born: East Ham, London, 20 February 1940
Club: Tottenham Hotspur. 5ft 8in, 10st 9lb

English football's most prolific goal scorer, he had played in England's opening three games of the World Cup but a gashed shin kept him out of the quarter and semi-finals. When he woke up on the morning of Saturday July 30 he had no idea whether he would be selected for the final and his 55th cap since making his debut in 1959 while with Chelsea. *Style of play:* The Artful Dodger of the penalty area, he could pickpocket goals in the blink of an eye. He had a low centre of gravity and was perfectly balanced, often electing to pass the ball into the net with either foot, but favouring the left. Arguably the greatest goal scorer in the history of the British game.

Bobby and Jack Charlton, the week before the 1966 World Cup final

9. BOBBY CHARLTON
Born: Ashington, Northumberland, 11 October 1937
Club: Manchester United. 5ft 8in, 11st 3lb

Bobby went into the final and his 74th international as England's most famous footballer. A survivor of the 1958 Munich air crash that decimated the Manchester United team, he had developed into a schemer-scorer while playing a deep-lying role after establishing himself as a blond bomber of a left winger. Now he was distinguishable for his comb-over hair. *Style of play:* Two footed, quick, clever, a rocket shot in either foot, the complete forward who could conduct a front line like a maestro with a baton. His passing was bold and inventive, and accurate to the point where he could land a ball on a duster from distances up to 40 yards. There have been few to match his shooting power, and most of his goals were of the spectacular variety. Feared and admired by opponents in equal measure.

10. GEOFF HURST
Born: Ashton-under-Lyne, Lancashire, 8 December 1941
Club: West Ham United. 5ft 11in, 12st 8lb

Converted by West Ham manager Ron Greenwood from ordinary wing-half into a powerful, international striker, Geoff came late to the party for his sixth cap. He did not make his England debut until a friendly against West Germany at Wembley in February 1966. England won 1-0 and the Germans had a goal turned down by a flag-waving linesman. The shape of things to come. *Style of play:* There was nothing flash or superfluous in Geoff's approach. He made it his duty to act as a highly visible target man for his team-mates to reach with passes that he would try to convert into goals by intelligent positioning and deft, two-footed finishing and glancing headers. Unselfish and dedicated to the team effort, he was expert at laying the ball off.

11. JOHN CONNELLY
Born: St Helen's, Lancashire, 18 July 1938
Club: Manchester United. 5ft 8in, 11st 3lb

Connelly was one of three wingers Alf Ramsey featured, playing him in the goalless draw against Uruguay that was one of the dreariest World Cup opening matches ever. This was John's 20th and final England appearance and the highlight of a successful career that started with the Burnley team he helped win the League championship in 1959-60. *Style of play:* John was a throwback to the traditional wingers who hugged the touchline, and he had the dribbling skill and acceleration to get past the most disciplined full-backs. Equally at home on either flank, he was a fierce finisher whose nose for goals persuaded United manager Matt Busby to take him to Old Trafford.

12. RON SPRINGETT
Born: Fulham, London, 22 July 1935
Club: Sheffield Wednesday. 5ft 10in, 12st 2lb

Ron had been England's No 1 goalkeeper until the emergence of Gordon Banks. All but five of his 33 games were under the management of Walter Winterbottom, including the 1962 World Cup when England were eliminated in the quarter-finals by Brazil. He started his career with Queen's Park Rangers and got a runners-up medal in the 1966 FA Cup final with Sheffield Wednesday, beaten 3-2 by Everton at Wembley two months before the start of the World Cup finals. *Style of play:* At his peak Ron was one of the finest shot stoppers in the game, and he continually pulled off seemingly impossible saves with a mixture of good handling, courage and anticipation. The only question mark over him was his tendency to dither over his positioning at set pieces.

13. PETER BONETTI
Born: Putney, London, 27 September 1941
Club: Chelsea. 5ft 10in, 11st 2lb

Making a name for himself in Tommy Docherty's young Chelsea team, Peter was in the squad as third-choice goalkeeper. He was at war with The Doc and was demanding a transfer. Alf Ramsey had blooded him at international level in Denmark during the warm-up tour leading to the World Cup finals. He had impressed with his handling and distribution in a comfortable 2-0 victory, and played with the confidence of a veteran. *Style of play:* Living up to his nickname of 'Cat', Peter had rapid reflexes and he was usually a thought and a deed ahead of oncoming forwards. His greatest asset was being able to catch blistering shots while in midair, and he was continually making spectacular diving saves. He bossed the penalty area and was quick and positive when coming off his line.

14. JIMMY ARMFIELD
Born: Denton, Lancashire, 21 September 1935
Club: Blackpool. 5ft 10in, 12st 12lb

Jimmy was understudying George Cohen after 43 England appearances in the No 2 shirt, fifteen of them as captain. A cultured and disciplined defender, Jimmy was a one-club loyalist with Blackpool, where he had started his long-playing career behind his idol Stanley Matthews. He was an intelligent, dignified man who brought composure to the squad. *Style of play:* More than any other full-back, Jimmy was a pioneer of overlapping runs. He had the speed and positional sense to know when to become an auxiliary attacker, and this in an era when full-backs were expected to concentrate solely on defensive duties. His crosses from out near the touchline often led to goals.

15. GERRY BYRNE
Born: Liverpool, 29 August 1938
Club: Liverpool. 5ft 10in, 12st 7lb

In the England squad as cover at left-back for 'Mr Reliable' Ray Wilson, Gerry was a key member of Bill Shankly's Liverpool defence. He had joined the Anfield groundstaff straight from school and was a true red-blooded Scouser. He had won two England caps before the World Cup, including in the 6-1 victory over Norway in Oslo. It was to be his final international game. *Style of play:* Quick and mobile, Gerry was a thoughtful and measured left-back, who could be incisive, even brutal in the tackle and had the speed to make recovery challenges if a winger had managed to get past him. He always looked to use the ball to launch counter attacks.

16. MARTIN PETERS
Born: Plaistow, West Ham, 8 November 1943
Club: West Ham United. 5ft 11in, 11st 9lb

Alf Ramsey had not yet made his startling statement that "Martin Peters is a player ten years ahead of his time," and when the World Cup kicked off he had played only three games for England. An artistic all-rounder with West Ham, he was promoted to the team for the second match against Mexico, and grew almost overnight into a major international player. *Style of play:* A natural-born footballing artist with balletic rhythm, Martin had the gift of being able to ghost into spaces that lesser players did not even realise existed. Time and again he would make blind-side runs that left opposing defenders tackling thin air as he glided past them. He had excellent ball control, and would continually come from deep positions to steal exquisite goals. Because his game relied on an element of surprise, not all fans really appreciated his subtle skill.

17. RON FLOWERS
Born: Doncaster, 28 July 1934
Club: Wolves. 5ft 11in, 12st 9lb

Ron was the oldest member in the squad and the first of the players to be capped, making the first of his 49 England appearances back in 1955. His Three Lions service included being an ever-present in the 1962 World Cup finals. He remained a powerhouse player with Wolves, and was in the 1966 squad as a stand-by for several defensive positions or as a midfield anchorman. *Style of play:* Brought up on the demands of Wolves manager Stan Cullis for muscular and disciplined defence, Ron was a utility defender who was a dead-eye specialist from the penalty spot. Always reliable and dependable under pressure, he had the perfect temperament and inspired his team-mates with performances that were poised and controlled.

From my scrapbook: Terry Paine, one of the last of Alf Ramsey's wingers

18. NORMAN HUNTER
Born: Eighton Banks, Gateshead, 29 October 1943
Club: Leeds United. 5ft 11in, 12st 6lb

Famed and feared throughout the game as 'Bites Yer Legs,' Norman was included in the England World Cup squad as cover for Bobby Moore and Nobby Stiles. A midfield anchorman for Don Revie's Leeds United team, he had won four England caps. When he made his debut as a substitute in Spain, Alan Ball said in mock prayer: "For what they are about to receive ..." *Style of play:* While Norman's reputation was as one of football's most notorious hatchet men, he actually had a lot more skill than many outside the game appreciated. He had an educated left foot that could send the ball zipping with great accuracy to his Leeds United team-mates, and he was intelligent with his support play, taking a prominent part in many swift counter attacks. But no matter how you paint his portrait, he was first and foremost a destructive force.

19. TERRY PAINE
Born: Winchester, Hampshire, 23 March 1939
Club: Southampton. 5ft 7in, 10st. 6lb

Terry was called into the England attack for the second World Cup final match against Mexico. It proved to be his 19th and last international appearance. A quick and clever winger with Southampton, he grabbed the headlines in 1963 when he became the first right winger to score a hat-trick for England since Stanley Matthews 26 years earlier. *Style of play:* Though a winger out of the traditional school, Terry was happy to often take on a scheming role for the Southampton team that he served so loyally. He had deceptive dribbling skills, and was always looking for the opportunity to drive into the penalty area to shoot with an accurate right foot.

20. IAN CALLAGHAN
Born: Toxteth, Liverpool, 10 April 1942
Club: Liverpool. 5ft 7in, 11st 9lb

The third winger tried by Alf Ramsey before he settled on his Wingless Wonders, Ian played in the third qualifying match against France. He was a vital cog in the successful Bill Shankly machine at Liverpool, but could not convince Ramsey that he should persevere with wingers. This was Ian's second international cap. He would have to wait a record 11 years for his next one! *Style of play:* Cally was a canny player, who could trick his way past tackling defenders before releasing the ball to better-placed team-mates. He had a good tactical sense and passing accuracy that enabled him to become an accomplished schemer at the back end of his distinguished career at Anfield.

21. ROGER HUNT
Born: Glazebury, Cheshire, 20 July 1938
Club: Liverpool, 5ft 9in, 11st 11lb
Roger came into the World Cup with many expecting that he would be second-choice striker to Jimmy Greaves, but he played in every match to take his caps collection to 19 and scored three goals in the group matches. He combined great industry to go with the finishing finesse that had made him such a powerful force in the Liverpool attack. *Style of play:* It is unfair and misleading to describe Roger as just a willing workhorse. Yes, he did run himself into the ground for the team, but he could be dynamic in a packed penalty area, finding space for himself and hitting the net with strong shots from either foot. He was also menacing in the air, and the perfect partner for Ian St John in Liverpool's first golden era under the mesmerising management of Bill Shankly.

22. GEORGE EASTHAM
Born: Blackpool, 23 September 1936
Club: Arsenal. 5ft 7in, 9st 12lb
The Matchstick Man of football was in the squad as understudy to Bobby Charlton but did not add to his collection of 19 caps. George followed his father into the England team, and helped revolutionise the 'soccer slave' system by taking on Newcastle United and beating them in a High Court case over the retain-and-transfer contracts that chained players to clubs. *Style of play:* One of the most technically gifted inside-forwards of his generation, George could pass the ball through the eye of a needle and created goals galore with his skilled service. He had a magical left foot, and always gave perfect weight to the ball. His one handicap was that he weighed little more than a featherweight, and he often struggled on the mud-heap pitches that were common in his era.

THEY ALSO SERVED
Alf Ramsey relied on a small, tight back-room team of trainers: Harold Shepherdson (Middlesbrough), Les Cocker (Leeds United) and Wilf McGuinness (Manchester United).

There were two medical doctors, Alan Bass (Arsenal) and Neil Phillips (Middlebrough), neither of whom took a penny for their services.

Ramsey was very much hands-on and demanded full responsibility for all the coaching and tactics. He was always working on new, inventive formations, and selected players that could make his plans work. No wonder he was known during his successful playing career at Tottenham as The General.

These were his troops and he was ready for his greatest battle, the World Cup Final on July 30 1966.

1
FOOTBALL'S
LONGEST DAY
KICKS OFF

The first person I saw as I walked from the Hendon Hall car park was Bobby Moore, taking a lone stroll through the hotel gardens at the start of the biggest (and longest) day of his life. We had known each other since serving our apprenticeships at West Ham, he with a ball at his feet and me as a reporter with a typewriter at my fingertips on the local newspaper.

We hugged like consenting adults, both of us knowing this was no ordinary day. "Good morning, Mr Moore," I said, slipping easily into our usual bantering conversation. "Got much on today?"

"Not a lot," he said. "Might nip down to Wembley later."

We talked boxing. Our friendship had at its foundation a mutual love of the fight game, and we often went together to the late-night closed-circuit cinema live broadcasts of the Cassius Clay/Muhammad Ali world championship contests.

"Choked we didn't get to meet the great man on Thursday," Bobby said. "I'm told he's coming to the game this afternoon."

I had arranged for promoter Jack Solomons to invite the England players to watch Ali train at the Haverstock Hill gymnasium for his upcoming August 6 title defence against Britain's Brian London at Earls Court. Everybody had been told except Ali, who was fast asleep at his hotel when the England squad arrived. (Something I learned when later working as a publicist for Ali fights in Europe was that no matter where he was in the world he kept his watch on American time. He ate and slept according to the demands of his US body clock. This explains why he slumbered through most of the final at Wembley, while slumped on a seat high up in the stands at the venue where Henry Cooper had dumped him on the seat of his pants three years earlier.)

Bobby and I studiously avoided talking about the only thing on our minds, the World Cup final against West Germany that was due to kick off seven hours later and five miles away down the North Circular Road at Wembley Stadium.

We scanned the sky as we walked together to the rear entrance of the hotel, and our conversation inevitably turned to the weather. A weak, early morning sun

From my scrapbook: Two days before the final and Bobby Moore (standing), Jack Charlton, Ray Wilson, Jimmy Greaves and Bobby Charlton wait at the gym to see Muhammad Ali train, but the champ was in bed!

was losing a battle to fight through a grey cloud cover. "There's a forecast for showers," I said, passing on what I had heard on the car radio during my drive round the North Circular from my Stratford home.

"Good," said Bobby. "It will freshen the pitch and the ball will zip like it did against Portugal."

This was in the semi-final on the previous Tuesday, when England won 2-1 with as good a performance as I'd seen in a Wembley international.

I allowed him to continue on his solo walk, leaving him alone with his private thoughts, his mind trained on the challenge ahead.

My parting shot: "Be lucky, Bob. The whole country's behind you."

He waved a hand and gave a thumbs up.

There was so much I wanted to say to Bobby, but this was not the time or place. I was one of the few who knew the mountain he had scaled to get to this Everest peak of his career.

It would be a long time before the secret came out that in 1964 he had a cancerous testicle removed.

Now he was ready to lead his country in the most important football match in their history. Nobody was better suited to the role.

8.10am
AVOIDING JIMMY GREAVES

During my brief conversation with Bobby I had deliberately refrained from mentioning our mutual mate Jimmy Greaves, who was sharing a room at Hendon Hall with the England skipper. Jimmy was the talk of the nation as we approached the final, with heated debates at clubs and pubs throughout the land as to whether he should play in this match of a life time.

My verdict that manager Alf Ramsey should select an unchanged side and leave out England's greatest ever goalscorer was splashed on the back page of the *Daily Express*, with my colleague Clive Toye agreeing with me and our colourful and controversial columnist Desmond Hackett voting for Jimmy to be selected instead of Geoff Hurst.

It was the hardest article I'd ever had to write, because I rated Greavsie the most artistic and accomplished England goalscorer I'd ever seen and, to make it even more difficult to compose, he was a close, personal friend.

I was from the old school that believed you should not change a winning team, and the collective display against Portugal in the semi-final had been so close to perfection that I did not see how Ramsey could gamble on a change now that Jimmy had recovered from the gashed shin received in the third match against France.

Let me confess here that as I walked into the foyer of the Hendon Hall Hotel I was hoping not to come into contact with Jimmy. I knew I would not be able to look him in the eye. I felt guilty of disloyalty, but I owed it to my newspaper to give an honest opinion. Back in those days the *Daily Express* sold 4.2 million copies a day and carried a lot of clout.

Eventually Jimmy came downstairs, and was engulfed by reporters from the news agencies and two London evening newspapers, the *News* and *Standard*, asking whether he was playing. "I know as much as you do," he said. "Alf's not said a dickie bird to me."

I kept hidden at the back of the posse of press men, and Jimmy disappeared through the folding doors behind which the England players and officials were having their breakfast. In or out? The debates continued.

8.30am RAMSEY'S JOYLESS BREAKFAST

Interview-shy Alf Ramsey did his best to walk past the reporters on his way to the private breakfast area, but 6ft 2in. Bernard Joy, former England and Arsenal centre-half and now distinguished football correspondent of the *Evening Standard*, man-marked him until he had to stop and make a comment.

"Is Jimmy Greaves playing?" Bernard demanded, chasing a deadline that would wait for no man. The most popular guesswork in the national newspapers is that Alf would play Greaves and Hunt, and leave out Hurst.

"You will have to wait and see," said Ramsey in that clipped, forced-posh voice that was the result of elocution lessons that had turned him into a Dick van Dyke sound-alike. "I am not going to announce the team until we get to Wembley, and I want the players to be the first to know."

This brought no joy to Bernard, who almost snapped his pencil as he noted down Ramsey's unhelpful quote.

"But surely if it's an unchanged team, you can tell us," Bernard said, in desperation for something to write for his pre-match edition that was due to go to press.

"I repeat," a bristling Ramsey said, "I want the players to know first. You will be told the team before the kick-off at Wembley. Now excuse me, gentlemen, my breakfast is getting cold."

Much later we learned that – the night before – Alf had told his players in an unchanged team that they would be playing, quietly passing on the news to each player in turn as they walked back from watching the film *Those Magnificent Men in Their Flying Machines* at a local cinema.

Can you imagine that today? The England players walking en masse through empty side streets on the eve of a World Cup final, and hardly an autograph hunter or photographer around. As they walked, Ramsey had gone up to each of the eleven players individually and said almost out of the side of his mouth: "Just want you to know you will be playing tomorrow. Please do not tell anybody else that you are selected. I just want you to have a good night's sleep."

Ramsey did not talk to Jimmy Greaves.

8.45am
ALAN BALL THREATENS WALK OUT

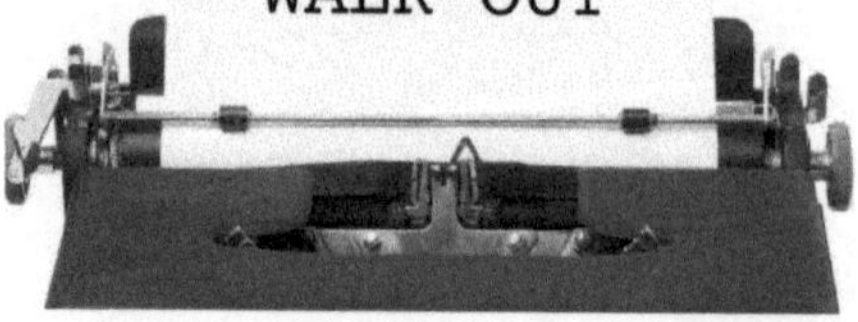

The Hendon Hall Hotel was an unlikely setting for the would-be football champions of the world. Built as a Georgian mansion in the 16th century and once the home of theatre legend David Garrick, it had been converted into a hotel in 1911 but still had more the feel and ambience of a posh country house than a hotel fit for heroes. It had been chosen as England's headquarters because of its close proximity to Wembley and the Bank of England training ground, which was just 12 miles away at Roehampton.

The squad had been ensconced at the hotel for five drama-filled weeks, and I was stationed there to report for the *Daily Express* on their health, moods and adventures virtually every day to the point where I felt I might have a shout at getting into the Ramsey team.

But Alf was so tunnel-visioned throughout the build-up that he managed to virtually ignore the journalists and photographers who grouped at the hotel each day, looking for news and gossip. We were in his eyes a nuisance, acknowledged and spoken to only when necessary. Communications were not exactly his strongest point. Goodness knows how he would have got on in this day and age of regular press conferences and PR handouts.

Despite the reluctance of Ramsey to cooperate, there were lots of stories to keep we reporters and our editors happy, but one that was kept buried is that Alan Ball threatened to walk out of the hotel in protest at being dropped after the opening drawn, goalless match against Uruguay.

When he was not picked for the second game against Mexico, the baby of the squad – 21 two months earlier – told his father in a tearful telephone call that he was coming home. His Dad, Alan Ball Senior, a demanding coach and about to manage Halifax Town, ordered his son to stay and "fight for your place like a man."

Jimmy Greaves and Ballie's room-mate Nobby Stiles also advised him not to walk out, and Alan stayed, and as he came bouncing down to breakfast on that July 30 morning he knew he had clinched his place for the most important game of his life. He would not let his father down.

Alan Ball was on his own when he came down the stairs – unusually without Nobby Stiles at his side like a Siamese twin. He called Nobby "my Northern brother." They were born 25 miles apart, and inseparable during the World Cup.

"Nobby's found a church down the road in Golders Green," Ball explained in his high-pitched Clitheroe Kid voice. "Being a good Catholic boy, he's gone to say a few prayers." George Cohen, "a fraction" Jewish, overheard as he was walking to the breakfast room. "Blimey, finding a Roman Catholic church in Golders Green," he said through his usual big smile, "is some miracle, my life."

At that moment Nobby arrived, after signing autographs for the handful of fans who had gathered at the hotel entrance. "Here comes pongo," said Ballie, holding his nose. "He's worn the same clothes, including socks and underwear, since the first match. He's not only superstitious but very smelly."

"Don't listen to him," said Nobby. "It's true I wear the same clothes on match days, but I do have them laundered."

Ballie and Nobby were the mischief makers of the squad, keeping team spirits high with practical jokes and off-the-wall humour. They were expert at making apple-pie beds, sending room service to the wrong rooms, and getting team-mates to take mock phone calls. You dare not leave your portable typewriter unattended. I had to fish mine out of the hotel swimming pool (in its case, thank goodness).

The only member of the squad they dare not try to trick was Alf, who had a very low humour threshold. He was known behind his back as 'The Sphinx' because he had an expressionless face that meant nobody knew what he was thinking.

But the two Lancashire jokers met their match in goalkeeper Ron Springett. He told them that the room they shared on the top floor of the hotel used to be the maids' quarters and that it was haunted by a female ghost.

They went late to their room one night after a marathon game of cards with team-mates (Alf insisting on a maximum of a shilling a point) to find a woman lounging on Nobby's bed. She was wearing a long blonde wig and a negligee that Nobby had bought earlier that week as a present for his wife, Kay.

The 'woman' was in fact joker Springett, making ghostlike sounds.

9.15am
BABY BLUES FOR JACK CHARLTON

Last down for breakfast was Jack Charlton, who had been on the telephone to his heavily pregnant wife Pat. He was always bright, upbeat and talkative, the complete opposite of brother, Bobby, who tended to look morose even when happy. “Looks like the baby’s coming next week,” he reported. “The missus says if it’s a girl she’ll be Victoria or, a boy, Victor if we win, and if we lose it will be Louise or Louie. I’ve told her there’s no chance of that, nor World Cup Willie.”

It would be their third child and Jack’s concern was that if the World Cup final went to a replay it was scheduled for the following Tuesday at Wembley. “I’ve talked it over with Pat,” he said, “and we’ve agreed I will stay with the team. She’s told me I was hopeless with the first two births, so it wouldn’t make any difference.”

Bobby and Jack were brotherly close during the World Cup build-up, with no hint of the estrangement that would come in later years, caused by personal family feuding. “If Our Kid plays against the Germans like he did against Portugal,” Jack told the evening paper reporters, “we have to be favourites to win. He was world class and even outshone Eusebio. I’m so proud of him. But then, he didn’t have Nobby sticking to him like plaster.”

In the far corner of the hotel foyer, two harassed Football Association officials had set up a desk where players were queuing to request match tickets for family and friends. All the wives and girlfriends had already booked into the Royal Garden Hotel in Kensington, and there was a cold fury among the players that they had not been invited to a cocktail reception given by Prime Minister Harold Wilson and neither to the after-match banquet at the Royal Garden. The acronym WAGS (wives and girlfriends) had not yet been born. Their husbands were less than happy.

Alf Ramsey shared their anger but told them: “Gentlemen, we are here to play football. We are here to play *winning* football. We are not here for cocktail parties or banquets. Push all that nonsense out of your minds. We have a job to do. We have a World Cup to win.”

It was a straight-between-the-eyes speech that stifled all protests.

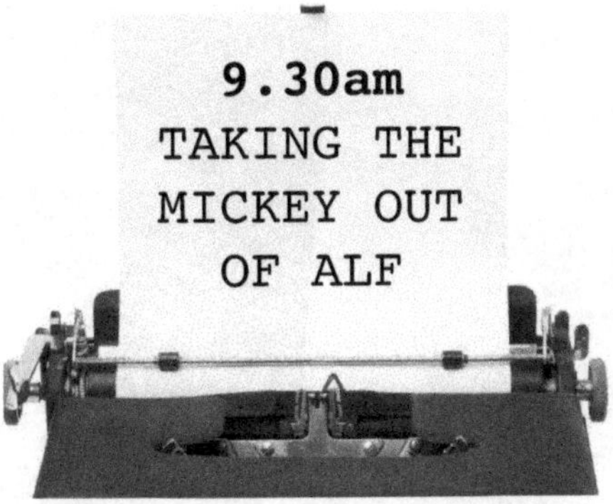

Bobby Moore had come in from his lone walk around the grounds of the hotel and joined his team-mates for breakfast. I gave a double take when moments later I thought I saw Bobby again, this time in the hotel foyer. I laughed when I realised it was Wolves defender Ron Flowers, who was not only Bobby's understudy but could have passed as his double.

He looked so much like the England skipper that on a summer tour one of the doddery FA blazered brigade had continually called him Bobby, which of course the players twisted to their juvenile advantage, pushing Ron alongside him at every opportunity and then listening to him talking about West Ham matters and Bobby's captaincy. Then Bobby would come and stand the other side of the confused official, with the players referring to him as Ron.

Moore was the ringleader of many pranks, and he and Jimmy Greaves went several bridges too far with their mickey taking of Alf Ramsey and his Dick van Dyke voice. Alf was a sensitive, proud man and he knew what they were up to. The England manager was overheard to say to trainer Harold Shepherdson: "Those two will take the piss once too often."

It was an open secret that during the European tour in the weeks before the World Cup Alf toyed with replacing Bobby with Norman Hunter. He left him out for two successive matches, but when Bobby was recalled he set his game up to top gear and it was clear to everybody that he was a class above not only Norman Hunter but every central defender in the world.

Alf knew better than anybody that Bobby was key to whether England could win the World Cup. They buried their mutual suspicion of each other and concentrated on the one objective of winning football's biggest prize. But there was never ever any real warmth between them.

Mooro and Greavsie, drinking pals and hoping to play together with Spurs after the World Cup, laughed at Alf's expense again on the Monday following the boring opening goalless match against Uruguay at Wembley on Saturday July 11. I joined the players on a guided tour of the Pinewood Studios, that had been arranged as a diversion from the pressures of the tournament.

Seen and heard at Pinewood Studios in 1966, Sean Connery and Yul Brynner with mischief makers Jimmy Greaves and Bobby Moore.

Sean Connery, who was shooting his latest James Bond film, *You Only Live Twice*, showed us around, along with Yul Brynner and Norman Wisdom, who were both also making films at the sprawling studios. At the end of the tour, Ramsey stepped forward to make a short thank you speech.

"I would like to thank," he said, in that distinctive, clipped posh-Cockney accent of his, "everybody at Pinewood Studios and in particular Mr Seen Connery."

I was standing with the mickey-taking masters Mooro and Greavsie. Bobby had us all falling about as he said in a stage whisper: "That's the funniest thing I've ever shawn or heard."

Alf sensed he was being laughed at, and shot a killer look in our direction.

England doctor Alan Bass, along with Harold Shepherdson one of the few who had the total confidence of the guarded Ramsey, joined Ron Flowers in the foyer on the morning of the final and told him: "Panic over."

It was later revealed that Ron had been warned by Ramsey to stand by to replace either Bobby Moore or Jack Charlton, both of whom had been struggling with sore throats after the semi-final.

But emergency treatment by Doc Bass had got them both fit for the match of their lives.

So Ron Flowers did not have to give a Bobby Moore impersonation.

09.35am JUST WHAT THE DOCTOR ORDERED

Bernard Joy, still hunting a story for his *Evening Standard* World Cup supplement, steered Dr Bass into a corner of the foyer. Doc Bass was everybody's friend and Bernard saw him as a saviour. "Doc," he pleaded, "is Greaves fit to play?"

Bass, always a cheerful, loquacious man, was unusually reticent to talk. "Much as I'd like to tell you," he told Joy, "Alf has sworn me to secrecy. He doesn't want anything leaking out about the team."

I knew that Jimmy was definitely fit. He had played in a secret match behind closed doors against an Arsenal team at their London Colney training headquarters the day after the semi-final victory against Portugal. All the England reserves had played as Alf kept them match fit, just in case of injuries to his first-choice players.

The players in the team that had beaten Portugal stood on the touchline cheering on their squad colleagues, much of it in joking tone, but Alf was in no mood for comedy. He kept a close watch on Greavsie's performance.

Jimmy was marked by Arsenal skipper Frank McLintock, who told me later:

> "There's no doubt that Jimmy was fit. He was his usual sharp self and popped in one of his typical solo goals. I was sure Ramsey would pick him for the World Cup final. I wouldn't have had the nerve to keep a world-class striker on the sidelines, not a player with Jimmy's unique finishing ability."

Later that day I heard loud, uncontrollable laughter coming from the team meeting at Hendon Hall. I peeped through the open door and saw Alf and all the players in hysterics as they watched film of their training matches leading up to the final. Projectionist Derek Cattani, official FA cameraman, was playing his film backwards. It was hilarious. The laughter was just what the doctor ordered.

But then the door was closed and Alf got down to the serious business of showing his players how they could beat West Germany and become champions of the world. The unanswered question: Would he be doing it with Jimmy Greaves in the team?

Les Cocker, Leeds United trainer and England assistant to Harold Shepherdson, was helping to keep nerves from jangling by talking cricket. in the hotel foyer. "Nobby Stiles," he told our gathering of pressmen, "would never get a place in Lancashire's cricket team."

He was referring to a knockabout game of cricket played the previous day, during a rare media conference at the Bank of England sports ground twelve miles away at Roehampton.

The highlight was Jimmy Greaves bowling a Chinaman – a left hander's googly – to batsman Nobby Stiles, who slogged it up in the air and watched incredulously as his Manchester United team-mate Bobby Charlton made an astonishing running catch. There seemed nothing this man could not do.

The press session was organised to help pass the time and give the media the chance for photographs and (stilted) interviews with Alf Ramsey and Bobby Moore. Notable absentees from the cricket match were the three best cricketers in Ramsey's football squad, Moore, Hurst and Peters.

It was still too fresh in their mind how during an identical cricket game on a media day at West Ham's training ground Alan Sealey had broken his leg in a freak accident.

I joined in that casual cricket match at their Chadwell Heath base after Fleet Street cameramen had taken team photographs of the West Ham side that had captured the European Cup Winners' Cup just two months earlier, with Sealey scoring the vital Cup-clinching goal.

The cricket ball was knocked high in the air and Alan sprinted after it, didn't see the bench that the photographers had used for the team picture and smashed his leg, an injury so bad that it virtually finished his career.

So it was understandable that the West Ham trio chose to sit out the cricket game on the eve of the World Cup final. It was switch-off day for the squad, and even Alf Ramsey relaxed to the point where he was again happy to say in front of the television cameras: "As I have been repeating since before the tournament started, England *will* win the World Cup."

It was after breakfast and out of sight of the growing army of newspapermen and broadcasters that Ramsey called a private team meeting. I later learned that he said, simply:

> "Gentlemen, it will be an unchanged team. I want to thank all of you for your efforts so far, and I know you'll all pull together this afternoon. It's our team spirit that makes us stronger than the rest. I don't want to announce the team until we get to Wembley, so please keep it to yourself."

Alf took his former skipper Jimmy Armfield on one side and told him: "I'm putting you in charge of the rest of the squad. There are seats reserved for you in the stand. Regardless of the score bring them down to the pitch side with five minutes to go. I want us all to be together at the end, no matter what the result."

In fairness to Ramsey, he was not keeping the team from the press so much as from the Germans. He did not want his rival manager Helmut Schoen to know his line-up until as late as possible. Alf was sure that the German boss – along with most good judges – would be convinced that Jimmy Greaves was certain to play.

In the German headquarters at the Homestead Court Hotel in Welwyn Garden City Schoen was holding a team meeting where it was not Jimmy Greaves on his mind but Bobby Charlton. He had watched Bobby's exceptional display against Portugal and decided to sacrifice his most talented player, Franz Beckenbauer, to man-mark the England schemer. It was a tactical decision that would have a huge impact on the final.

The England players had sat in a darkened room at Hendon Hall watching television film of West Germany's victory over Russia in their semi-final, with Alf continually stopping the action and giving each of his players specific instructions how to play them. He ordered Bobby Charlton to shadow Beckenbauer. Two of the most creative players in the world were about to cancel each other out.

Alf was a man with a plan, and his fellow Dagenhamite Jimmy Greaves was not part of it. And neither were any wingers.

Jimmy Greaves had guessed he was out, and without a word to anybody he had packed his bags ready for a quick getaway once the match was over. Hendon Hall had become Heartbreak Hotel.

He smuggled the cases to his brother-in-law Tom. They would be leaving with their wives the next day for a Caribbean holiday. For Jimmy, the World Cup campaign was over.

Greavsie would give his team-mates his full, sincere support at Wembley, but inside he felt sick and empty. For months he had been telling people, including me, that England would win the World Cup. He just did not envisage being a non-playing spectator.

Alf did not see fit to say a word to him. He considered there were ten other excluded players who would then also deserve an explanation.

I felt I had betrayed a good pal by writing that Alf should leave him out of the biggest game that any footballer could play.

And over the next 50 years Jimmy never ever let me forget what I had written in the *Express* on the morning of the match. He has always done it in jest, but deep down I know he must have felt I was putting the boot in on a friend.

It was 12 years later, when we were writing the first of our twenty books together, that Jimmy conceded that he was playing below par in the 1965-66 season. The hepatitis that put him into hospital in the autumn of 1965 had robbed him of a vital half yard of pace.

He worked harder than at any time in his career to get his match fitness back, and was still considered England's major striker going into the World Cup finals. But a wild kick from a French defender – picking on Jimmy rather than the fearsome Nobby Stiles – opened a deep gash on his left shin that required twelve stitches.

"I had no idea how bad it was until I looked down and found that my white sock was blood red," he told me. "An alarm bell went off in my head at that moment that maybe my World Cup was over."

For Jimmy, it was a life-changing moment ... as it was for Geoff Hurst.

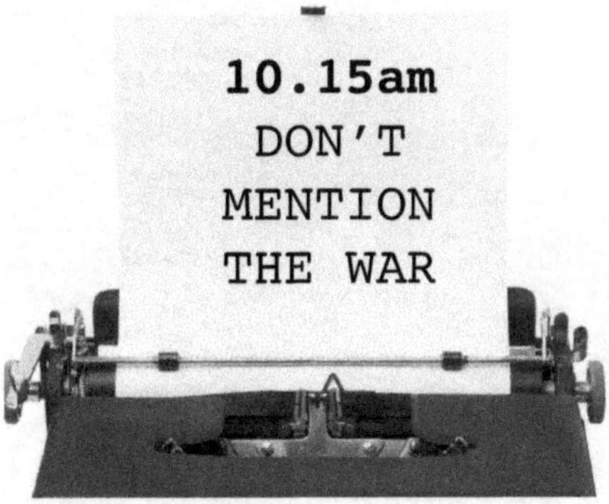

10.15am DON'T MENTION THE WAR

Martin Peters and Geoff Hurst came out of the breakfast area together, and I wished them luck as they went up to their room to prepare for the coach ride to Wembley. It was astonishing how their lives had turned round. When the year started neither of them had won a single England cap, now here they were with West Ham club-mate Bobby Moore on the brink of footballing history.

Both had been sworn to secrecy the night before by Alf Ramsey when he told them they were playing against West Germany. But those of us with our ear to the ground knew they were in, and Geoff and Martin had confided in their wives, Judith and Kathy, who were best friends.

Dennis Signy, the 'King of Hendon', editor of the local paper and the best-informed freelance football reporter in the land, had told me that all three West Ham players were in the side. We met for breakfast every morning at Hendon Hall during the World Cup, which was an easy assignment for Dennis, because he and his new bride, Pat, lived just a couple of hundred yards from the hotel.

He and *News of the World* sleuth Reg Drury were among the few who had the full confidence of Ramsey, and knew before most that Alf had decided on an unchanged team. So I got confirmation that Jimmy Greaves was out while eating my toast and marmalade. It was not easy to digest.

Ramsey reluctantly and briefly gave an interview in front of the BBC and ITV cameras. He and the squad were fuming with the BBC and ITV over what they saw as less than friendly coverage. After the opening goalless draw with Uruguay Jimmy Hill had told the nation: "England will not win the World Cup, but don't blame Alf. No one could win with this lot."

Ramsey welcomed the chance to build a 'them and us' siege mentality, and the England players closed ranks. They were particularly upset with BBC pundit Danny Blanchflower's blistering criticism of Nobby Stiles after the match against France. He said Nobby's tackling had ruined the tournament for him and that he could not care less if England won if they were going to play the game in that spirit. He crucified Ramsey's tactics to start a feud between him and his predecessor as

Helmut Schoen, the West German master coach, with Franz Beckenbauer, the player he was about to sacrifice to nullify the threat of Bobby Charlton

Spurs captain that lasted the rest of their lives.

"Everyone is fit," Ramsey tersely told viewers, "and we are ready to do our best. The Germans have a very good team, but I remain confident we will win the World Cup. I will confirm the team when we get to Wembley."

"Is Jimmy Greaves playing?" the interviewer asked in vain, as Alf walked off camera without another word. He was always a miser with his words, and today of all days he was giving nothing away.

Helmut Schoen gave an almost identical interview from the German headquarters in Hertfordshire. He had earlier become agitated over an article I wrote in which I compared Ramsey with Montgomery and him with Rommel on the eve of El Alamein.

The German tabloid *Bild Zeitung* described me and my British sports writer colleagues as "chaps who write their copy in steel helmets and gas masks."

When judging us from this distance, remember that all the journalists representing Fleet Street in the Wembley press box lived through the war, and the legendary *Daily Sketch* columnist Laurie Pignon had been a prisoner of war, with bayonet scars to show for it.

Schoen asked me to identify myself at a press conference and, while admonishing me, said: "You should refrain from using wartime metaphors. This is not war, young man. This is sport."

Anybody who could see the glint in the eyes of 'The General' Alf Ramsey – who as Sergeant Ramsey had captained the Palestine Services XI while fighting the war in the Middle-East – would have doubted that.

12.10pm ENGLAND'S LUCKY CHARMS

There was a strange ritual of England players checking each other's clothing as they gathered in the hotel foyer ready to board the team coach, first of all making sure that usual 'lucky mascot' driver Sid Brown was at the wheel.

Superstitions run deep with many footballers, and the England team were leaving nothing to chance. The usual dress code for the players was FA-issued England blazers or charcoal-grey Hardy Amies-designed, Burton-tailored sponsored suits, but Ramsey relaxed the rules on match days.

He himself was caught up in the whirlpool of superstition, and underneath his 'lucky' blue tracksuit he wore the same underwear, shirt, socks and shoes for every game at Wembley.

On the first day of the finals Jimmy Armfield had borrowed Norman Hunter's red sweater. He'd worn it every match day since, regardless of the summer heat. Hunter always carried a folded raincoat that he held on to through every match, never ever putting it on, even if it rained.

> **JIMMY ARMFIELD:** "I was never really caught up in football superstitions, but after I had worn Norman Hunter's ghastly red sweater on the first day of the finals I dare not break the spell. Norman would have bitten my legs! Like all Leeds United players, he was very much a player of habit. If you see any photographs of Alf on the bench at the final whistle you will see me bending over him wearing Norman's red sweater, even though it was a sweltering summer's day. I was doing my bit for my country. We won, so it must have worked."

Room-mates Bobby Charlton and Ray Wilson went for an after-breakfast stroll to the local shops, not because they wanted anything but because it is what they had done each match day. While they were out Ray decided on the spur of the moment to buy a new pair of black leather shoes to wear later in the evening at the after-match banquet. This on the morning of a World Cup final, and hardly a soul recognised them.

Jimmy Greaves with trainer Les Cocker leaves Hendon Hall – Heartbreak Hotel – on his way to Wembley to watch the 1966 World Cup final. The unknowing porter wished Jimmy good luck.

They were back in time for the same light-snack meal they always had, and they then sat on the same seats on the coach. The same card schools were started as on every other match-day coach ride, even though none of the players had the appetite for their usual hands of poker, brag and rummy. Groundhog Day with bells on.

In the dressing-room before each match superstitions ran riot. Gordon Banks had to rub chewing gum into his gloves, while Nobby Stiles rubbed olive oil on his chest with exactly the same number of hand strokes every time. He always handed his false teeth to Ian Callaghan wrapped in the same handkerchief. It had to be Cally, who would place them in the same jacket pocket. Then Nobby would stand in front of the same mirror and insert his contact lenses.

Jack Charlton was eaten up with the same regime that he always used to follow in the Leeds dressing-room, where manager Don Revie was the king of superstition. Jack gave up the Leeds captaincy because he was convinced that he only played well if he was the last player to come on to the pitch. He had to sit on the toilet for exactly five minutes before every game, and habitually changed studs at the last minute and would always take a sniff of Vic vapour to clear his nostrils just before leaving the dressing-room. Finally, he could not end the pre-match warm-up without shooting the ball past Gordon Banks and into the England net. Gordon knew better than to try to save it.

The strangest ritual involved West Ham team-mates Bobby Moore and Martin Peters. It had always been Bobby's superstition for club and country that he should be the last to put on his shorts. As a wind-up before his first World Cup finals match against Mexico Martin had waited for his skipper to put on his shorts and had then taken his off. Bobby responded by removing his, and then Martin put his back on and whipped them off again as Bobby pulled his shorts up.

They played this on-off game of chicken until the time came for them to walk out into the tunnel, and continued to do it throughout the World Cup match-day preparations, both reluctant to stop in case it upset the football gods.

The important thing is that at the end of the charade it was Bobby who was always last to pull up his shorts. This doubtless sounds juvenile to non-football people, but I have rarely known a major team in any sport that is not in some measure the puppet of superstition.

> **MARTIN PETERS**: "It will seem ridiculous to people outside the game, and they will think we were off our rockers. But it was important to us that we followed the same routine for every match. Bobby and I also did it when we played for West Ham, and I always used to let him win because he was the captain. We did it for a laugh to release the tension in the dressing-room, but deep down we knew it was a ritual we dare not stop."

The Metropolitan Police got caught up in the illogical formalities, and the same two motor cycle outriders were assigned each match day to lead the sweep of the coach around the North Circular Road to Wembley, and mascot driver Sid Brown always parked the coach in exactly the same spot.

Sid was an important part of the England routine. Each player touched him as they got on to the coach, and he always wore the same clothes when driving on match days. He was considered one of the squad, to the extent that Alf Ramsey insisted he went to Mexico with England for the 1970 finals, and an identical team bus was shipped across the Atlantic, much to the anger of the Mexican World Cup organisers who considered it disrespectful that the FA would not trust their local buses and drivers. But Alf had the strength to make demands then, a position of power that ended with England's exit in the quarter-finals. But that's another story for another day. Back to the special 1966 day.

Sid Brown's brother got married on this July 30 Saturday, and to compensate for not being at the wedding he gave an England No 16 shirt presented to him by Martin Peters to the bride and groom. Years later it fetched £8,000 at auction.

A couple of hundred fans waving rattles, scarves and Union Jacks had gathered at Hendon Hall to see the team off. Not a flag of St George in sight. How times and habits change. There was polite rather than wild applause as the players filed on to the coach, each one making sure he sat in the exact same seat as when they went to Wembley for the previous five matches against Uruguay, Mexico, France, Argentina and Portugal.

Alf and trainer Harold Shepherdson always sat together at the front, Shep taking the window seat. He would hand a stick of chewing gum to Alf, and he would chew the same piece of gum throughout the journey and the match.

> **HAROLD SHEPHERDSON**: "Alf and I didn't think of it as superstition as much as keeping the same routine. I'd been doing the England trainer's job since 1957, and I never knew anybody as well organised as Alf. He liked everything to work like clockwork. He planned what was going to happen on and off the pitch like a military campaign, and I got to understand why his Tottenham team-mates used to call him The General in his playing days. It was a privilege to be his right hand man. In all the years I worked with him – over one hundred matches – I never knew him drop that mask of his. People, including me, never knew what he was thinking. It was one of his strengths. He was thinking all the time."

The police outriders kicked their powerful motorbikes into life, and the tension and excitement at Hendon Hall suddenly started to rise as the last of the players filed out to the coach. The entire hotel staff – chefs, waiters, maids, bar and reception staff and porters – turned out to wave off the squad that had been made to feel at home for the past five weeks from the end of England's warm-up tour.

Jimmy Greaves passed just six feet in front of me on the way to the coach, wearing a forced fixed smile on his face. One of the hotel porters, not privy to the team selection, shouted: "Good luck, Jimmy boy. Pop one in for me."

I could not find any words and just gave him a friendly nod. The nation was yet to know that Alf had decided to gamble on leaving out the most prolific scorer in the history of English international football, and I felt as if I had been party to it.

Much later, Jimmy told me he had no recall of the drive from Hendon to Wembley. He admitted:

> "I was in a daze. This was the game I had dreamt about playing in, and now I was going to watch it. I am the world's worst spectator at the best of times, and I knew it was going to be torture looking on from the stands. I'm not going to lie. I was as jealous as hell of all the boys playing for England that day, but they had my full, unstinting support. They were my mates and all of them great footballers. A year later they would have allowed substitutes, and no doubt I would have got on. It's a funny old game."

2

JULY 30 1966

THE ROAD TO WEMBLEY

1.10pm MATCH OF THE CENTURY

THE North Circular Road was jammed with flag-bedecked cars heading for Wembley, mostly Union Jacks but plenty of black, red and gold of West Germany. Even with a police escort, the England coach was delayed on the final mile to the stadium as 96,924 spectators, including dignitaries and the world's media, converged on the stadium, with its iconic twin towers, "hallowed" turf, famous 39 steps to the Royal Box and seating for more than 45,000 people.

"We all tried to treat it just like any other match," defender George Cohen recalled. "But the nearer we got to Wembley the more the pressure and the importance of the occasion hit us. The feeling was one of mounting excitement, nervous anticipation and a sort of fear of the unknown. Let's face it, this was the biggest sporting event our country had ever known. It was an ordeal but one I would not have missed for the world. I looked around the coach and realised I was surrounded by strong, talented mates. I knew we'd be all right."

George would have seen Gordon Banks, now established as one of the world's great goalkeepers, Ray Wilson as stylish and reliable a left-back as there was in the tournament, Nobby Stiles looking almost angelic with his teeth in but an assassin of a player once released into battle.

Then there was big Jack Charlton, a centre-half with a heart bigger than his head, 'our captain' Bobby Moore, regal looking and exuding cool confidence, and there's little Ballie, a baby but with an old football head on his shoulders and with more energy than a nuclear power station.

Playing cards at the back of the coach were Roger Hunt and Geoff Hurst, England's new striking partners who had been so impressive against Argentina and Portugal, while Martin Peters was a latecomer to the England camp but proving his right to be there with elegant football that Alf Ramsey would describe as ten years ahead of its time.

And there, holding all the cards, the impassive Bobby Charlton, one of the most famous footballers in the world who was the on-field general able to find any team-mate with a 30-yard pass and the net with a thunderbolt shot from either foot.

Yes, George thought, England would be all right.

His heart bled when he looked at the forlorn figure of Jimmy Greaves, Greavsie his mate since they played against each other in East London v. West London schoolboy matches. He could not find any words to comfort the best goal scorer he had ever clapped eyes on.

"I didn't know what to say to him," George recalled. "So I said nothing. He gave me a hug before the game. It spoke volumes."

George went along with most people in the game on the Greavsie debate: "What a call it was by Alf to leave him out. To be honest I would have found a way of playing him. That's why I would never make a manager. There's no room for softness or sentiment in football. I'm soft and I'm sentimental."

Danny Blanchflower, Jimmy's former Totenham team-mate and godfather to his son, Danny, did not try to sheathe his anger when the team was announced from Wembley. He reached for a metaphor fit for the occasion:

> **DANNY BLANCHFLOWER:** "That's like The Beatles leaving Lennon out of the recording studio. You should always select your best players. Ramsey wants a team of robots. To leave a player of Jimmy's quality on the sidelines is a sad indictment of Ramsey's philosophy. He is happy to have a player in the team like Stiles who is purely destructive, yet omits a footballer with world-class skills and the finest goalscorer these islands have ever produced."

Danny, who had joined me on *Express* newspapers, was consistent and never ever changed his view of Ramsey's selection.

I tried to follow the England coach from Hendon Hall to Wembley in my Austin 1100, but got engulfed in the traffic jams and finally arrived at snail's pace at the stadium car park.

Then it was up in the lift to the galleried press box high in the main stand, looking down on the Royal Box and the white-helmeted Royal Marines Band marching in perfect formation on what would soon be the stage for England's football match of the century.

More than eight-hundred international reporters from around the world were covering the match, with the overflow given seats in the stands, many from tickets returned by countries whose teams had been knocked out on the way to Wembley.

My *Daily Express* colleagues Desmond Hackett and Clive Toye were reporting the match, while my brief was to gather quotes and note any off-beat incidents.

Cleverly and craftily, I manoeuvred my seat so that I was adjacent to legendary Wembley press officer Len Went, a long-time pal of mine through our mutual love of boxing. I knew I would need him at the final whistle.

Alf Ramsey was not the only man with a plan.

2.00pm
A HARVEST FOR THE TICKET TOUTS

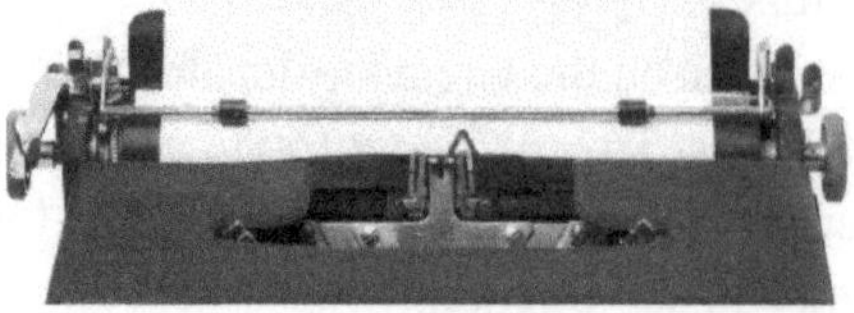

Many of the tickets – unused by overseas fans going home early with their teams – ended up in the hands of the London network of ticket touts. Standing tickets, that cost as little as ten shillings (50p), were changing hands at £10 each, and £5 seats in the stands fetched what was then an astronomical £50.

In an interview I got for the *Express*, 'Fat Stan' Flashman – leading tout, or ticket stockbroker as he called himself – told me: "This match is like a harvest. People are willing to pay the earth to see England in the final, and hundreds of Germans have come over without tickets. We'll oblige them at the right price. It's getting us out of trouble. We lost fortunes on matches in the sticks (provinces) because people would not pay over the odds. We've only made money on England games ... but big, big money."

For England's semi-final against Portugal, you could stand and watch in the west enclosure for seven shillings and sixpence, 37.5p. The ticket spivs were selling them for £10. It probably does not sound a lot, but remember this was in the days when the average weekly wage was £15.

People went to extraordinary lengths to get to the final to support England and say 'I was there.' Few could match the efforts of a coal miner colleague of Tommy Charlton, youngest of the footballing family brothers. "Bobby and Jackie arranged for me to have a ticket," he said, "but I was working a shift down the mine and I didn't feel as if I could bring them any luck. They'd done all right without me being at the World Cup games, so I decided to watch the match on TV. I gave the ticket to my foreman who cycled to and from the game. Said it was the best day of his life."

This was the little matter of a round trip by bike from Ashington in Northumberland of 580 miles.

The parents of Bobby and Jack, Bob and Cissie Charlton, were put up at the Royal Garden Hotel. Cissie, from the legendary Milburn footballing family, knew the game inside out. Bob had other things on his mind, and said his main concern was having to leave his pigeons unsupervised.

Would he approve of Ramsey's 'Wingless Wonders'?

2.10pm
TV HISTORY IN BLACK AND WHITE

Adjoining the press box were glass-fronted booths for dozens of commentators stationed in front of their microphones, and describing the action in thirty different languages. There were 381 TV reporters, and hardly a woman in sight.

With the BBC and ITV as the co-host broadcasters, the match was being shown live to North and South America, Africa, the Middle East, Asia and across Europe. There would be an estimated worldwide audience of 400 million in 40 countries.

It was the most-watched international broadcast since the launch of inter-continental television, and it would be the last final shown in black and white. But there were colour versions being shot by Pathé News, Movietone and for the official Fifa film, *Goal*, superbly scripted by Brian Glanville and narrated by distinguished English actor Nigel Patrick. Well worth seeing. It was pilloried at the time for being too arty-crafty, but is now recognised as a cult classic. It has a wonderfully dramatic jazz score by master bassist Johnny Hawksworth.

There were demands by politicians in Buenos Aries to pull the plug on the coverage because of the anger that followed Alf Ramsey's description of the Argentines as "animals" after their ill-tempered quarter-final. Disgraced skipper Antonio Rattin led his team back to a delirious welcome-home as if they had won the World Cup. He said England's finest player was Fifa President Stanley Rous.

I had never known Ramsey so angry, and later learned that he lost his famous cool because Argentinian players spat at him and his team as they returned to the dressing-room, and a chair was thrown through the glass window above where the England footballers hung their clothes.

Alf called a team meeting and hushed everybody up, and it was weeks before the story got out. That's how tight security was around the Wembley dressing-rooms. Imagine what the social network would make of it today!

There were another 213 commentators working for home and overseas radio stations in a long line in front of the press box, including young BBC staffman Brian Moore, who was my best buddy. He shared 'live' commentating duties on the BBC Light Programme with former BBC Northern head of sport Alan Clarke. Ex-England amateur star Maurice Edelston was alongside them as summariser.

BBCtv's commentary team for the 1966 World Cup finals, back row, left to right: Frank Bough, Alan Weeks, David Coleman, Walley Barnes; front: Ken Aston (head of the Fifa referees panel), Kenneth Wolstenholme and former League referee Arthur Ellis, later of 'It's A Knockout' fame.

The BBC television commentary was trusted to the experienced larynx of Kenneth Wolstenholme, who had been the Voice of Football for more than ten years. He had won the DFC during the war for flying more than one hundred missions over Germany as an RAF bomber pilot.

And how about this for a little bit of trivia: Ken went to the same Farnworth, Lancashire, grammar school as the 'baby ' of England's team, Alan Ball.

I had a gin and tonic with Wolstenholme at the press bar before he took up his commentary position. "I've done all my homework," he said, as meticulous as ever. "Now I just hope I get the names right. It's the commentator's nightmare, calling the wrong scorers." He and the Birmingham-based, silver-tongued ITV commentator Hugh Johns were about to address a record combined audience of 32.3 million viewers, the majority tuned to the BBC. There were 20 TV cameras trained on the pitch, and another dozen cameras shooting colour film.

The press bar could not cope with all the thirsty journalists. There were officially 1,392 media reporters and photographers on duty.

The 1966 World Cup final would be well recorded. Take my word for it.

George Best, in the early stages of his glittering career, arrived at Wembley to watch the match from the stands in the company of his Manchester United team-mate David Sadler and Manchester City winger Mike Summerbee. "I'm British so obviously I want to see England win, and I'm here to support my United team-mates Bobby and Nobby," George said. "But the Germans have some world-class players, particularly Beckenbauer. There's nothing to choose between the teams. Wouldn't be surprised to see it go to a replay."

One Manchester United legend who would have been happy to see his Old Trafford team-mates on the losing side was Scottish international striker Denis Law. He could not face the prospect of watching 'the auld enemy' winning the World Cup, and elected to be on the golf course at kick-off time. It is well documented that he threw his clubs when he heard the result.

Higher up in the Wembley stands world heavyweight champion Muhammad Ali, still known to most as Cassius Clay, had gone almost unnoticed to his seat immediately alongside the press box. He was with his brother Rudolph Clay, about to adopt the Muslim name Rahaman Ali.

"I would have been happy to miss the match," Ali confided to me years later when I was working as publicist on his fights. "I only went 'cos promoter Jack Solomons told me tickets were going slow for my defence against Brian London the next week. We needed the publicity. It was unthinkable there could be empty seats when The Greatest was performing. Couldn't get in the papers 'cos of the soccer. I had no interest. Back home it's a game for little gals." He dozed virtually throughout the match (and the poorly attended fight cost Solomons a small fortune).

The Royal Box was packed with dignitaries waiting for the arrival of the Queen and Duke of Edinburgh. Prime Minister Harold Wilson's seat was glaringly empty. He was dashing back from a flying visit to Washington for crisis talks with American President Lyndon Johnson over the state of the British economy that would soon lead to a devaluation of the pound. The match was just about to kick off when he arrived at Wembley. For the next few hours the country would forget the mess we were in.

2.30pm
MAN WHO KEPT ALF IN THE PICTURE

I liked to think I was close to the England camp and with an ear to the men that mattered, but I could not compete with brilliant young photographer Derek Cattani. He was employed by the Football Association as their film and picture librarian, and had his library next door to Alf Ramsey's cubby hole of an office at Lancaster Gate.

Alf relied heavily on the photographs he took at all England's matches, and used to base his team talks on Derek's pictures magnified on a large screen at Hendon Hall. Derek worked the projector for Alf, who was to film and camera technology what Einstein was to ladies' hairdressing.

Derek attended all training sessions, even when they were behind closed doors at the Bank of England ground at Roehampton. He also had the privilege of being allowed on the team coach, and provided exclusive pictures for the *FA News* magazine.

His huge collection of off-beat pictures from the World Cup was a collector's treasure chest, but a fire in his library later destroyed 98 per cent of the photographs and a priceless record of the finals was lost for ever.

The one thing he was rarely allowed to do was take pictures in the dressing-room. Alf considered it a journalist-free zone.

I am always being told my memory is playing tricks when I say there were no still photographs taken in the England dressing-room after the final. If they exist, I have never seen them. Have you?

Even the *Goal* film cameraman, working on the official Fifa movie, had to have an argument at the dressing-room door before he was allowed in for fleeting shots of the players celebrating.

Derek was one of more than twenty people, including the eleven reserves, turfed out of the dressing-room by a taut Ramsey with 40 minutes to the kick-off, after Bobby Moore had complained that it had become like Piccadilly Circus.

The FA's man of record went out on to the pitch and took up his position behind a goal. There was to be no photograph or film record of Alf giving his final team talk. Where was the sense of occasion?

2.32pm
SCHOEN TAKES A SHINE TO CHARLTON

Across the corridor from England's 'lucky' South dressing-room Helmut Schoen was giving his final instructions to a West German team that had reached the final on the back of four victories and a draw. They topped their group stage with victories over Switzerland (5-0) and Spain (2-1) and a brutal, bad-tempered goalless draw at Villa Park with Argentina, who had key player José Albrecht sent off in the 65th minute.

In their quarter-final at Hillsborough they cruised past the Uruguayan team that had frustrated England in the opening match of the tournament. The Germans won 4-0 in a bitterly fought clash in which English referee Jim Finney sent off two Uruguayans. This on top of the Rattin dismissal against England at Wembley triggered 'Europeans fix the World Cup' headlines across South America. All four semi-finalists were from Europe.

West Germany overcame the Soviet Union in the semi-final at Goodison Park, winning 2-1 after Dynamo Moscow midfielder Igor Chislenko had been sent off just before half-time. Franz Beckenbauer, rated the most exciting young prospect in the tournament, scored the decisive second goal with a rasping shot past great Russian goalkeeper Lev Yashin in the 68th minute.

England were originally meant to play their semi-final against Portugal at Goodison, but it was switched to Wembley for what Fifa described as economic reasons.

It added to the catalogue of criticisms that everything in the tournament was loaded in England's favour. They were the only finalists in World Cup history to play every single game on their national stadium turf.

Schoen would not bite when asked by the media to comment on the controversy. "The English FA can be very proud of the way they have organised the tournament," he said diplomatically.

A courteous, controlled man, he was much more approachable than Ramsey, who was suspicious of all newspapermen. Alf had been given a rough ride by a faction of the Fleet Street reporters who objected to his off-hand treatment and, more so, to tactics that turned the England side into a functional, defence-minded team that gave them little to get excited about. But by the time England were through to the final, the reporters and pundits were behind him to a man, with the notable exception of BBC team member Danny Blanchflower, who said the Ramsey style of football was "far too negative and neurotic."

Schoen, an East German from Dresden who had escaped from the Soviet-occupied East zone in 1950, was, like Ramsey, a brilliant tactician, who over the following 12 years would prove himself one of the game's most successful World Cup coaches. He was still at foundation-building stage with the team he had inherited in 1964 from the legendary Sepp Herberger.

After the semi-final win over the Soviet Union, he selected his strongest side for the showdown with England and they remain the youngest team ever to play in a final:

Hans Tilkowski (Borussia Dortmund, 31)

Horst-Dieter Höttges (Werder Bremen, 22)

Wolfgang Weber (Cologne, 22)

Willi Schulz (Hamburg, 27)

Karl-Heinz Schnellinger (AC Milan, 27)

Franz Beckenbauer (Bayern Munich, 20)

Helmut Haller (Bologna, 27)

Wolfgang Overath (Cologne, 22)

Uwe Seeler (captain, Hamburg, 29)

Siegfried Held (Borussia Dortmund, 23)

Lothar Emmerich (Borussia Dortmund, 24)

Schoen had already made up his mind that he would build his future team around Bayern Munich's multi-talented Franz Beckenbauer, who played with the maturity of a veteran even though he was four months younger than Alan Ball, the 21-year-old baby of England's side.

When he watched the England semi-final victory over Portugal Schoen was deeply impressed by the influence of two-goal Bobby Charlton, who arguably gave the greatest performance of his 106-cap England career.

He decided, stop Charlton playing and we stop England playing.

Franz told me years later when I was working with him on the production of a TV programme: "Helmut took me on one side and told me he wanted me to shadow mark Bobby wherever he went on the pitch. Bobby and I are now good friends and he told me that he got exactly the same instructions from Alf Ramsey. We stopped each other playing. How crazy is that?"

An unmarked police car pulled up in the Wembley Stadium tunnel and out stepped a policeman holding a locked box containing a fairly important trophy, the solid silver, gold-plated Jules Rimet World Cup that would be presented by the Queen to either Bobby Moore or Uwe Seeler. It had enjoyed quite an adventure on the way to the final. The Football Association became a worldwide laughing stock when four months before the tournament the most coveted prize in sport was stolen while on public display at a stamp exhibition at Westminster Central Hall, the largest Methodist church in London and just 50 yards from police headquarters at New Scotland Yard. Definitely a job for Inspector Knacker of the Yard.

The lid of the Cup and a ransom note were sent to FA chairman Joe Mears, demanding £15,000 for the return of the trophy. While he and the police were negotiating with the thief the trophy was recovered in South East London, when a black and white collie dog called Pickles nosed it out. The foot-high Cup, wrapped in newspaper, lay abandoned under a garden hedge and was fished out by the pooch's owner, David Corbett. For the full harrowing and at times hilarious story I recommend you read Martin Atherton's well-researched book, *The Theft of the Jules Rimet Trophy.* Pickles became a national hero, and collected total reward money for Mr. Corbett of £6,000, and for himself a life time's free dog food, a walk-on part in the film *The Spy with the Cold Nose* and an invite to the post-match victory banquet, from which the England wives and girlfriends were banned. My claim to fame, on Final day I stroked Pickles and touched the World Cup.

Sadly the tasty Pickles perks did not last long. He died in 1967, strangled by his own lead while chasing a neighbour's cat. His name lives on in football trivia history, as does that of Edward Betchley, the petty thief who got a two-year jail sentence for stealing the trophy, although he denied the charge.

Following on behind the policeman bound for the Royal Box with the Jules Rimet World Cup was another policeman. He was carrying an exact replica of the trophy. The FA were taking no chances on losing the Cup again. Within an hour of the game finishing the real Jules Rimet trophy was secretly on its way to a safe at FA headquarters, and from then on usually only the replica was seen in public.

The dog Pickles threatened to steal the thunder of the cartoon lion that was the official mascot of the tournament – World Cup Willie, the creation of freelance children's book illustrator Reg Hoye, who got paid just a flat fee and not a penny in royalties, including from the hit song by king of skiffle, Lonnie Donegan (a Scot).

Masterminded by two promotion specialists – Walter Tuckwell and New Zealander Richard Culley – there were over 125 World Cup Willie licenses granted, including in France, Germany, Italy, Denmark and Holland, and more than 10 million items of merchandise were produced, ranging from mugs, T-shirts and key-rings to children's dolls and tea towels. More than £4-million was raised by what was a pioneering mascot that set the merchandising targets for future World Cup tournaments.

©The Football Association

But it was not the World Cup Willie song that was coming from the massed choirs of England supporters as the kick-off to the final approached after a hail storm followed by bright sunshine. The most popular vocals were When the Reds Come Marching In, sung to the old jazz standard When the Saints. Leading up to the final it had been bellowed out as When the Whites Come Marching In, but the Germans had won the toss to select their traditional white shirts.

There were also lots of ee-aye-adio chants borrowed from Merseyside, and Wembley thundered to German klaxon horns and rhythmic clapping building up to choruses of "Eng-er-land, Eng-er-land". The England supporters were out-singing the Germans, but outside in Wembley Way there were scores of ticketless German supporters making a lot of noise. How many knew Wembley Way was built by German Prisoners of War for the 1948 London Games?

2.45pm
THE REFEREE AND 'RUSSIAN LINESMAN'

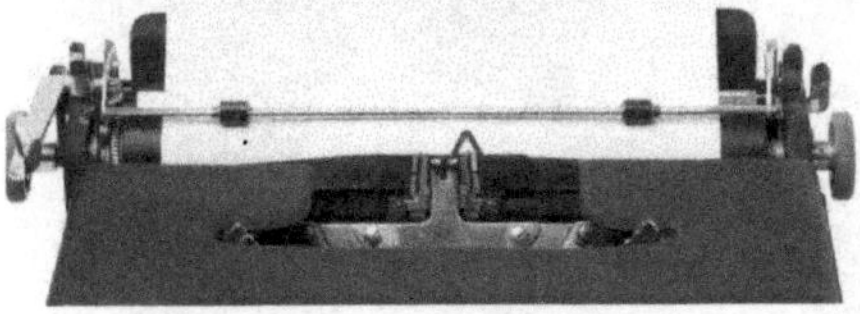

The referee – elected by the Fifa committee under the chairmanship of Ilford primary school headmaster Ken Aston – was Switzerland's Gottfried Dienst, one of the most respected match officials in the game, who had been in charge of the 1961 and 1965 European Cup finals. He was noted for his firm and authoritative control, and respected by players throughout Europe.

His linesmen were Dr Karol Galba, an intellectual from Czechoslovakia who was a prominent football administrator in his home town of Bratislava, and the moustachioed Tofik Bakhramov, from the Soviet Union. He was a former player who turned to refereeing after injury forced his retirement. By the time the afternoon was over he would be the most famous – or infamous – match official in the world, known across the globe as "The Russian Linesman," when in fact he was proudly from Aghjabadi in Azerbaijan.

Both Bakhramov and Dienst were multilingual but did not speak each other's tongue, and communicated with sign language and common football phrases. Referee overlord Ken Aston, who was to later introduce the yellow and red card system, said: "Football is an international language. We all understand each other."

The three officials shared a square dressing-room, 12ft x 12ft, situated up two flights of marble steps leading off the huge tunnel that ran down a long slope from the pitch to the players' dressing-rooms, and wide enough for the parking of both team coaches. Their cramped room, with its small en suite shower and two mirrored dressing-tables, had no windows and was a claustrophobic cell-like setting. A loudspeaker high on the wall picked up the stadium announcements, making it sound like Waterloo Station.

The tunnel in the two hours leading up to the final was a heaving hive of activity, thronged with bandsmen waiting to march on the pitch, scores of uniformed police officers, TV and film camera crews and St John's ambulance men.

Along the corridor from the referee's room was the control centre occupied by the organising committee headed by Fifa President Sir Stanley Rous, FA officials Denis Follows, E.K. (Sandy) Willson and Dickie Bird, press officer Harold Mayes, Ken Aston, and the unsung hero, Alan Leather. He was on loan from his backroom

Captains Uwe Seeler and Bobby Moore exchange mementoes, watched by referee Gottfried Dienst and linesmen Tofik Bakhramov and Karol Galba.

job at Tottenham Hotspur, and was the liaison officer who got the teams to the right places at the right times. The logistics were a nightmare.

Wembley was virtually full an hour before the kick-off, with sunshine and showers making more than 90,000 spectators unsure whether to wear shirt sleeves or put up umbrellas. They had plenty of reading material. The match programme – covering the entire tournament and with updated result supplements added after each round – was a hefty sixty-four pages, and sold for 2s 6d (12.5p). Purchasers had to hand write the teams as they were announced over the loudspeakers. It was edited by brittle-tempered press officer Harold Mayes, and contained a welcoming message from FA chief Joe Mears, chairman of Chelsea, and written just before he died of a heart attack on June 30 while on England's warm-up Scandinavian tour. Stress caused by the Jules Rimet trophy theft had taken its toll.

The Royal Marines band played a tune representative of each of the sixteen finalists before the two teams walked out side by side for the match of their lives, England in rarely worn red shirts, the West Germans in traditional white shirts and black shorts. Then the roof was nearly lifted off Wembley as the crowd, now with the Queen in attendance, sang the national anthem with extra pride and gusto, before Deutschland Uber Alles echoed around the historic stadium.

It was kick-off time and the battle was on.

3
JULY 30 1966
THE
FINAL
REPORT

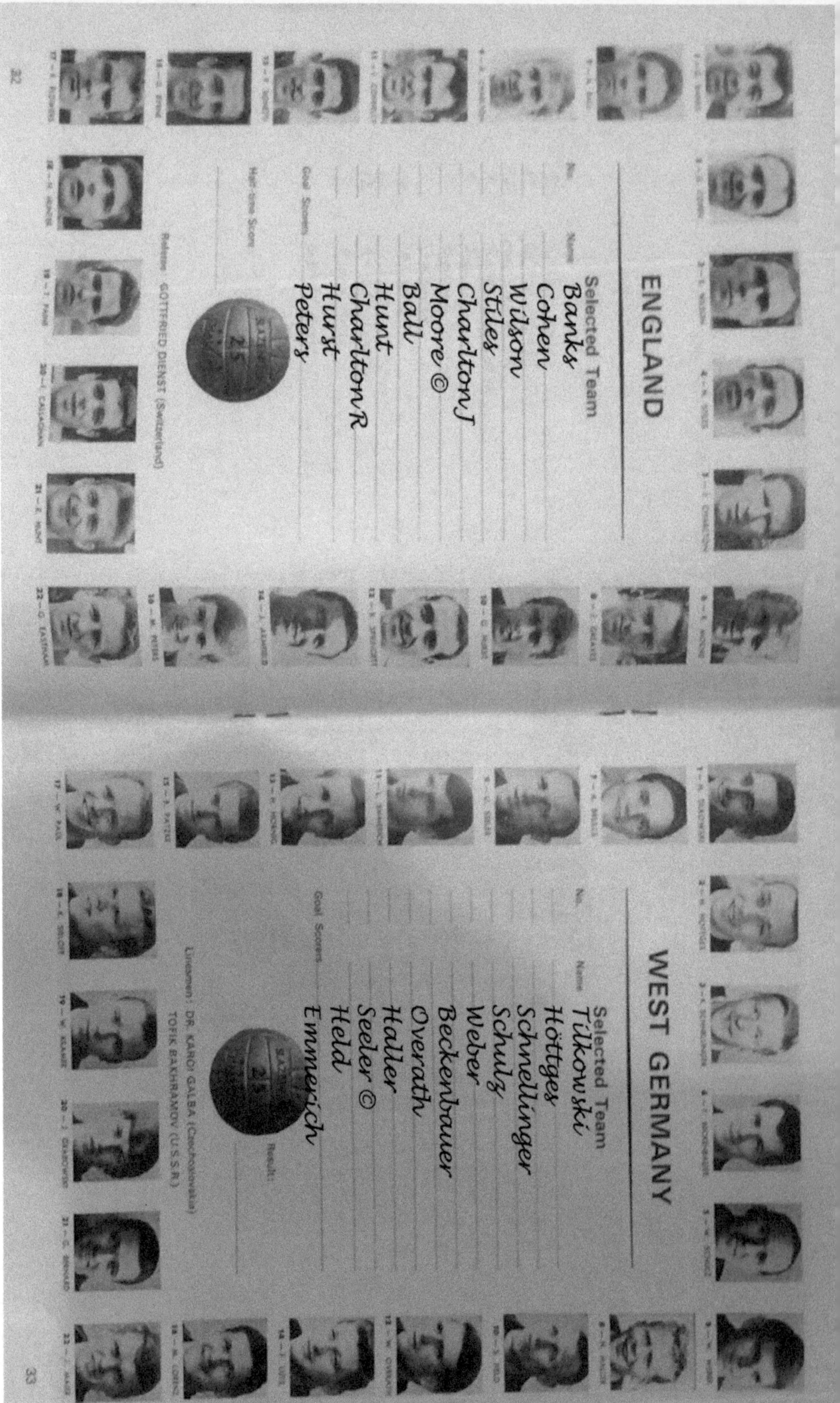

Scanned from my original World Cup final programme on which we had to fill in the teams ourselves as they were read over the Wembley loudspeakers.

3.00pm
THE 90 MINUTE DEADLOCK

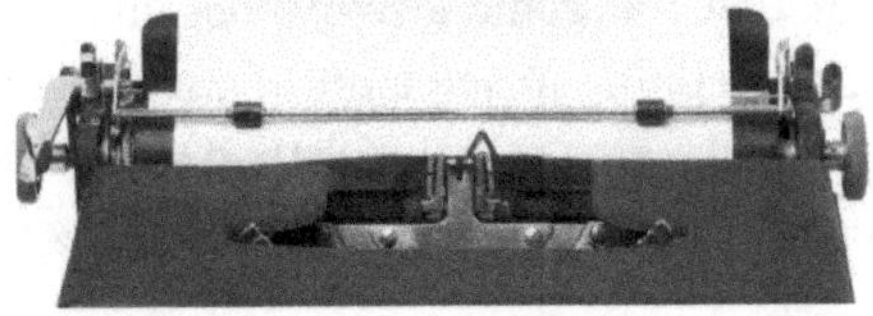

FOR all my experience of watching and reporting football from European Cup finals, FA Cup finals to crucial League games, I was not prepared for how I felt as Siggi Held kicked off for West Germany to set the ball rolling on this eighth World Cup final. I was fighting to catch my breath as I became engulfed in the explosion of excitement and expectation of it all. So goodness knows how the players must have been feeling.

> **GEORGE COHEN**: "To be honest it was easier for us than the spectators. We had a job to do and so all our concentration was on simply playing the game to the best of our ability and not letting the side down. Little the fans could do but shout, cheer, moan and groan, while we got on with trying to win the most important game we were ever likely to play. I was as nervous as hell waiting for the match to start, but once the ref blew the whistle I was in full control and cut everything out of my mind except what I needed to be doing for the team. There was a constant wall of noise and we could hardly hear each other as we tried to shout instructions."

It was England who pieced together the first meaningful attack as one of several short sharp showers soaked the players. Martin Peters and Bobby Charlton exchanged passes down the left, and the ball was steered inside to Nobby Stiles. He was not exactly renowned for his shooting and his attempted instant pot shot at goal from 20 yards was comfortably blocked.

The ball broke loose to Peters, who ghosted to the edge of the German penalty area in the third minute but could only screw the ball wide as a posse of defenders descended on him. The Germans threaded the ball on a conveyor belt of passes to Emmerich, who off-loaded it to Held as he advanced deep into England territory.

The shriek of hundreds of German klaxon horns filled the Wembley air as the idolised Held shaped to shoot, but he snatched at the ball with his weaker right foot and put the first decent chance of the game wide.

Now we knew why 'klaxon' was Greek for shriek. The noise was ear piercing.

The Wembley pitch had been saturated by heavy rain during the hours leading up to the kick-off, and the pitch was already starting to cut up and was not the usual famously smooth surface. Players were leaving footprints behind them as they ran on the soggy green lawn and it looked as if they were being followed by ghosts.

Even this early in the match it was clear that the game's two most creative players, Beckenbauer and Bobby Charlton, were going to see a lot of each other. They seemed tied together by an invisible rope and were rarely more than ten yards apart. It was only afterwards that we learned that both were under instructions to mark each other.

Geoff Hurst, racing full-pelt to meet a lobbed centre from Bobby Charlton in the ninth minute, collided with goalkeeper Hans Tilkowski, who fell to the ground as if pole-axed by a punch from the watching Muhammad Ali. One of three Borussia Dortmund players in the side, he got up after cold sponge treatment from the German trainer, but was staggering around in obvious pain and holding his jaw ...

> **HANS TILKOWSKI**: "I was briefly knocked out, and I felt as if I had been punched in the mouth. I was spitting blood. It was an accidental collision, and Geoff and I have often talked about it in our many meetings since. He got a black eye from it, and it took me several minutes to recover. I was playing in a daze. Because it was a World Cup final I forced myself to concentrate and not think of the pain."

Tilkowski proved he had recovered when in the next attack the eager Peters tested him with a fierce cross shot from the left that he managed to push off target with a scrambled dive across his goal. Two minutes later Alan Ball made huge inroads into the German defence with an energetic 20-yard run before releasing the ball to Peters, whose third shot of the match flew just a foot the wrong side of the post.

All the signs were that England had settled down quicker than their opponents, yet it was West Germany who took a surprise lead in the 12th minute. It all happened as if in sleepwalking time, and looking on from the press box with its wide-sweeping bird's-eye view I was able to see the danger before goalkeeper Gordon Banks could react.

The goal was self-inflicted by, of all people, Ray Wilson, who had been the epitome of defiance and reliability all through the tournament .

Siggi Held fired a hopeful high cross into the England penalty area, but over-hit it right towards Wilson, who seemed to have time to bring it under control and play it to a team-mate, the sort of routine clearance he could make in his sleep.

But there was a sharp intake of breath from at least 60,000 of the spectators

Gordon Banks appears to lose his head as Haller shoots West Germany into a 12th minute lead, and Jack Charlton is already giving the culprit Ray Wilson a mouthful. Then it was on with the game. No time for recriminations.

as Mr Reliable Ramon had a brainstorm and elected to head the ball away with nobody in challenging distance. It went straight to the feet of Germany's Italian-based striker Helmut Haller, who did not need a second invitation to crack it first time past the despairing dive of Gordon Banks from 15 yards. Gordon later admitted he was slow to react because he thought Jack Charlton was going to block the shot.

> **RAY WILSON**: "I knew I'd played it wrong the second I headed it, but it was an instinctive thing. Just my blooming luck that the ball went to their deadliest finisher. Big Jack and Nobby had a bit of a go at me, but we were professional about it and got on with the game and were even more determined to beat the Germans. We knew we were the better team, and now had even more incentive to prove it. I felt sick that I'd helped give them a goal start. But it was no good dwelling on it."

For the millions watching their televisions at home, they were startled to see a slow-motion action replay of the goal, and many wondered if their sets had gone wrong. BBC had hired the revolutionary system from an American company, and this was for many viewers the first time they had seen an instant replay. The shape of things to come.

I have recently been in a BBC editing suite and watched the entire match as live, and the slo-mos of each of the goals, just one each time with a laboured voice-over from co-commentator Walley Barnes, almost clunk on to the screen compared with today's slick instant replays.

In the Royal Box lip readers were able to see that the Queen said: "Oh dear, how disappointing." FA President, the Earl of Harewood, later revealed he turned to Her Majesty, his cousin, and said: "Don't worry, it's a fact that in all post-war World Cup finals the first team to score first loses."

The Earl knew his football history. However, the England players were not thinking of the past. They were weighed down by the present, but kept their composure after absorbing the shock of the Haller goal.

It took just six minutes to cancel it out with a made-in-West-Ham equaliser. Wolfgang Overath upended Bobby Moore in midfield to concede a free-kick. The quick-thinking England skipper immediately flighted the ball into the heart of the German defence, where unmarked Geoff Hurst met no opposition as he steered the ball perfectly with his head wide of the grounded Tilkowski for a goal that put Wembley in party mood.

> **GEOFF HURST**: "I knew exactly where to position myself as Bobby prepared to take the free-kick. It was the sort of thing we'd rehearsed hundreds of times in training with West Ham and England. Bobby couldn't have delivered better if he'd run forward and put it on my head with his hands. Perfection."

With Bobby Charlton and Franz Beckenbauer following orders and cramping each other's movement, the game lacked rhythm and direction. The two best passers on the pitch could not escape each other's attention, and it was like watching an orchestra with the two main soloists playing out of tune.

It was left to Alan Ball and Martin Peters for England and the German pair Wolfgang Overath and Lothar Emmerich to emerge as the chief playmakers, but they lacked the passing precision and penetration of Charlton and Beckenbauer.

For a brief moment Bobby Charlton escaped the warden-like attentions of Beckenbaur with a determined run across the face of the goal from the right and climaxing with a trademark left foot shot. It almost had Tilkowski beaten, but he gathered it at his second attempt.

The Germans retaliated through Haller, who advanced dangerously into the England penalty area, but the alert Banks came off his line to win a race for the ball.

In the press box the clatter of typewriters and chatter of reporters dictating their stories in dozens of different tongues and mixed with the chants of the fans and the klaxon horns gave a unique soundtrack to the football. It was nothing I had experienced before and added to the intense excitement of the occasion.

Geoff Hurst heads the first of his goals, guiding in a perfectly flighted free-kick from his West Ham United skipper Bobby Moore.

Down below Bobby Moore was in his element, playing with supreme control and assurance, and driving his team forward with passes that were both positive and precise. He wore his confidence as comfortably as most of us wear our casual clothes.

We later learned from the statisticians that an incredible 96% of Bobby's passes found their target. Perfection personified.

Off to the right of the press box high in the stands the England reserve players were as nervous and neurotic as the supporters.

> **RON FLOWERS**: "We were as involved as anybody in the crowd, and were kicking and heading every ball. Even though we were not playing we felt part of the team. We were a very tight-knit squad and were desperate for our team-mates to win the World Cup not just for England but for us. It was nerve-racking to watch, torture."

Back on the pitch, the human dynamo Alan Ball was lectured by the referee for showing dissent, and then continued his wholehearted input by figuring in one of England's more effective attacks. George Cohen fired in a high cross from the right and Hurst rose athletically to power in another header similar to the one that had brought his equalising goal. Tilkowski could only scramble the ball away from his right hand post, and Ball was on the spot to turn it back into the goalmouth. The German defenders were exposed to the perils of panic until Overath came dashing in to scoop the ball away for a corner.

Just as we were thinking that England had gained command, back came the Germans with a series of thrusting attacks. Jack Charlton had to intervene with a do-or-die tackle to halt a dangerous Siggi Held run. It cost a corner from which the Germans very nearly scored. From the corner-kick the ball was guided into the path of Overath, known in Germany as the man with the golden left foot. From 20 yards he drove it in fiercely at chest height. Banks parried it and then, when Emmerich powered it back in from close range, Gordon caught it in both hands with the aplomb of an acc England slip fielder.

The game had little pattern but lots of passion and fluctuating fortunes, and next it was Tilkowski's turn to feature when he blocked a left foot volley from Roger Hunt after Hurst had headed the ball down to his feet.

Moments later it was Germany back on the attack. Again it was Overath exercising his left foot with a stunning shot from 20 yards that Banks turned over the crossbar just as it seemed the ball was dipping beneath the bar.

After a breathless first half, the consensus was that 1-1 was slightly flattering to the Germans. Tilkowski had been flapping at the ball but England had failed to take advantage of his loose clearances. It was not classic football as in England's semi-final against Portugal, but the action was fast and competitive and worthy of the occasion. Half-time was a relief to the players who had run their socks off and deserved a breather.

Alf Ramsey walked tight-lipped back to the dressing-rooms, threading his way through the ranks of the oncoming Royal Marines band with tactics rather than music on his mind.

> **JACK CHARLTON**: "Alf was composed and controlled as ever at half-time, the complete professional. He told us to just continue playing as we had in the first-half, and instructed us to keep putting the pressure on Tilkowski as much as possible because his handling was so dodgy. Alf suggested that our kid (Bobby Charlton) go off to the flanks and so take Beckenbauer with him. Franz was following him as if they were glued together."

Early in the second-half Bobby Charlton, moving quickly through on to Moore's pass, went tumbling in the penalty area after being tackled by Schulz, but being the first gentleman of football he made no complaint while England supporters vociferously demanded a penalty that would have been harsh on the Germans.

Big-hearted Cohen was making regular runs on the right wing but his centres were being swallowed up by Schulz and Weber at the heart of the German defence. Karl-Heinz Schnellinger had been prominent and productive as an attacking full-back in Germany's matches on the way to the final, but he had his hands so full

It's like a numbers game as Martin Peters (16) hammers England into a 2-1 lead

trying to contain the full-of-running Ball that he could not take time off from his defensive duties.

As torrential showers soaked the players the game became a stalemate, with neither side able to break down each other's well-drilled defence.

It was Ball, showing nuclear energy, and the barking, aggressive Stiles – room-mates and both competitive beyond the call of duty – who started to give England the edge as they took control of the midfield engine room.

Referee Dienst had to reprimand Stiles after the Toothless Tiger had bounced the ball in protest at a disputed decision. In today's 21st-century game Nobby would have been a certainty for a yellow card, but the card system was not introduced until the 1970 World Cup at the instigation of Ken Aston (inspired to come up with the idea when sitting at traffic lights watching the amber going to red. Not a lot of people want to know that).

There were 76 minutes on the clock when Roger Hunt fed the ball through to Ball, whose low shot was pushed wide for a corner by the diving Tilkowski. It was the irrepressible Ball who raced to the corner flag with the ball and took an instant kick that flew to Geoff Hurst lurking on the edge of the penalty area. He tried to fire a shot through a forest of bodies and the ball ran loose into the path of Martin Peters, who studiously hammered (what other word to use?) the ball into the net from six yards.

> **MARTIN PETERS**: "It was the greatest moment of my career. The ball just sat up beautifully for me and I hit it with all the accuracy I could find in a crowded penalty area. For the next ten or so minutes I was thinking I had scored the goal that had won the World Cup for England. What a fairy tale. I had not even been near the team at the beginning of the year."

The Germans were down but not out. A free-kick awarded against Stiles was

Wolfgang Weber, on the ground left, starts to celebrate his last-gasp equaliser

aimed accurately above the English defenders by Emmerich, and Weber should have done more than head tamely past a post.

With five minutes to go Jimmy Armfield, following Ramsey's instructions, appeared in the players' tunnel leading the non-playing members of the squad from their seats in the stand. The countdown was on for England to be declared world champions when – into injury time of the 90 minutes – referee Dienst awarded the Germans a hugely debatable free-kick 20 yards from the heavily guarded England goal.

Siggi Held, a canny pro who had been born in Nazi-occupied Czechoslovakia in 1942,, exaggerated a coming together with Jack Charlton and stumbled forward as the England centre-half rose to head the ball clear. It's a trick known in the game as 'making a back.' Herr Dienst fell for it hook, line and stinker and ruled that it was a foul and a free-kick to West Germany.

Emmerich powered the ball through the English wall. As it ricocheted around the goalmouth as if on a pinball machine, the ball appeared to hit Schnellinger on the elbow before Weber at the far post was able to drive it home for a dramatic last- kick equaliser.

Bobby Moore and Gordon Banks led futile protests to the referee that Schnellinger had handled the ball, Jack Charlton carried on his moan that the free-kick should not have been awarded, and the majority of the Wembley crowd were in a state of shock.

The Germans were dancing like men on death row being given a sudden reprieve just as the switch on the electric chair was about to be pressed.

The as-ever alert Alan Ball ran into the goal, collected the ball and sprinted back to the centre-circle, urging his team-mates to follow him. England just had time to kick-off when the referee blew to signal extra-time. So near, yet so far.

To my left every German reporter was up on his feet cheering the Wolfgang Weber goal as if it had won the World Cup. Press box neutrality had been kicked into touch. This truly was The Great Escape. Where was Steve McQueen and that motorbike?

To my right, Laurie Pignon of the *Daily Sketch* and still carrying the scars of having been a prisoner of war, almost bit through the stem of his ever-present pipe as he said aloud: "The bloody Krauts never know when they're beaten."

This was no time for political correctness.

At the front of the press box I saw Bernard Joy almost pulling his hair out in frustration. His *Evening Standard* report had to go to press with the score at 2-2, and his London readers would not know the result.

England's reserves emerged from the players' tunnel looking bemused and confused. They were sharing the pain and disappointment of their team-mates on the pitch, who had been literally seconds away from celebrating the winning of the World Cup.

Like the rest of us, they now had 30 extra minutes of punishment to come. Watching can be harder than playing.

> **JIMMY ARMFIELD:** "Most of the reserves didn't see the German goal. They were still in the lift on the way down to the tunnel when Weber banged it in. As far as they were concerned England were still leading 2-1. We felt so sorry for the lads, and we knew just how exhausted they must have been. It's a tough ask at the best of times, but for it to happen in a World Cup final!"

Let's be honest, if the game had finished with a 2-1 England victory and Weber had not snatched the last-kick equaliser, this would have gone down as one of the most ordinary, most uneventful and most unexciting of all the World Cup finals.

But the best was yet to come, and the game was about to be lifted into the unforgettable category.

The scene was set for the most dramatic extra-time period in World Cup history.

In the BBCtv commentary box, summariser Walley Barnes – former Arsenal and Wales skipper – looked down on to the Wembley pitch and made the knowing comment: "This will be the survival of the fittest. This Wembley surface is unforgiving and will test every players' endurance to the limit."

Walley knew better than anybody what he was talking about. In the 1952 FA Cup final he limped off the Wembley turf with a badly damaged knee after just 35 minutes, leaving Arsenal having to play with ten men against eventual winners Newcastle United.

Commentator Kennth Wolstenholme took a quick gulp from his glass of gin and tonic, grateful that Walley was allowing him the opportunity to rest his voice before the challenge of extra-time.

> **KENNETH WOLSTENHOLME:** "Obviously it was exhausting for the players, but spare a moment's sympathy for the commentators. It was a match played at break-neck speed and you had to be alert for the full 90 minutes. Little did we expect that there was much greater drama and excitement to come."

Next door in the ITV commentary booth, Hugh Johns was taking a breather while Dave Bowen – like Walley Barnes a former Arsenal and Wales skipper – gave his expert summary.

> **HUGH JOHNS:** "When it was all over I remember being as limp as a wet rag. I had no words left. I was a wreck. The rest of our commentary team went out celebrating, but I quickly went back to the Hendon Hall hotel where I was staying, had three quick gins and got myself off to bed. I was completely wiped out."

My good pal Brian Moore was at the BBC Light Programme microphone, and mimed wiping his brow to me as we waved to each other at the end of the exacting 90 minutes.

> **BRIAN MOORE:** "I'd kept it secret that I had been negotiating to join the BBC television team, but talks had broken down before the World Cup kicked off. I could have been sitting in Ken Wolstenholme's seat and then there would not have been his famous last line. All commentators would have given the crown jewels for that. A stroke of ad-libbed genius."

Let extra-time commence ... it's nearly all over ...

4
EXTRA
TIME
DRAMA

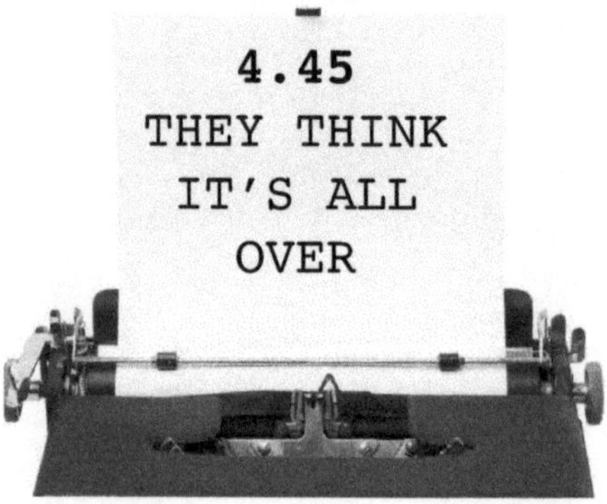

4.45 THEY THINK IT'S ALL OVER

Cometh the hour, cometh The Man. ... and that man was the stoical Alf Ramsey. As the referee blew his whistle at the end of the 90 breathtaking minutes, he came striding on to the pitch full of purpose and positivity. His players were still in a state of distress and disbelief after the late-late equaliser by Wolfgang Weber, and with their socks down to their boots and sodden by the rain they looked a tired, beaten bunch.

But Alf had no thoughts of surrender in mind. As his players started to sink to the ground he ordered them to their feet, and then pointed towards the West Germans, who were looking even more exhausted and out of gas.

"Look at that lot," he said. "They have nothing left. You've beaten them once. Now go and do it again."

> **BOBBY CHARLTON**: "It was a short, sharp speech. But it was just the motivational words we needed to hear. Suddenly we realised that the Germans were out on their feet. They had given everything getting back into the game. That equalising goal was their victory. Now Alf had convinced us we could beat them. Again."

With the game about to restart, the England reserves either squatted down or grabbed the few seats left on the bench behind Alf, who – for superstitious reasons – remained squashed between team doctor Alan Bass and trainer Harold Shepherdson, with trainer assistant Les Cocker two away to his right. This is the bench formation they had followed throughout the World Cup finals.

Buoyed by Ramsey's words, England got off to a quick start to the first extra-time period. The tired Germans fell back into desperate defence under an avalanche of attacks in which Alan Ball was always prominent as he gave his impersonation of Superman.

If you ever get the chance, watch the full unedited version of the match and monitor Ballie's input. It was nothing short of astonishing. The little red-headed terrier covered the pitch like a fire engine on emergency call. Truly, a Ball of fire.

The Geoff Hurst goal that triggered a 50-year argument. In or out? Roger Hunt starts to celebrate. Over to "The Russian Linesman."

I know I have gone off into the world of hyperbole but this is what Alan's performance did to reporters, making them reach for superlatives to try to capture his contribution to a never-to-be-forgotten game.

Five minutes into extra-time Bobby Charlton escaped the suffocating attentions of Beckenbauer and unleashed a shot that struck a post, and then he produced another shot that whistled just wide.

Then Ballie, speeding past Schnellinger for the umpteenth time, found Geoff Hurst with a cross from the right 11 minutes into extra-time. The West Hammer, his back to the goal, swivelled and with his right foot shot all in the same movement. The ball flashed above Tilkowski and thundered against the underside of the bar.

What happened next turned it into the most hotly debated moment in World Cup history. Depending on whether you had English or German eyes, the ball came down off the bar, on to or just behind the goal-line and spun out. Roger Hunt, following up, instantly raised an arm to celebrate a goal as Weber hurriedly kicked the ball behind the goal for what he expected to be a corner.

On the goal-line or behind it?

In the press box, many yards away from the incident, English journalists screamed 'goal' along with the majority of the Wembley crowd. It was as much in hope as expectancy. The German media men were equally insistent that the ball had not crossed the line. Truth is none of us could be sure.

Referee Gottfried Dienst at first appeared to signal no goal, but then decided to consult "the Russian linesman" Tofik Bakhramov.

With three quick, vigorous nods of his head and a wave of his flag towards the centre-circle, he signalled that it WAS a goal to trigger an argument that has lasted for 50 years, and to which there can never be a satisfactory answer.

Early in 2016 SkySports, using state-of-the-art camera techniques, declared that it was definitely a goal and that the whole of the ball had crossed the line, conveniently forgetting to mention that just a few months earlier a team of specialist engineers at Oxford University – also using "state-of-the-art" measuring devices – had declared that the ball had NOT crossed the line. At the last count, German television had investigated the incident at least twenty times and had always come to the conclusion that the ball had hit the line and come out.

According to the Laws of the Game the definition of a goal is when "the *whole* of the ball passes over the goal line".

How linesman Bakhramov managed to see it clearly enough to give a goal remains a mystery. His angle from level with the 18-yard line seems all wrong on television and film replays, and he was surrounded by German players screaming protests at him. Wearing a distinctive white belt, he looked like a St John's Ambulance man, and it was the German players in need of a stretcher.

It all got nasty to the point where he was accused of getting revenge for wartime atrocities, and it was claimed that – asked on his death bed why he gave the goal – he replied: "Stalingrad." It's apocryphal, of course. Stalingrad was one of the most bitter battles of the war, but Bakhramov, who fought with the Red Army on the Eastern Front, was nowhere near it.

Geoff Hurst has reached the stage where he is reluctant to go out socially because he knows at some stage a complete stranger will come up to him and ask – for the millionth time – "Was the ball over the line?"

> **GEOFF HURST**: "I now have the stock answer of saying, 'What was the score before the ball hit the bar? 2-2. And afterwards 3-2. So it must have been a goal.' I could not see because Tilkowski was in the way. Roger Hunt had the best view and he immediately raised his arm and turned round celebrating. It definitely was a goal. Just look in the record books. At least it has given people something to talk about for fifty years."

Credit the Germans for swallowing their disappointment and dragging their weary limbs back into the contest in a bid to come from behind again. They had to gamble everything on snatching an equaliser, and this meant pushing everybody

Geoff Hurst completes his historic World Cup final hat-trick

up into the England half during the second draining period of extra-time. Could they come up with a repeat of the Wolfgang Weber goal that had dragged them into this extra-time period? An equaliser would have meant everybody coming back to Wembley the next Tuesday for a replay. Penalty shoot-outs had not been created.

There was a last-minute German raid on the heavily defended England net, but they lost possession and the ball broke loose to the imperious Bobby Moore eight yards from his own goal.

He calmly exchanged passes with Roger Hunt while behind him Jack Charlton was screaming: "Get rid of the f***ing thing. Put it in the stands."

Bobby, blessed with ice in his veins, strode forward with the ball at his feet as if in an exhibition match, looked up and saw his club-mate Geoff Hurst motoring into the German half ahead of the pursuing Wolfang Overath. He stroked the ball with his right foot and it arrowed 30 yards into the path of the galloping Hurst.

Alan Ball – who else? – was running parallel with Hurst and demanding a pass in his high-pitched Clitheroe Kid voice. But Geoff had tunnel vision and at the end of that tunnel was the German net.

BBCtv's Kenneth Wolstenholme was keeping pace with Hurst with his commentary as half a dozen spectators started to run past stewards on to the pitch, thinking the referee had blown the final whistle:

> *"And here comes Hurst. He's got... some people are on the pitch, they think it's all over. (Hurst lets fly with a ferocious left foot shot from 15 yards that whooshes past Tilkowski) It is now! It's four!"*

Geoff had completed the perfect hat-trick. Head, right foot, and now left foot. And the first (and still only) treble in a World Cup final!

Moore-Hurst-Peters entered footballing folklore for club and country

JACK CHARLTON: "That Bobby Moore! He put years on me. I was shouting for him to belt the ball away. But what does he go and do? Plays it as if in a training match. As long as I play this great game I'll never be able to be as cool and as controlled as that. I'd have had the ball in Row Z. That pass he made to Geoff was as good as you'll ever see, particularly when you consider the circumstances. Mooro is like our kid. Class. Sheer class."

ALAN BALL: "I was screaming for Geoff to pass the ball to me. I was unmarked and had a clear run to goal. As I recall, I even called him a greedy b*****d. But he just kept running and then hit the sort of shot that no goalkeeper on earth could have saved. I then stopped moaning at him. It was the best way to put me in my place."

GEOFF HURST: "I've always said I hit the ball as hard as I could so that if it missed the target it'd fly so far beyond the goal that by the time they got the ball back the final whistle would have blown. In truth, I knew exactly where the ball was going. It was the perfect end to a perfect World Cup for me. Like everybody in the squad, I really felt for Jimmy Greaves, a far better footballer than I'll ever be. But I was grateful to get a chance to play and was determined to make the most of my opportunity. To have my mates Bobby and Martin in the team was the icing on the cake. It was like a dream and, as George Cohen kept saying, pinch me. It really was true. I'd scored three goals in a World Cup final!"

Startling stats note: England had 40 attempts on goal, West Germany 37; 21 on target. Each of the four goals that found the net (or the goal-line) had manufactured-in-West-Ham stamped on them, and watching with a beam of pride and satisfaction was Hammers manager Ron Greenwood. One of the game's great thinkers, he was on the Fifa World Cup technical committee, and he had educated all his players to play football more with brains than brawn. "I owe Ron so much," said Hurst. "It was he who had the vision to see me as a striker rather than, let's be honest, a pretty pedestrian midfield player."

Another happy man was soon-to-be Foreign Secretary George Brown, a West Ham devotee who sat within shouting distance of Harold Wilson. The Prime Minister, a Huddersfield supporter, later reported that he had to remind his Cabinet colleague that he was in the Royal Box and not on the terraces at Upton Park.

Wilson said as he went into the Wembley hospitality lounge: "George has just told me that West Ham have won the World Cup."

Moore-Hurst-and-Peters had played themselves into English football folklore.

As referee Dienst really did make it all over with a triple blast on his whistle there were two dozen cameos being played out before our eyes down on a soaked, cut-up pitch now bathed in evening summer sunshine.

Bobby Charlton, survivor of Munich, national treasure, was in a flood of tears as his Nemesis Franz Beckenbauer sportingly gave him a congratulatory hug. As happened right through the match, they were still locked together. It was the start of a close friendship that has gone on for the rest of their lives.

> **FRANZ BECKENBAUER**: "It was a pity that Bobby and I had to take each other out of the game. He is a wonderful player and a great sporting competitor, who is a perfect ambassador for football and his country. We are close friends, but I never let him forget that I know the ball did not cross the line for Geoff Hurst's crucial second goal. The linesman surely deserved a knighthood from the Queen."

Jackie Charlton fell to his knees, his hands clasped in front of his face in what looked silent prayer, and then got up and found his 'kid' brother. They hugged and then joined in an untidy but delirious team celebration.

> **JACK CHARLTON**: "As our kid and I fell into an exhausted cuddle, Bobby was crying and he had me blubbing too when he said, 'We've done it. Nobody can ever take this moment away from us. Our lives will never be the same. We're the best.' I have never felt such a mixture of total exhaustion and extreme elation. Those steps up to the Royal Box looked like Mount Everest."

Alan Ball was closest to Geoff Hurst when the referee blew the final whistle. He jumped into the hat-trick hero's arms, and then went scampering off to find his best mate Nobby Stiles, and the two buddies rolled around on the pitch like kids in the playground. Ball was a rival even to Geoff Hurst as the man of the match after

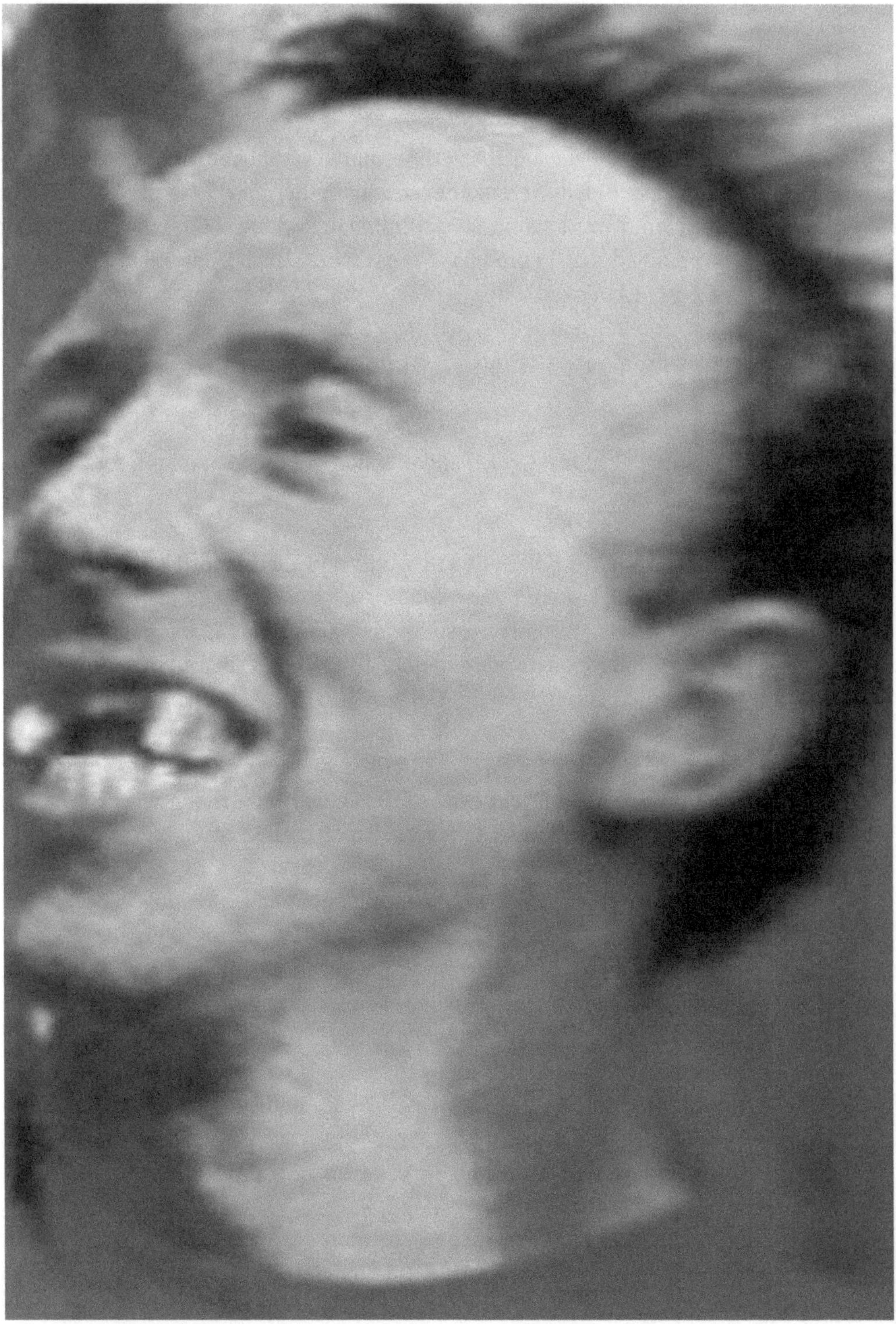

Nobby Stiles, the Toothless Tiger with a tackle like a clap of thunder

a staggering physical display that later brought the compliment from manager Alf Ramsey: "Young man, you will never play a better game of football in your life."

> **ALAN BALL**: "I don't think I could have run another step. I gave every ounce that I had, and then some more. I kept remembering what my Dad had said, that I would never get another chance to play in a World Cup final. It was a game in a million. He told me not to come off feeling disappointed that I could have done more. I was happy that I had done my best. I believed along with Alf that we were invincible. The only slight doubt I had was when they scored their late equaliser, but Alf picked us up for extra-time."

Gordon Banks came running off his goal-line, hugging every one of his England team-mates in turn. Then he stopped and scanned the crowd, looking for his wife, Ursula.

> **GORDON BANKS**: "All the wives and girlfriends were together up in the stand. I waved and blew kisses in the direction of Ursula and wondered what my inlaws would be making of it all back in their home in Germany. My wife gave me her full support, but a little of her must have wanted her home nation to win."

West Ham wives Tina Moore, Judith Hurst and Kathy Peters sat alongside each other, watching the ebb and flow of the match with mounting excitement, experiencing every high and low as their husbands battled down on the pitch.

> **TINA MOORE**: "I sat next to Judith Hurst and we clung to each other throughout the match, pinching each other's arms with the tension, hugging when Geoff kept putting the ball in the net and screaming with Kathy Peters when Martin scored. There were a lot of German supporters immediately behind us, and when Geoff's second goal hit the bar Judith and I stood shouting, 'It's in ... it's in.' The Germans came back with 'Oh no it isn't ... oh no it isn't.' It was like a Christmas pantomime! I was busting with pride that it was my Bobby who was leading the England team, and as with everything he ever did he was just immaculate."

The only person not taking part in the party on the pitch was the main orchestrator of England's triumph, Alf 'The General' Ramsey. It became a point of discussion that as the final whistle blew he did not get off his bench seat as the referee signalled it was all over. Even when the crowd started to yell 'Ramsey,

Ramsey, Ramsey' he did not acknowledge them, and sat staring almost blankly as the reserve players started slapping his back.

> **ALF RAMSEY**: "The only reason I didn't stand up at the end of the match is because Doc Bass and Jimmy Armfield were pinning me down, and shouting that we had done it. I was as excited as everybody else but could not move. Eventually I managed to stand up and as I made my way towards the pitch the players came walking off to go up to the Royal Box to collect the trophy. I had carried the pressure for months of saying that England would win the World Cup. Most people, particularly in the press, did not believe me, but I got the players to have faith in my conviction. Now my job was done. It is the players who deserve all the credit. I just showed the way it could be achieved."

As Bobby Moore led his troops towards the 39 steps that he knew so well Alf stood and greeted each player before they started the climb. He shook their hands in turn, almost formally, first skipper Bobby Moore, then hat-trick hero Geoff Hurst, a weeping Bobby Charlton, an exhausted-looking Roger Hunt, the still elegant Martin Peters, big Jack Charlton who stumbled on the steps, Ray Wilson now forgiven for his early mistake, Mr Perpetual Motion Alan Ball, good old reliable George Cohen, Toothless Tiger Nobby Stiles, and bringing up the rear the man now acknowledged as equal to Lev Yashin as the world's No 1 goalkeeper, Gordon Banks.

Only Bobby Moore would have had the innate awareness to realise that the Queen was wearing white gloves as he approached her to receive the trophy, and he carefully and deliberately wiped the palms of his muddy hands on the velvet cloth decorating the royal balcony.

The roar as he received the Jules Rimet World Cup was unequalled in my experience of attending many major events at Wembley, and the chants of 'ee-aye-adio we've won the cup' might have been heard back in Liverpool, birthplace of the chorus.

Then came unforgettable scenes deposited into the memory bank as the players took turns holding the Cup aloft while they made a carnival circuit of the pitch, accompanied by a score of photographers, Wembley security guards and uniformed police officers, who were making sure nobody nicked the Jules Rimet trophy again before it could be switched with the replica, secretly hidden away in the care of a police custodian.

Most memorable of all was seeing Nobby Stiles, red socks down to his ankles and his front teeth still missing, skipping like a drunken hobgoblin on tired legs as he gave his impression of a victory jig.

The final whistle, left to right, front: Les Cocker, Doc Bass, Alf Ramsey, Jimmy Armfield, Harold Shepherdson. Reserves in the background, Gerry Byrne, Ian Callaghan, Ron Flowers and a distant-looking Jimmy Greaves

> **NOBBY STILES**: "It was not until I saw the TV film and newspaper photographs later that I realised what a plonker I looked. But everybody seemed to enjoy the sight, except my wife Kay. She gave me a right telling off for not putting my teeth in before going up to get my medal from the Queen. In the excitement of it all I forgot about them, and it was much later before I could find Ian Callaghan among the crowd on the pitch. Cally, as always, had been looking after them wrapped in my lucky handkerchief."

Ballie grabbed hold of his mate and pointed to a large banner being waved in the crowd that read: "Nobby for Prime Minister." The huge toothless beam from Stiles showed that he approved and he gave a double thumbs up in the direction of the banner holder.

What a turnaround from the third match against France when Fifa officials were trying to get him banned from the tournament because of the ferocity of his tackling. "I'll never forget that Alf backed me all the way," said Stiles.

What we did not know at the time is that Alf threatened to walk out on his job rather than give in to demands to drop Stiles, the main protests coming from FA executives who claimed he was a disgrace to the England shirt.

Nobby had the last toothless laugh.

5

AFTER THE BALL WAS OVER

5.30pm THE ANGUISH OF JIMMY GREAVES

It was impossible not to focus on the lonely figure of Jimmy Greaves as he wandered among the celebrating players, giving genuinely warm hugs to his squad-mates yet managing to look like a man who'd wandered into a party to which he was not invited. Jimmy and I were later to write twenty books together, so you could say I knew him reasonably well. I could read him like – uh, well – a book. He did a good job hiding his disappointment at not playing, but deep down he had a dull ache and the feeling that he'd rather be any place in the world apart from Wembley.

He had already plotted his escape and at the first opportunity he would be off and away on a Caribbean holiday with his wife, Irene, brother-in-law Tom Barden and his wife. His bags had already been packed and smuggled to Tom, and it was just a question of time before he would disappear from sight, refusing all interviews and smiling uncomfortably as team-mates tried to make the right noises.

What do you say to a man who has had his dreams crushed? Ask any one of the footballers who were around in the 1960s to name their top striker, and very few would not have had Jimmy's name immediately on their tongue. There were four genuine world-class England players in the game at the time: Gordon Banks, Bobby Moore, Bobby Charlton and Greavsie. I told Jimmy before his recent violent stroke that I was writing this book.

> **JIMMY GREAVES:** "Leave me out of it. It's all history. Everything about that day is a blur, so I can't give any worthwhile memories. Just write that I was delighted for the team and that they were all my good mates and deserved to win the Cup. I wanted to be part of it but fate – and Alf – decided otherwise. Just one thing I will admit – if I hadn't been struck down by severe hepatitis in the autumn of 1965 things might have been different. But then, if my aunt had balls she'd be my uncle."

England had won the World Cup without their greatest scorer. And it was his replacement Geoff Hurst who scored the historic hat-trick that had knighthood written all over it. Yes, a funny old game.

Jimmy Greaves, masking his true feelings, congratulates Alan Ball

The beaten and bitter Germans made as swift an exit from the Wembley pitch as possible after collecting their runners-up medals and acknowledging the support of their fanatical followers. It was generally accepted by most neutrals that the better team on the day had won, but the Germans would forever claim they had been cheated by the goal they insist should not have been awarded.

Fifa and the German FA had to warn 'Russian' linesman Tofik Bakhramov not to show his face anywhere near Germany after flagging that Geoff Hurst's second goal had crossed the line. He had made himself millions of enemies in Deutschland. Any dubious goal in Germany is still referred to as a 'Wembley Tor', Wembley Goal.

> **HELMUT SCHOEN**: "If we could play the game over again I would not be so restrictive with Beckenbauer. He did a fine job curtailing Bobby Charlton's influence, but it also meant he could not impose himself as an attacking force. You will never get any German observer of that match to agree that the ball crossed the line for England's crucial third goal. I will never understand how the linesman could be so certain when nobody else in the world could be sure. That goal took the wind out of us after we had done so well to come back after we had gone 2-1 down."

While Geoff Hurst was celebrating his hat-trick, Helmut Haller quietly and craftily made off with the match ball. The tradition had not then started of a player automatically keeping the ball after scoring three or more goals, but it was widely agreed that if anybody deserved it that man was Hurst.

Fast forward thirty years and Geoff was reunited with the ball when the *Daily Mirror* won a bidding war with *The Sun* to get Haller to return it. Their cheekily clever front page headline read:

"World exclusive. They think it's all over ... it's his now.
The Daily Mirror *gets Geoff his ball back"*

The ball now resides in the National Football Museum in Manchester.

5.50pm
IN AND OUT OF THE DRESSING-ROOM

I watched all the on-field celebrations from up in the press box, where the cream of the world's sportswriters were sending their reports over the telephone and telex lines to millions of readers across the globe. The thunderous clackety-clack of their typewriters was a symphony to a World Cup final that would not be remembered as a classic, yet never forgotten for its drama.

While they were concentrating on telling their stories of an extraordinary match I put my plan into operation. I was determined to try to get into the England dressing-room.

It was considered mission impossible.

Security at Wembley had never been tighter. The fracas following the quarter-final against Argentina and death threats made by South American fanatics plus the globally-reported robbery of the World Cup had prompted a doubling up of police and stewards to keep everybody – including the media, especially the media – away from the dressing-rooms.

Shrewdly, I tied myself to Wembley public relations officer Len Went, who talked and walked me past all the jobsworth stewards. I got to the door of the England dressing-room just as Bobby arrived carrying the gleaming, real Jules Rimet trophy. In a repeat of our meeting and greeting at Hendon Hall that morning, we hugged each other and I got to touch the World Cup.

All the England players were in a state of exhaustion as they pushed their way down the tunnel, yet Bobby looked immaculate without a bead of sweat showing.

I followed the proud skipper into the cavernous dressing-room and was just about to hug a hugely grinning George Cohen when Alf Ramsey came in, having reluctantly given after-match interviews when he became irritated because so much emphasis was put on the disputed goal. No choreographed conferences like today.

I was quickly x-rayed out by Alf's famous and feared baleful stare. He did not have to say a word. I was not welcome and neither were any of the photographers trying to battle their way through the wall of security.

There was a row at the doorway when the cameraman filming the official Fifa

"Look what we've won, Alf ... the World Cup!" Ramsey didn't want to come on to the pitch. "This moment belongs to the players," said the shy hero.

Goal film was refused permission to enter, but he finally managed to convince the stewards that he had the blessing of the big chief, Sir Stanley Rous. If you get a chance to see the excellent *Goal* film you will notice that there are just very brief shots of champagne being drunk and a fleeting glimpse of the England players laughing and shouting in the large communal bath.

The champagne the players were sharing was from a case of Heidsieck produced specifically for the team. Eleven bottles were supped and Alf gave the remaining one to dressing-room assistant Jim Green, who had the good sense to get all the players to sign the label. It sold at auction for £2,000 thirty-six years later.

The last England player back to the dressing-room was Jack Charlton, turning the air blue with his language as he fumed over being drug tested for the fourth time during the tournament. But his mood softened when the chief of the testing team later presented him with a baby's potty that had a label stuck to it that read: "Presented to Jack Charlton, who gave his best for his country."

"They've been taking the piss out of me right through the finals," said Jack, leading the laughter at his joke.

The drug tests had been carried out randomly, and Big Jack's name kept coming out of the hat. He was always declared clean.

Forty-five years later, in 2011, it was revealed that three players in West Germany's team in the dramatic 1966 World Cup final failed drug tests after the game, and it was covered up to save Fifa from a scandal. (After the 1954 final won by the Germans, the beaten Hungarians alleged they'd used high-energy drugs).

Historians found a letter from Fifa revealing the 1966 test failures while sorting through documents at Berlin's Humboldt University. The letter, which was dated November 29 1966, was written by Fifa's Mihailo Andrejevic and sent to Max Danz, the president of the West German Athletics Federation.

In the correspondence, the Fifa medical chief drew attention to the use of the banned substance ephedrine by three unnamed German players, which he conceded could have been contained in a cold remedy.

That's what they all say.

> **GEORGE COHEN:** "All of us in the England squad are astounded. We always wondered where they got their energy from in extra-time! Maybe this news will stop the Germans questioning whether our third goal crossed the line. This is a much bigger scandal. Just imagine if the result had been affected by whatever it was the Germans were taking. What would Fifa have done if Germany had won? It's extraordinary that this has been covered up for so long."

Fifa in a corruption scandal? I don't believe it!

6.15pm
THE BONUS AND LATE TEAM PHOTO

Trainers Harold Shepherdson, Les Cocker and Wilf McGuinness, on the instructions of Ramsey, started to usher out all dressing-room visitors. Left inside and forming a semi-circle around the England manager were the 22 players who had been together as a tight-knit squad since the start of the European warm-up tour eight weeks earlier. They were now showered, bathed and dressed, and eager to get to their families and loved ones.

George Cohen had his team-mates falling around laughing as he kept saying: "Will somebody pinch me? Am I dreaming? Have we just won the World Cup? Shouldn't I feel different to this? I feel just the same. We are the world champions. Champions of the world. Pinch me someone."

Meantime, a suited and booted Geoff Hurst quietly nipped out and walked alone back to the pitch and looked up at the large Stadium scoreboard. It read England 4, West Germany 2. "I just wanted to make sure my third goal had counted," Geoff confided. "In the hullabaloo I was not sure if the ref had blown the final whistle before I shot. It's all like a dream."

I later learned that behind closed doors Alf raised a glass to his players and said: "Gentlemen, mission accomplished. I want to thank each and every one of you for your efforts. You did England and yourselves proud. I know you now all want to go to your wives and families but we have an official banquet to attend. After that you will be free to go your own way, but remember we have two diary engagements tomorrow, first to a cinema to see your great performance and then a lunch at ITV that I wish we didn't have to attend, but it was agreed months ago and they are paying a fee into a football charity. Then we can all go our separate ways with the satisfaction of knowing that we have won the World Cup for England. We're now heading back to the Hendon Hall Hotel, dress code our official England suits. Let's look the part when we arrive at the Royal Garden Hotel for the banquet. World Champions."

Alf then applauded his players who in turn applauded him.

"One more thing, gentlemen," he added, "I have been instructed by the FA to tell you that there is a £22,000 bonus, that they suggest should be shared among

Four months after the triumph at Wembley, the official team photograph, back row: Harold Shepherdson, Nobby Stiles, Roger Hunt, Gordon Banks, Jack Charlton, George Cohen, Ray Wilson, Alf Ramsey. Front: Martin Peters, Geoff Hurst, skipper Bobby Moore, Alan Ball, Bobby Charlton.

you on a sliding scale according to appearances."

Straight away skipper Bobby Moore spoke up for the players and kicked that idea high into touch. "I know I'm speaking for all the lads, Alf," he said, "when I say we want the money to be split equally between all twenty-two of us. We've been in this together from day one and will stay in it together."

Months later the players learned their £1,000 bonus was being taxed. Bobby, on behalf of all the squad, took the Taxman to court and won. They would each receive an uncut thousand pounds, a third of what the German runners-up earned. What a way to treat our heroes.

The bonus was on top of the £60 match appearance fees. So the eight ever-presents in the six games – Banks, Cohen, Wilson, Stiles, Jack Charlton, Moore, Roger Hunt and Bobby Charlton – picked up £1,360 each. Alf was paid £5,000, taxed.

In the excitement of it all, it was suddenly remembered there were no team photos. All the hundreds of pictures taken out on the pitch were of wild celebration, and there was no official, formal photograph for posterity. It was not until the following November, on the eve of an international match against Czechoslovakia at Wembley, that the team photograph that you see on hundreds of walls was taken at the Roehampton training ground. And they allowed the REAL Jules Rimet trophy out of the safe for the occasion. Not a lot of people know that.

7.15pm
JUST LIKE VE-DAY FOR THE FANS

It was only when I got out on to the North Circular Road and headed for the Royal Garden Hotel in Kensington via Hendon Hall that I realised what impact the World Cup victory had made. Way beyond Wembley, there was patriotic fervour and fever unequalled since VE-Day, with Union Jack flags and bunting the whole way and virtually every car driver honking their horns to a da-da da-di-da da-di-da-da da-da beat, imitating the rhythmic chants that had filled Wembley throughout the match.

I did my best to follow the England coach but quickly got trapped in the convoy of cars trying to keep up with the team as the players waved almost in wonder at the thousands of people lining the route, instinctively drawn there to be part of the great celebration.

I decided to drive on past Hendon Hall where the players stopped to change into their smart, charcoal-grey Hardy Amies-designed, Burton-tailored suits with a red English rose in the lapel, and I managed to get to the Royal Garden Hotel Fifa headquarters just as the team coach, with faithful Sid Brown at the wheel, arrived for the banquet.

There was an arms-linked cordon of police doing their best to keep a crowd of at least 7,000 on the opposite side of the road, but as the coach pulled up they broke through and mobbed the players as they stepped down on to the hotel forecourt, looking happily bewildered and bemused by the mass hysteria.

"I'm over the world!" shouted Captain Moore. He was determined to avoid the footballer's cliché of 'Over the moon.'

Cries of "England", "Ramsey", "Moore", "Stiles", "Hurst", "Charlton" greeted each one as they were recognised. Alf steered the players into the foyer like a concerned shepherd herding his sheep.

Reports reached us in the hotel that traffic in the West End was at a complete standstill. Thousands of cars and pedestrians battled for space around Leicester Square, Piccadilly Circus and, of course, Trafalgar Square, where hundreds had gathered, many of them dancing in the fountains, drunk with delirium.

An AA spokesman reported: "It's like VE Day, election night and New

Strictly come dancing in the Trafalgar Square fountains

Year's Eve all rolled into one." The theatres and cinemas were empty, the pubs full to bursting. In the famous Windmill Theatre the nude models performed an impromptu 'dance of the seven Union Jacks.'

As the players pushed their way into the comparative peace of the hotel they were ushered into a side room, where they were reunited with their wives and girlfriends. Quite a few of the players got earache from wives complaining about their treatment. They had been shunted off to see the Black and White Minstrel Show at Victoria Palace the night before (imagine that today!), and were now going to be sent upstairs to a burger house for a meal while the players were downstairs at the official banquet. The wives were quick to spot that Pickles the dog got in, while they were barred.

> **ALAN BALL:** "I hadn't seen my wonderful childhood sweetheart Lesley for eight weeks, and now they were keeping us apart while we listened to a load of boring old farts. Not to sit our wives and girlfriends with us was a heartless decision. It added a touch of bitterness to the greatest day of our lives."

The players had to sit through speeches by the Earl of Harewood, Sir Stanley Rous, and a string of overseas officials. Adding to the formality was the presence of Prime Minister Harold Wilson and his Cabinet colleagues George Brown, Jim Callaghan and Minister for Sport Denis Howell.

A cake shaped and decorated like a football pitch was presented to the England team by the Earl of Harewood, who said to Alf: "After you've cut it would you mind going out to the enormous crowd outside. To lend you a little moral support the Prime Minister is prepared to take you there." As if the beleaguered PM would miss this dream photo opportunity.

The naturally reserved Ramsey was reticent, but Mr Wilson took his arm and pulled him towards the balcony. "It's only once in a lifetime you know," the PM said. Fifty pot-less years on, we know what he meant!

There was a huge roar from the crowd as Alf led the players out, each in turn holding up the (replica) World Cup. Inside the banqueting hall, the players of West Germany, Portugal and Russia were looking bored stiff.

They escaped once Eusebio had collected his tournament top-scorer award, and all stood in genuine appreciation of Bobby Moore when he was named the 'Player of Players' by the overseas press. Following the banquet, with an empty Jimmy Greaves seat, Alf – knowing my closeness to Greavsie – asked: "Is Jimmy okay?"

"You know, Jim," I replied. "He just doesn't want any fuss, so he's nipped away." Alf was a relieved man. His gamble of leaving out England's greatest goal scorer had come off. If the Germans had won, he knew he would have been crucified.

11.15pm
DANCING AND DRINKING THE NIGHT AWAY

Free at last from the stiff formalities, the players, their wives and partners found contrasting ways to enjoy what was left of the night. Just like they had forgotten to plan a team photograph, the FA did not have anything booked for celebrations and it was left to our heroes to find their own entertainment.

Jack Charlton, his wife Pat at home waiting to give birth, set the tone. He scrawled on a sheet of hotel notepaper: "If found, please return this body to Room 308 Royal Garden Hotel," and slipped it into the top pocket of his Hardy Amies suit.

He then grabbed his long-time friend James Mossop, exceptional *Sunday Express* sportswriter, and told him: "Jimmy, we're going out on the town."

James said: "But I've only got a tenner."

"Don't worry," said Jack, "I've got enough to keep us in drink for a month." He took a wad of £5 notes from his pocket – £100 in all – that had been paid to him for wearing a branded pair of boots.

They swam in champagne in the swish Astor Club in Mayfair, with well-heeled people fighting to buy them drinks, and not a penny of the £100 was needed. Eight hours later they woke up side by side on a sofa in the lounge of a terraced house in Walthamstow, East London, neither of them knowing how they got there. Apparently it had been a good party.

Jack walked out into the back garden to get some air and a middle-aged woman called over the neighbouring fence in a thick Geordie accent: "Aren't you young Jackie Charlton? I used to live in the same street as you in Ashington. How's your mam?"

Not surprisingly, Jack wondered if he was dreaming it all.

Hat-trick hero Geoff Hurst felt that everything was falling flat and decided they all – particularly the wives and girlfriends – deserved a good night out. He telephoned Danny La Rue's West End nightclub at Hanover Square, explained who he was and after convincing them he really was 'the' Geoff Hurst he was promised a VIP table.

Headline star at the cabaret that night along with Danny La Rue was Ronnie Corbett, a Scottish football fanatic.

Bobby and Tina Moore toast Eusebio at the Royal Garden Hotel, where the African-born Black Panther of Portugal picked up a cheque for £1,000 as the leading marksman at the 1966 World Cup finals with nine goals in total.

> **GEOFF HURST:** "I suddenly found what fame was all about. In the past I had always said I was a friend of Bobby Moore when I was booking a table for a restaurant. Now they were asking me if I was the *real* Geoff Hurst. I invited Nobby Stiles, Alan Ball, Martin Peters, John Connelly and their ladies to join Judith and me. Only Martin said no, and he and his wife Kathy went to their room on their own with a bottle of champagne. They didn't open it and settled for a cup of tea. But I thought a good night out was the least we could do for our wives. We'd been away for eight weeks and had virtually ignored them. Everybody at Danny La Rue's stood and applauded as we came in. It was a night to remember for all of us. For me, it was a day I would never forget."

Ronnie Corbett, who once had a trial as a winger for Hearts, remembered the night well when we talked about it before his passing in 2016:

> **RONNIE CORBETT:** "I thought it was a leg-pull when I was told Geoff and his England team-mates would be in our audience. I'd watched the match in the afternoon and thought it one of the most dramatic games I'd ever seen. When they arrived we made sure they had the best table in the house and everybody stood and roared. We played When the Saints. There was Danny, an Irishman, and me, a Scot, weeping with joy for these wonderful footballers. Danny, one of the best ad-libbers in the business, kept dropping references to the England team into his songs. It was a riot. I always remember Alan Ball introducing his lady to me as 'the future Mrs Alan Ball, wife of a World Cup winner.' I thought that was lovely. Geoff Hurst was the one the audience demanded stand up and take a bow. Three goals in a World Cup final. Nobody in history has been able to match that. Not bad for an English footballer!"

It was chaos back at the Royal Garden Hotel as everybody tried to escape the boredom of the banquet at the same time. Footballers throughout the ages have been notorious for not wanting to sit through boring speeches by long-winded officials seeking to hog the limelight.

Bobby and Norma Charlton, accepting an invitation from Bobby Moore to join his party at the Playboy Club in Park Lane, were caught in a crush of people pushing into the main hotel lift, and suddenly the alarm bells started ringing.

"The lift was overcrowded and got stuck," Bobby reported later. "My wife Norma hates being in claustrophobic crowds at the best of times and this was a nightmare for her. The doors were stuck and we manually had to prise them open. It was pretty scary for a while, and certainly not what I'd planned for my long-awaited reunion night with Norma. Eventually we managed to get out and catch up with Bobby's party and we had a memorable night."

Skipper Mooro and his wife Tina led a small group including not only the Charltons but also Ray Wilson, George Eastham and their wives at the Playboy Club, where American composer Burt Bacharach was a guest and played the piano for the World Cup winners.

As much as I wanted to enjoy the West End night life, I stayed behind in the Royal Garden Hotel in the hope of getting an interview with man-of-the-moment Alf Ramsey. No chance. He had been given a brutal time by many journalists, and was savaged across the world for his "animals" outburst after the quarter-final war with Argentina. He was in no mood to forgive and forget.

Laurie Pignon, larger than life columnist with the *Daily Sketch* and with the sort of cut-glass English accent Alf clearly pined for, held out his hand as Ramsey left the banquet hall and said: "Alfred, I just wanted to say on behalf of myself and all my Fleet Street colleagues, thank you for all your co-operation during the World Cup."

Alf gave him that cold-eyed stare of his and replied: "Are you taking the piss?" He then disappeared into the night with his charming, always-protective wife, Victoria.

Thanks to the influence of gallivanting manager Malcolm Allison, I had a press pass membership for the Playboy Club and got there just in time to see a well-oiled Mooro and Ray Wilson – completely out of character – joining in the singing and dancing on stage. Ray stole the show with his Al Jolson impersonations.

I got a boozy after-midnight hug from Bobby, which was how we had started the historic July 30 day at Hendon Hall.

It was nine hours later that morning when Alf led his hungover players and the yet-to-be-called WAGs to Wardour Street to watch an edited colour film of the final at the Pathé headquarters. Then, many of them in grumpy mood, they went to ATV's Borehamwood studios in Hertfordshire for a televised lunch hosted by Eamonn Andrews. It fell as flat as a Gordon Banks cap.

Top Fleet Street football writers Brian James (*Daily Mail*), Clive Toye (*Daily Express*), Ken Jones (*Daily Mirror*) and Peter Lorenzo (*The Sun*) had been Ramsey's staunchest supporters throughout the World Cup campaign, and they waited patiently for an interview while Alf ate his lunch.

As he came out of the studios he nodded curtly when they chorused their congratulations. "Can you give us your considered thoughts on the final, Alf?" asked Brian James.

Alf looked at the four scribes, wrinkled his beetled brow and said: "Gentlemen, you know full well this is my day off. I never ever give interviews on a Sunday."

And he walked off, leaving them wordless.

6
ALF RAMSEY'S ENEMIES WITHIN

1974
THE TRUTH ABOUT THE SILENCES

WE travel forward eight years for the truth from Alf Ramsey – by then, of course, Sir Alf – as to why he was so moody and uncooperative on the greatest day of his footballing life. But first of all allow me to indulge myself with an anecdote that will explain how I got the exclusive facts from the man himself.

When I tunnelled my way out of the *Daily Express* in January 1974 I teamed up with broadcaster Peter Lorenzo in a sports PR agency, and to keep my reporting hand in wrote a weekly match report for the *Sunday Mirror*. And it was the *Sunday Mirror* that was involved in the greatest scoop I never had.

By this time I had been chief football reporter at the *Express* for eight years, and had chiselled away through Alf's tough exterior to become as close as you could get to a complex man. He was rumoured to be from Romany stock, but would never be drawn on it and would clam up if anybody asked him why his Spurs team-mates called him 'Darkie Ramsey,' in those pre-politically correct days a nickname for those of 'gypsy' heritage.

His Cockney-as-they-come best mate at Spurs, England schemer Eddie Baily, told me: "Alf was one of the lads, and we used to go to the dogs together. Then one day I met him after he'd gone off to manage Ipswich and I said, 'Why are you talking with a plum in your mouth?' From then on, we hardly spoke. He was never the old Alf again."

There were snobs among the hierarchy at the Football Association who never fully accepted him, and they gave him a rabbit hutch of an office as they tried to belittle him and hold on to their power base. He got his own back by keeping them all distant from his players, and he disbanded the amateur selection committee that used to pick the England team before he took charge.

His enemies at the FA finally got the chance to get rid of him when Poland stopped England getting to the World Cup finals in West Germany. Peter Lorenzo and I were closer than most to Sir Alf, and when he got the sack in the spring of 1974, we placed him under lock and key.

First, we put out a smokescreen that he had gone off to Spain to consider his future, while all the time he was tending his beloved garden at his modest home in Valley Road, Ipswich.

Then Peter and I sat with him for hours, tape recording his memories of managing England and his running battle with the frugal FA, who rewarded his services with a paper-tissue handshake of £6,500. We assured Alf that we would get him four times that for newspaper serialisation of his story, this at a time when £25,000 could buy you a decent semi-detached house.

I burned the midnight oil to get Alf's searing revelations down into three parts, 4,000 words each chapter. Then I packaged it in those pre-computer days to look as professional as possible, and I talked Peter into letting the *Sunday Mirror* have first bite.

Their sports editor, a Cockney Max Wall lookalike by the name of Tony Smith, was all but dancing on his desk when we gave him a strictly confidential look at the bullet points. This was at a time when there was a huge circulation war going on in Fleet Street between the tabloids, and Peter and I knew we were offering him gold dust. Everybody had been hunting for Ramsey ever since the Football Association had axed him, and we had his story tied up.

Tony went "upstairs" and 10 minutes later came down with an opening bid of £20,000. We told him that we had promised Alf four times his redundancy payoff.

Tony went back "upstairs", and returned with a £25,000 offer, which we finally pushed up to £26,500, to include our own £1,500 fee.

Once we had agreed the deal with Smithy, we let him read the full serialisation.

I sat facing him as he went through it with an excitement that could be measured on the Richter scale. At the end of every page he said, "This is f***in' brilliant, Norm … f***in' brilliant …"

As he reached the end of part two, he called in his loyal No 2, Dave Ellis, and said: "Get a smudger down here to take a picture of Norm. We're going to put his mush on the back page this Sunday. We'll knock spots off the opposition …"

The words were hardly out of his mouth when he was summoned back "upstairs".

Ten minutes later he came back ashen-faced and looking like a man who had been hit by a bus.

"The f***in' bastards have taken it away from us," he said quietly, struggling to get the words out. "They have got a push on for the *People* and they've got to take it."

The story was serialised by the *Mirror's* stablemate and run under the byline "Exclusive by Mike Langley". Mike, the man I replaced at the *Express*, was one of the finest football writers of his generation, but he had as much to do with that story as I had in helping Hillary conquer Everest.

And I never did get my picture on the back page of the *Sunday Mirror*.

Alf Ramsey gets shirty with George Cohen as he attempts a jersey swap with Argentine Alberto Gonzales. "We don't give our shirts to animals," said Alf.

This all brings me to why Alf was so reluctant to give interviews after the 1966 World Cup triumph. Here's what he told me in 1974:

> **SIR ALF RAMSEY:** 'I was hauled over the coals following my outburst after the quarter-final against Argentina. Some members of Fifa and our own FA wanted me disciplined and fined because I called the Argentines animals. I could have called them much worse, the way they behaved. They spat at me, tried to break into the dressing-room to start a fight and threw a chair through the window. It was appalling behaviour, and I was fuming when I was asked why I had stopped George Cohen swapping his shirt. I instinctively told the truth and said we would not give our shirts to animals.
>
> This became the story rather than the football match. All hell broke loose and the Foreign Office got involved, saying that back in Buenos Aires they were threatening to set fire to the British embassy. The previous week I had threatened to walk out when the FA tried to make me drop Nobby Stiles following a hard and poorly timed tackle against the French. I told them either Nobby plays in the quarter-final against Argentina or I walk and they could pick the team.
>
> They climbed down, but I vowed I would in future bite my tongue rather than give an interview that would allow my enemies at the FA the chance to stab me in the back. Many in the press crucified me and my tactics throughout the World Cup, and then they expected me to be as nice as pie to them after we had achieved what we had set out to do. I refused to be a hypocrite and so ignored them.'

1974
A MOUSE BRINGS THE HOUSE DOWN

Alf Ramsey was fiercely loyal to his players, and I have rarely come across any of his former footballers with a bad word to say about him. He had the gift of being able to talk their language, but the handicap of not being able to communicate with the media in an era when the likes of Desmond Hackett (*Daily Express*), Peter Wilson (*Daily Mirror*), J.L. Manning (*Daily Mail*) and Laurie Pignon (*Daily Sketch*) were brutal with their criticisms.

My business partners Peter Lorenzo, Malcolm Rowley and I organised a testimonial dinner for Sir Alf at London's Café Royal to try to make up for the fact that the Football Association had kicked him out with a derisory pay-off. We labelled the evening "British Trade and Industry Salutes Sir Alf," underlining how England's 1966 World Cup win did wonders for the home spirit when the Labour government was about to devalue the pound.

Every member of the 1966 playing squad was there, except Greavsie.

Prime Minister Harold Wilson, the main speaker, made the point that the triumph gave the country a morale boost when confidence was low.

I will never forget that during the course of the Prime Minister's speech a mouse ran the length of the top table. Its Speedy Gonzales sprint was cut off by Henry Cooper, who caught it in his hammer of a left fist. Henry handed it to the chef, who instantly stamped on it.

Mr Wilson had no idea this was all going on, and as the audience roared, he thought his speech was going down a bomb.

How do you follow that? Only master sportswriter Geoffrey Green could. One of the most entertaining after-dinner speakers in the land, the Man from *The Times* was next to pay tribute to Sir Alf. He announced that he would now play the mouse organ. I have often wondered if he released the mouse so that he could use that joke.

He turned to Sir Alf and said: "As you are now out of work, perhaps you would like to join me in a street busking team?"

Geoffrey then produced a harmonica and proceeded to play Moon River. I don't know who was the more bemused and amused, Sir Alf or the PM.

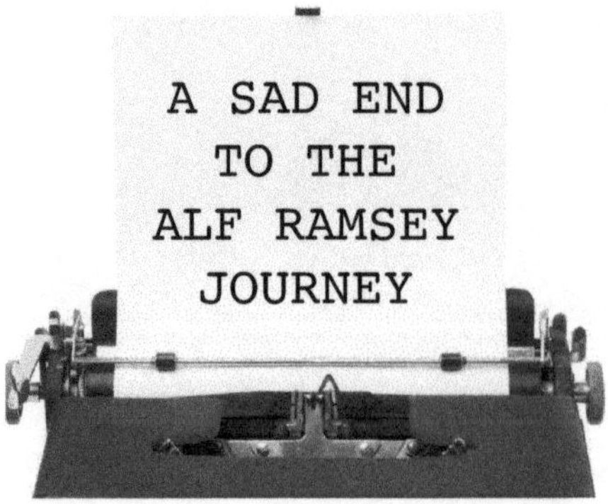

The last time I met Sir Alf Ramsey in the mid-90s he did not recognise me (I am easily forgotten), but the fact he could not place my companion either rang loud alarm bells about his health. It was Jimmy Greaves who was with me, and we came across Sir Alf relaxing in the lounge of the Suffolk golf club where he spent many hours of his retirement time.

For all the controversy over Ramsey leaving Greaves out of the 1966 World Cup final, they were not – as widely suggested – sworn enemies. In fact they quite liked each other, but Alf could never compete with Jimmy gently taking the mickey out of him and so he used to duck out of conversations that were not purely football based. Don't forget Greavsie had the sharpest tongue in the game, and could cut anybody down with his quick wit and raucous Cockney humour. It's a funny old game.

Nigel Clarke, well-connected football reporter on the *Daily Mirror*, was first to warn me that Alf was having memory problems. He ghosted a column Sir Alf "wrote" in the *Mirror*, and confided that he was having to make a lot of it up because Ramsey had lost his famous recall. I have never met anybody in the game who could match what was Alf's photographic memory of the style of play of just about any footballer he had ever seen. But by the mid-90s he could hardly recall a single member of his 1966 World Cup winning squad.

I had been discussing with Lady Victoria Ramsey, Alf's delightful but very defensive wife, the possibility of writing an honest, in-depth book on her husband's life and achievements. I knew if I could get her on my side, Alf would relax and allow me to pry deeper into his private life than he had ever allowed. My objective was to get him to admit pride in what he had achieved from his poverty-trap background, and rid him of the impression he gave of being ashamed and secretive about where he had come from.

Since being disgracefully removed from the England manager's job by jealous, feuding Football Association old farts, Alf had been largely ignored in the football world where he had established himself as one of the great tacticians. He had brief encounters with Birmingham City and Greek club Panathinaikos, but had lost his

Sir Alf Ramsey, 'The General' who won football's greatest battle

appetite for the cut and thrust of the game and became a virtual recluse in his small, unpretentious home in Ipswich.

It was only when Jimmy and I found him in a confused state at the golf club that we realised he was in the early stages of Alzheimer's, the footballer's curse that claims the lives of so many giants of the game.

I have campaigned with little success for Premier League clubs to set up a fund to help pre-2000 footballers in their old age. If the 20 Premier League clubs each put £5m into the kitty that would raise £100m to help veteran ex-footballers who are struggling in their senior years. Let's face it, £5m would not even buy a second-rate forward these days. Clubs could easily afford it out of the their golden television windfall.

It would then avoid the indignity ex-players like Jimmy Greaves have experienced, having to go cap in hand for help with their medical expenses when ill health strikes.

Alzheimer's is the biggest problem for our old heroes. Sir Alf joined a long queue of ex-managers and players struck down by the disease, including Arthur Rowe, Bob Paisley, Stan Cullis, Ron Greenwood, Dave Sexton, Billy Liddell, Danny Blanchflower, Dave Mackay, John Charles, Jeff Astle, Tony Hateley, Jimmy Hill and so many more. All of them passed on not knowing what they had achieved on the playing fields of England, and Alf's old World Cup rival Helmut Schoen also passed on lost in the fog of dementia.

Football must look after its own, and I hope the fate of these masters of the game inspire you to bring your voice to the call for the hierarchy to open their treasure chests and help the old players, most of whom missed the gravy train in which the modern footballers are swimming.

Sir Alf suffered a stroke on June 9 1998, during the World Cup finals in France, and he died less than a year later in an Ipswich nursing home on April 28 1999.

He passed on with no memories of his glorious achievements as a player, Ipswich Town miracle worker or World Cup-winning manager.

The cause of his death was a heart attack following on from the dual problems of Alzheimer's disease and prostate cancer. He was 79.

His deliberately low-key funeral was in Ipswich rather than a grand farewell in London, because it was well known that he had never forgiven the Football Association for their shabby treatment, and he did not want any of their bigwigs present. Alf was always proud never to be a hypocrite. If anybody deserved a Westminster Abbey send-off, it was Sir Alfred Ramsey, Master Football Manager.

Before he got lost in the maze of dementia, Sir Alf told me when looking back on his greatest triumph, the World Cup victory in 1966:

> ‘The most reckless thing I did was saying so early on that we would win the World Cup. It gave the media the chance to beat me around the head with the prediction at every opportunity. I had no doubt that we could win it, but nothing is ever certain in football. We were the fastest, fittest and the strongest side in the World Cup, but I do not think we will ever match the individual techniques of the Latin-Americans or the Latin-Europeans. We play a different kind of football, more physical and in a more positive way, but we do not have their instinctive skill on the ball. I was lucky to have three world-class players at the core of the team in goalkeeper Gordon Banks, the wonderfully skilled Bobby Charlton and, in Bobby Moore, a captain with the perfect temperament, who could carry my orders and see that they were followed on the pitch. My objective from day one was to build a team with a club spirit, and I achieved this by selecting players with the right personalities as well as the necessary skills. There were some very talented players who I preferred to ignore because there was a selfish, egotistical edge to their game. Give me a team player any time ahead of the exhibitionist. I moulded the players together as a team, and it was as a team that we became world champions. The players deserve all the credit. I just gave them the plan, and they made it work.’

Alf insisted that he never meant to get rid of wingers. “If I'd had a Matthews and a Finney, or a George Best and a Cliff Jones,” he told me, “I would have come up with tactics to utilise their skills. But I played to the strengths of the players I had at my disposal, and we got the job done.”

Fifty years on, Alf – The General – remains the only manager to have lifted the World Cup for England.

Not a bad epitaph.

7
BOBBY MOORE
CAPTAIN
MARVEL

Next to Alf Ramsey, Bobby Moore was comfortably the most important cog in the England World Cup wheel. They did not particularly like each other but had a deep, mutual respect. Bobby played 108 times for England, 100 of his caps won under Ramsey, 90 of them as captain. Without defensive master Moore, Alf knew he would not have captured the biggest prize in football. He was not a bawling, fist-brandishing skipper, but inspired by example and set such high standards that all his team-mates felt motivated to try to match them.

I speak from pleasant experience when I say if you were in Bobby's company you somehow felt six inches taller. And this was how it was with his team-mates. He had an aura about him that you could never manufacture. My old Fleet Street chum Jeff Powell captured him perfectly for the inscription on his Wembley statue: 'Immaculate footballer. Imperial defender. Immortal hero of 1966. First Englishman to raise the World Cup aloft. Favourite son of London's East End. Finest legend of West Ham United. National Treasure. Master of Wembley. Lord of the game. Captain extraordinary. Gentleman of all time.'

> **JACK CHARLTON:** "Bobby Moore was magnificent throughout the 1966 World Cup. Alf used to say to me, concentrate on marking your opponent and always if you're in trouble give the ball to either of the Bobbys. He meant Mooro or our kid. Like everybody else, I knew Bobby Moore but didn't know him. He was always friendly and would say, 'All right, Jacko ... how's the wife and kids.' Then he'd go into football-only mode and inspired us all by the way he played and approached the game. I don't think he had a nerve in his body. He was always immaculate and never seemed to sweat, while the rest of us were breaking our necks to do our job. Alf was very lucky to have him as captain. You could put your house on him to do whatever was required to put England in command. He was a real thoroughbred, and made the rest of us reach for our best. A supreme footballer."

Bobby Moore on top of the world, with England team-mates Martin Peters, Geoff Hurst, Ray Wilson, George Cohen and Bobby Charlton. Roger Hunt is half hidden

Bobby went into the World Cup under a cloud of confusion. He was in a contract dispute with West Ham and had refused to re-sign in the hope that Tottenham would follow up on their barely secret interest in him. Both Terry Venables and Jimmy Greaves had quietly tipped off Bobby that manager Bill Nicholson wanted him at White Hart Lane, but Hammers were determined to hold on to their captain. The Football Association made it clear to Alf Ramsey that an unregistered player would not be eligible to take part in the World Cup. Ron Greenwood, with whom Bobby now had a frosty relationship, was summoned to the England team Hendon Hall headquarters at the last minute to sign his skipper on a one-month contract.

> *BOBBY*: •You have to remember that at the time Spurs had one of the best teams in Europe, and I was concerned I was getting stale at West Ham. I felt almost as if I was being blackmailed into signing a contract, but we compromised and agreed to renegotiate once the World Cup was over. I wanted to give the finals every ounce of my energy and concentration. Let's face it, for me it was the biggest challenge of my life.•

I got Bobby to give his judgment on each of England's matches in the World Cup finals for a brochure that I edited for the Alf Ramsey tribute night. No apologies for repeating some of the facts. They warrant a second telling:

OPENING GAME

Uruguay, World Cup, Wembley, 11.7.66. Drew 0-0

Banks Cohen Wilson Stiles Charlton J. Moore*
Ball Greaves Charlton R. Hunt Connelly

Summary: A dull and uninspiring start to the World Cup left neutrals wondering on what Alf Ramsey based his confidence that England would win the Cup. Uruguay played with nine men back in defence and defied all England's attempts to break them down. It was the first time in twelve matches that England had failed to score. John Connelly was Alf's one winger. The Uruguayans celebrated at the final whistle as if they'd won. They squeezed exactly what they wanted from the game.

> *BOBBY*: •We were very flat at the end of the game because we knew we hadn't delivered. There was only one team trying to play, and it wasn't Uruguay. They just came to stifle us and did not allow our forwards time or space to breathe. I remember Ballie throwing his boots on the dressing-room floor in disgust and saying in that high-pitched voice of his, 'If I go for a sh*t, I'm expecting two Uruguayans to come with me.' It could only get better.•

SECOND GROUP MATCH

Mexico, World Cup, Wembley, 16.7.66. England won 2-0

Banks Cohen Wilson Stiles Charlton J. Moore*
Paine Greaves Charlton R.[1] Hunt[1] Peters

Summary: Alf Ramsey had not yet completely abandoned wingers. Terry Paine was preferred to Connelly in this second game, with Martin Peters taking the place of Alan Ball in midfield. Bobby Charlton unleashed one of his magnificent twenty-five yard specials for the first goal, and Roger Hunt clinched victory after having what looked a good goal ruled offside. After the frustration of the opening match against Uruguay, this victory convinced many people that England could live up to Ramsey's expectations. Mexico were not allowed to create a single goalscoring chance by an England defence in which Bobby Moore was at his commanding best.

> *BOBBY*: ❛We made a stuttering start but our nerves settled once Bobby Charlton scored with one of his rockets. Ballie was heartbroken to be left out and we had to rally round him to stop him walking out. We knew there was plenty more to come from him. We were really feeling the pressure of being the host country, but this victory helped lift us and the supporters.❜

THIRD GROUP MATCH

France, World Cup, Wembley, 20.7.66. England won 2-0

Banks Cohen Wilson Stiles Charlton J. Moore*
Callaghan Greaves Charlton R. Hunt[2] Peters

Summary: Two smartly taken Roger Hunt goals gave England a confidence booster on their way into the World Cup quarter-finals. Ian Callaghan became the third winger tried by the England manager. Jimmy Greaves finished the match with a deep gash on his left shin, and Stiles was warned for a crunching tackle on French striker Simon. He was fortunate not to be sent off, and Ramsey defied calls from Football Association officials that he should drop Stiles because of his competitive nature.

> *BOBBY*: ❛Alf was furious when the Blazers tried to put pressure on him to drop Nobby. He knew how vital his ball-winning performances were to the team in an era when fierce-tackling midfield players were necessary. The way Alf stood by Nobby helped strengthen the bond in the England camp.❜

Scanned from my Daily Express *scrapbook, Argentina captain Antonio Rattin gets his marching orders from referee Rudolf Kreitlein in the World Cup*

QUARTER-FINAL

Argentina, World Cup, Wembley, 23.7.66. England won 1-0

Banks Cohen Wilson Stiles Charlton J. Moore*
Ball Hunt Charlton R. Hurst[1] Peters

Summary: Argentina shelved their superior skills and instead concentrated on what seemed a premeditated policy of disrupting England with a spate of petty fouls. Their captain Antonio Rattin arrogantly challenged just about every decision that the referee made and was waving his arms around like a traffic policeman. Finally the referee, a balding, little West German called Rudolf Kreitlein, could take no more of Rattin's cynical tactics and ordered him off. It was almost comical to see the tiny figure of the referee staring up at the tall, stately looking Rattin and demanding that he leave the field. It was also very sad. It took nine minutes of argument and touchline interpretations before Rattin finally walked. At one stage the entire Argentine team was threatening to walk off with him. It was mutiny, and the South American players had lost the plot. Geoff Hurst, making his World Cup debut in place of the injured Greaves, headed the winning goal from a Martin Peters cross to the near post. It was a classical creation that had made-in-West-Ham written all over it. For Gordon Banks, it was a record seventh successive England appearance without conceding a goal. This was the first World Cup match in which England played without a recognised winger. Ramsey's 'Wingless Wonders' were off the launching pad. Alan Ball, so disappointed to miss the previous two matches that he considered walking out, gave a perpetual motion performance that confirmed that he was in the side to stay. Alf Ramsey described the Argentines as 'animals', a heat-of-the-moment description that had diplomatic repercussions. The sad fact is that Argentina were the most skilful side in the tournament, but they allowed their tempers to overrule their talent.

> *BOBBY*: ❛I'd never known Alf as angry. He nearly blew a gasket when George Cohen tried to swap shirts with one of the Argentines. They attempted to break into our dressing-room afterwards for a fist fight, and they were trying to kick the door down. I was thrilled with the part my West Ham team-mates had played in the victory. Geoff's goal came from a move that we had perfected playing together at Upton Park and was the trademark of our manager Ron Greenwood. Rattin was a flawed genius, a marvellous footballer but he lost his discipline. I had learned long ago to control my temper after I'd got sent off early in my career when playing for West Ham at Manchester City. I stupidly retaliated and got my marching orders. It almost wrecked my international career before it had started, but from then on I always tried to retaliate with skill.❜

SEMI-FINAL

Portugal, World Cup, Wembley, 26.7.66. England won 2-1

Banks Cohen Wilson Stiles Charlton J. Moore*

Ball Hunt Charlton R.[2] Hurst Peters

Summary: This was THE classic match of the 1966 World Cup. It lacked the drama of the Final, but the football played by both teams had rarely been bettered at Wembley. The match belonged more to Bobby Charlton than anybody. He moved with the grace of a Nureyev on grass and the power of a panther. His reward was two superb goals, one drilled low into the net from a rebound after a Roger Hunt shot had been blocked, and the second, a real beauty, rifled high into the net from twenty-five yards. West German manager Helmut Schoen was so impressed by Bobby's display that he decided he would sacrifice his most talented player, Franz Beckenbauer. He ordered him to concentrate on a man-to-man marking job on the England playmaker in the final. Seven minutes from the end of a sumptuous semi-final England's magnificent defence conceded their first goal of the tournament when Eusebio scored from the penalty spot after Jack Charlton had needlessly handled a header from Jose Torres. Nobby Stiles performed a disciplined containing job on the great Eusebio, fresh from his stunning four-goal performance against North Korea in the quarter-final at Goodison after the Koreans had rushed three goals into the lead. Eusebio left the Wembey pitch in tears as the two teams got a standing ovation for producing a match that would live long in the memory. "This," said Alf, "is the football I knew we could play if we met opponents prepared to play the game in the right spirit. Portugal deserve a lot of credit for helping to make this such a wonderful advertisement for football."

> *BOBBY*: ❛This was the performance that finally convinced our critics and our supporters that we had the skill, the determination and the all-round talent to win the World Cup. The game belonged to Manchester United. Bobby scored two cracking goals and Nobby did a brilliant job snuffing out the great Eusebio. Nobody could complain that he kept Eusebio quiet with anything but good old-fashioned man marking, always snapping at his heels and making sure he had no room for his electric spurts. There was nothing in the slightest bit dirty or violent about the job he did. It was just great, disciplined defending. We were disappointed to concede a goal, but had still not let one in in open play. Jacko's handball was just an instinctive action. Banksie was having a magnificent tournament and apologised for not saving Eusebio's penalty! I had a bit of a worry after the match when I was diagnosed with tonsilitis, but some tablets from team medic Doc Bass quickly cured it.❜

THE FINAL

West Germany, World Cup Final, Wembley, 30.7.66. England 4-2 (aet)

Banks Cohen Wilson Stiles Charlton J. Moore*

Ball Hunt Charlton R. Hurst[3] Peters[1]

Summary: Alf Ramsey decided to stick with an unchanged team. No place for fit-again Jimmy Greaves, who spent the morning of the match packing his bags for a quick getaway to a family holiday. Alf had said nothing to him, but he guessed he would be missing out on the game of a lifetime. West Germany took the surprising approach of putting Beckenbauer on man-to-man marking duty against Bobby Charlton, so the two most creative players on the pitch cancelled each other out. This was manager Helmut Schoen's reaction to Charlton's spectacular show against Portugal. in the classic semi-final.

A rare Ray Wilson mistake on a wet surface let Helmut Haller in for a 12th minute goal, which was equalised six minutes later when the alert Hurst headed in a perfectly flighted free-kick from his West Ham team-mate Bobby Moore.

In the 78th minute a Hurst shot was blocked and it was another West Hammer, Martin Peters, who smacked the rebound smartly into the net to make it 2-1.

England were just one minute from winning the World Cup when Jack Charlton was adjudged to have fouled Germany's skipper Uwe Seeler. During the goalmouth scramble that followed the free-kick defender Wolfgang Weber forced the ball into the net, with skipper Moore insisting there had been a handball.

It was a cruel blow to England, but a determined Alf Ramsey refused to let them feel sorry for themselves and rallied them to make a superhuman effort to get the better of the Germans. There were deafening roars from the crowd as England took the lead again with one of the most talked-about goals in football history.

Ten minutes into extra-time, the inexhaustible Alan Ball made one of his many scampering runs past left-back Schnellinger and centered the ball. Hurst brought it under instant control, turned and fired a first-time shot against the underside of the bar. As it bounced down England claimed the ball had crossed the goal-line. Referee Gottfried Dienst awarded a controversial goal after consulting the Azerbaijan linesman Bakhramov. To this day, the Germans dispute the decision. It all happened so quickly that it was impossible to be sure if the ball had crossed the line, but the referee awarded a goal and England were back in control at 3-2.

Hurst ended all arguments in the final seconds when he ran on to a perfect pass from Moore and hammered a left-foot shot past goalkeeper Hans Tilkowski to complete the first ever World Cup finalΔ110 hat-trick. It presented the BBC's Kenneth Wolstenholme with one of the most memorable of all commentary lines: "Some people are on the pitch ... they think it's all over ... it is now!"

England were champions of the world.

It's all over now ... Geoff Hurst unleashes his last-minute hat-trick goal

BOBBY: 'I was heartbroken for my room-mate Greavsie that he missed out, but at the same time pleased for my club-mate Geoff. My opinion was that Jimmy would have frightened the life out of the Germans with his finishing skill, but I knew there was no way Alf could change a winning team after our performance against Portugal. The game should never have gone to extra-time. Their last minute free-kick should have been awarded to England because Siggi Held made a back for Jack Charlton. Then as the ball bounced around the penalty area like a pinball Schnellinger definitely handled it before Weber bundled the ball into the net. Alf was magnificent. He wasn't panicking or shouting. He just said, plainly and simply, 'You've won the World Cup once ... now go out and do it again.' He pointed to the German players. 'Look at them,' he said. 'They're out on their feet. Now finish them off.' I was too far away to judge whether Geoff's extra-time shot had crossed the line, but Roger Hunt was on the spot and immediately turned in celebration of a goal. He's a good honest man, and that convinced me it was right to award the goal. Then Geoff settled all arguments with his fantastic hat-trick goal.'

The always meticulous, always calculating, always immaculate Bobby Moore was even thinking better than anybody else as he climbed the 39 steps at Wembley for a third successive year. He noticed the Queen – waiting to present him with the Jules Rimet trophy – was wearing white gloves, and he had the presence of mind to wipe his hands on the velvet drapes decorating the Royal Box rather than get mud on them. Talk about On Her Majesty's Secret Laundry Service.

After all the shooting and the shouting was over the world's press were invited to vote for the outstanding player of the tournament.

The explosive Eusebio was top scorer with nine goals.

Both Gordon Banks and Russian Lev Yashin had been marvellous goalkeepers.

Bobby Charlton was exceptional with his finishing, and young Franz Beckenbauer outstanding in the German team.

But there could be only one winner, a player who had led the England team with dignity, elegance and a composure and confidence that put him on a pedestal above all others.

The Player of the 1966 World Cup was, of course, the blond boy from Barking, Bobby Moore. His reward was a £1,000 bonus from the vote organisers, Radox Bath Salts. He was forever blowing bubbles.

At the after-match banquet, the great Eusebio said: "Bobby Moore is the greatest defender in world football. He is also an outstanding gentleman and sportsman, a credit to football and to England."

The Master.

Long before Saint and Greavsie there was another double act that was every bit as entertaining and enchanting: Mooro and Greavsie. Who better to call as an eyewitness of the footballing life and times of Bobby Moore than his best mate in football, the one and only Jimmy Greaves.

They were inseparable on England tours and late in their careers became team-mates at West Ham. Several years earlier they were close to teaming up at Tottenham.

Jimmy and I have collaborated on twenty books, and I spent many happy hours in the company of Mooro and Greavsie when they were footballing masters on the pitch and drinking partners at the bar. Here's Greavsie on Mooro, speaking before his violent stroke in May 2015:

‘Every time I think of Bobby, the memories of our experiences and adventures together – off as well as on the pitch – fill me with warm nostalgia. This is then overtaken by feelings of hot anger for the way he was treated after he'd hung up his boots. It was disrespectful, and in my opinion nothing short of disgraceful.

They have erected statues to him at Wembley and at West Ham, named a stand after him, television docos have lauded him, and people who barely knew him have compiled books and websites galore about the master. To top it all the Football Association – the f****** sweet FA – in 2003 named him their ‘Golden Player’ of the last 50 years.

Where the f*** were all these fawning people when Bobby was alive? Why couldn't the FA have let him know how precious he was to them before cancer claimed him? They turned their back on him after he had captained his country 90 times in 108 appearances, and played a key role in winning the World Cup for them in 1966.

He climbed the 39 steps at the old Wembley for three successive years to collect major trophies, and later had to climb down and almost beg for jobs in the game he had served so well. What a way to treat our greatest hero.

Captain Bobby Moore with the man who would eventually overtake his 108 caps record, goalkeeper Peter Shilton, understudy to Gordon Banks at Leicester in 1966

Surely it was obvious that the blazered brigade at their then headquarters at Lancaster Gate could have employed him in an ambassadorial role. He was known and admired throughout the world of football, and would have been welcome anywhere as representative of all that was best about our country. Instead of that, when he applied for the England manager's job he didn't even get the courtesy of a reply.

One of the greatest defenders the world has ever seen was forced to scratch a living on the periphery of the game after a few business projects had gone belly-up. He went to Denmark, Hong Kong and those soccer hot-spots of Oxford and Southend to earn his bread and butter. He then became 'sports editor' of a daily paper that peddled soft porn before winding up as a pundit-commentator alongside Jonathan Pearce on London radio station Capital Gold, giving his expert opinions on football in between the pop songs.

What a way to treat one of England's finest sportsmen; ignored when alive, acclaimed and applauded in death. It was like reducing Admiral Lord Nelson to the job of looking after the rowing boats at the local park, and then erecting a statue to him. The hypocrisy makes me sick.❞

Yes, Jimmy was fairly angry! I gave a lot of thought to how best I could represent them both in this World Cup anniversary book, a date that Jimmy would for obvious reasons rather forget. I decided to dig out an interview I had with them after I had helped launch Jimmy's TV career through Greg Dyke at TVam. They talked about the good and bad times they had together on and off the pitch. So, if you're sitting comfortably, I shall begin ...

JG: What a jammy git you were, Mooro, to last 90 matches as England captain. I did my best to cost you the job.

BM: There were a couple of times when Alf was on the point of giving me the chop after incidents involving you, James. He went ballistic in New York in 1964 after you'd talked me into breaking a curfew to sneak away from the team hotel to see Ella Fitzgerald at Madison Square Garden.

JG: Dear old Alf. When we told him we'd been to see Ella he thought it was an elephant at the circus. All he knew about was football and westerns.

BM: Yeah, he loved his westerns. Remember when we were in East Germany and Alf found out there was a western showing with subtitles? He rounded us up and we all went off to the cinema. The film was dubbed in German, and the subtitles were in Polish!

JG: We pissed ourselves. Alf loved us to do things together, to go round as a team as if tied by a rope. It was always a togetherness thing.

BM: You were too much of an individualist for him, Jim. Don't forget that we were together on the best day of my life and the worst of yours.

JG: Knew you'd bring that up. We were room sharing in the Hendon Hall Hotel during the 1966 World Cup. It was weird when we woke up on the morning of the final because you *knew* you were going to captain the side and I *guessed* I wouldn't be playing. Alf had not said a dicky bird to me, but I sensed I'd been given the elbow.

BM: What could Alf do, Jim? You'd been injured for the quarter and semi-final and the team had been magnificent in both games If there had been substitutes then you would have got on, and Geoff probably wouldn't have got his hat-trick.

JG: That's all blood under the bridge, Mooro. I always knew we would win the World Cup but, to be honest, I never envisaged that I'd be a spectator. Remember the first Monday after the opening match of the finals when we went to Pinewood film studios. Sean Connery was making the Bond movie *You Only Live Twice,* and showed us around the set.

BM: I know what's coming. The famous Alf speech. He said, "On behalf of the team, I'd like to thank Seen Connery for his guided tour."

JG: And you said quick as a flash, "That's the funniest thing I've ever shawn or heard." I fell about laughing and Alf was not best pleased with us taking the pee. I wonder if people realise how close you came to not playing in the finals?

BM: Oh, you mean the West Ham contract business. I was virtually blackmailed into signing a new contract with the club just before the first match against Uruguay. Ron Greenwood came to the hotel with all the papers, and it was made clear to me that as I was out of contract with West Ham I would not, under Fifa rules, be eligible to play for England. I'd been hanging out for a hoped-for move to join you at Tottenham, but West Ham kept copping a deaf ear to their approaches. So I put my name to a short-term contract. I wasn't being greedy. I just knew I was getting paid half of what many of the players at other clubs were earning. Anyway, after the final they offered me a generous new contract and I agreed to stay.

JG: You'd have loved it at Spurs. Bill Nick never made a secret of his admiration for your talent, and if you'd joined us in those mid60s I reckon we could have got the League title to go with the FA Cup we won in '67.

BM: Don't rub it in, Jimbo. I was always a fan of that Tottenham team's style of play under Bill Nick. I got several pulls on the old hush-hush including from you that Bill wanted me, but West Ham would not budge. No disrespect to West Ham, but the overall strength of the Spurs squad was far superior back then to what we had at Upton Park.

JG: Thinking back to the Hendon Hall days, I remember the funniest thing

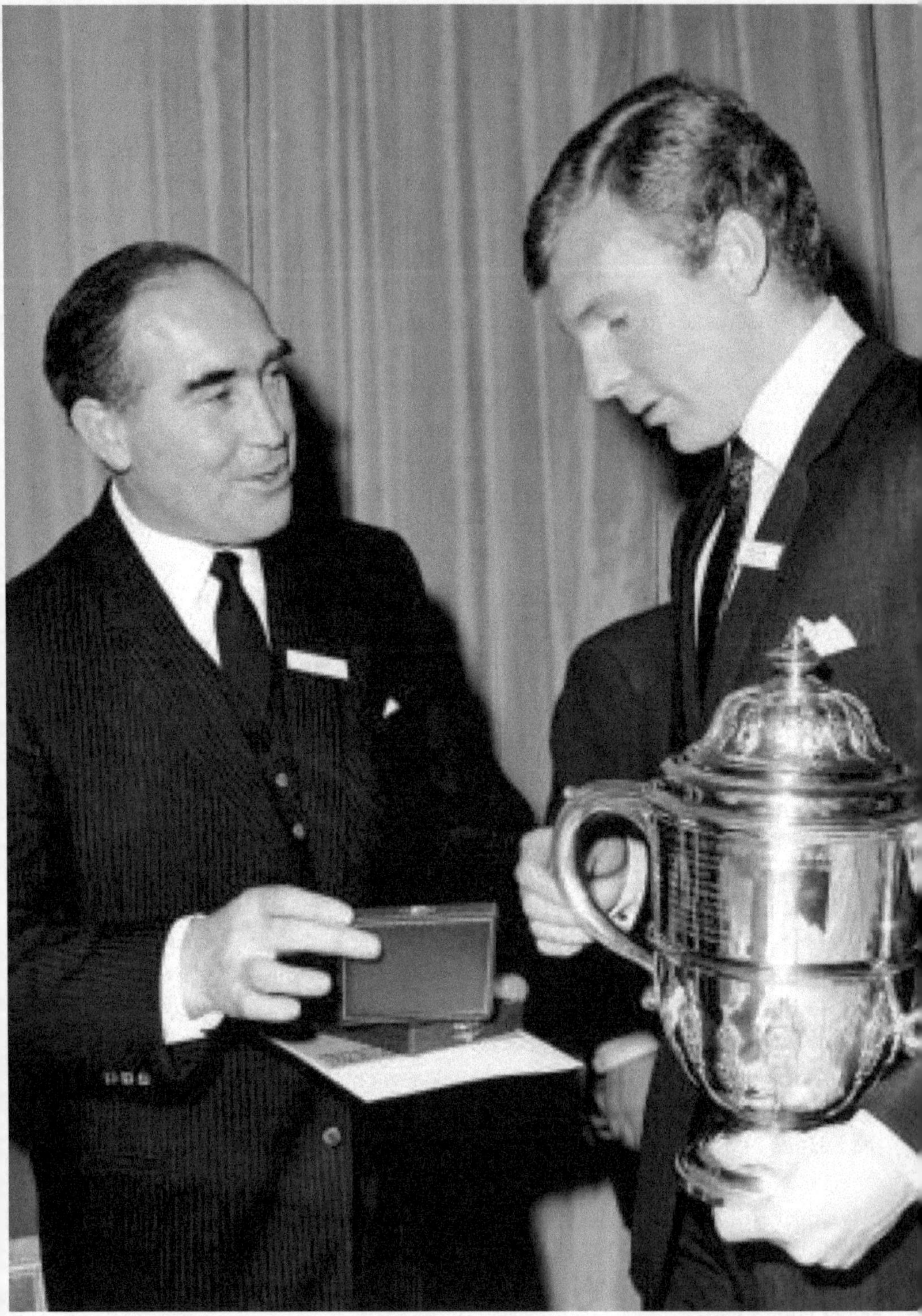

Sir Alf Ramsey presents his captain Bobby Moore with the Daily Express *Sportsman of the Year award at the Dorchester Hotel in December 1966.*

was when you complained about all the smoke in the meeting room when Alf was giving one of his team talks. Jimmy Armfield and I were puffing on our pipes, Ray Wilson. Ron Springett and Jackie and Bobby Charlton were dragging on their fags, and you said it was like being in Smokey Joe's. Alf, who liked a crafty cigarette himself, said: "Gentlemen, out of respect to your team-mates, please put out your fags."

BM: Yeah, I remember it well, because about half an hour later that pompous FA bloke Professor Harold Thompson walked into the room smoking a huge cigar. Alf went potty and told him never to dare smoke anywhere near his players.

JG: They hated each other's guts. Thompson used to call Alf just plain Ramsey. He was always on about the Oxbridge team Pegasus being the greatest English side of all time. Just didn't rate professional football.

BM: That was what was wrong with the English game. The FA was run by a bunch of amateurs. They did their best to make Alf's job as difficult as possible, and never ever forgave him for stopping them selecting the team. Poor old Walter Winterbottom always had a selection committee poking their nose in.

JG: You were England captain for Alf Ramsey's greatest triumphs, but also for the bad times. There were, for instance, the cock-ups he made with the substitutions in Mexico in 1970.

BM: Yes, it was the one weakness with Alf apart from his lack of communication skills with the media. He hated the substitute rule because it had never been part of his thinking in all his time in the game. He never experienced it as a club player or manager, and just didn't feel comfortable with the rule. His decision to take off Bobby Charlton, who was motoring nicely in the 1970 quarter-final against West Germany, was a shocker. Beckenbauer was standing near me as Bobby got the hook, and his eyes lit up. He'd suddenly been given hope that Germany could save the game.

JG: And you were involved in Kevin Keegan's embarrassing exposure at Wembley.

BM: That was in the 1974 World Cup qualifier against Poland. I'd been dropped after I'd had a bit of a nightmare in the game in Poland. I sat alongside Alf, and had never seen him so lacking in ideas as England struggled to get the ball into the net. I kept on at him in the second-half to get a substitute on to mix things up a bit. But the longer the game went on he just seemed to freeze. Sitting to my right were our subs, including Ray Clemence, Kevin Keegan and Kevin Hector. Suddenly, with just five minutes to go and with me nagging him, Alf finally decided he should send on a sub. 'Kevin, get stripped,' Alf ordered. This was the moment when the drama on the bench turned to farce. Ray Clemence helped Kevin Keegan off with his tracksuit bottoms, but was so eager he tugged his shorts down to his knees. While

Scanned from my Daily Express *scrapbook, Greavsie puffs on his pipe and Mooro dozes at Hendon Hall Hotel during a lull in the 1966 World Cup*

Kevin was suffering this overexposure he became even further embarrassed when Alf made it clear he meant Kevin Hector not Keegan. I helped Hector off with his tracksuit bottoms, but by the time he got on there were just 100 seconds left – the shortest ever England debut. England went out of the World Cup, and it eventually cost Alf his job.

JG: The most shocked I'd ever known you, Bob, was when I dropped in from nowhere to see you in Mexico City when you were under lock and key in the British ambassador's villa.

BM: That was when I'd been sent back from Colombia after being arrested on that crazy charge of stealing a bracelet from a jeweller's shop in Bogota on the eve of the 1970 World Cup. Talk about a stitch up.

JG: I'd arrived in Mexico at the end of the World Cup rally to find out you'd been nicked. Our mutual mate Norman did some detective work and found out where you were being held until allowed to rejoin the England squad. I climbed over the wall of the villa to avoid all the press and photographers at the front, and the ambassador's snooty wife caught me wandering around the garden. She gave me a right bollocking and demanded I go to the front door. When I rang the doorbell it was she who let me in!

BM: She almost fainted, Jimbo, when your first words to me were, 'Show us the bracelet then, Mooro.' I was so pleased to see you after the nightmare I'd been through. We cleared the ambassador out of all his drink that night.

JG: Once we'd settled down your larger-than-life neighbour from Chigwell, Lou Wade, was allowed to join us, remember? He stood six foot seven and wore a garish check jacket that made him look like a Las Vegas gambler.

BM: The look on the face of the ambassador's wife when Lou walked in was one of total disbelief. He helped give the drinks cabinet a real hammering.

JG: It was disgraceful the way Alf and the rest of the Football Association freebie-chasers left you out to dry in Colombia. You could have got thousands out of the jewellery shop for destroying your reputation with a false charge.

BM: I thought of going down that road, Jim, but it would have cost a fortune in legal fees, and knowing what crafty people they were I ran the risk of them inventing some witness who would have pointed the finger at me. Bobby Charlton was in the jewellery shop with me at the time of me supposedly stealing the bracelet. Can you imagine him having anything to do with anything that dodgy!

JG: Or anything dodgy. You could trust him with your last bottle of water in the desert. Remember our dance, Mooro?

BM: You, you silly sod, suddenly grabbed hold of me in the penalty area during a First Division match between West Ham and Spurs. You twirled me around as if it was a Cockney knees-up. It was hilarious. Can't imagine that happening in today's game. It's all so bloody serious. As we danced you said, 'See you later at the Black Lion', one of our watering holes.

JG: Happy days. Of course, we wound up together at West Ham.

BM: Yes, and you got me in trouble again. New Year's Day 1971.

JG: Here we go. I'm going to get blamed for the "Blackpool Affair".

BM: Well it was you, Jim, who called the cab to take us to Brian London's nightclub when you heard one of the hotel porters say there was no chance of the Cup-tie being played the next day because the pitch was under snow.

JG: Let's be honest, Mooro, Eskimos couldn't have played football in those conditions. And by the way, I didn't call a cab. Two arrived for a TV crew who only needed one. On impulse we took the spare cab.

BM: I felt sorry for Clyde Best, who we dragged along with us at the last minute.

JG: Yes, Clyde came along for the ride and Stag (Brian Dear) for the drink. We were not pissed when we got back to the Imperial, but we had been seen having a few pints in the nightclub by a supporter. He reported us to the club after we had lost to Blackpool on a skating rink pitch that should have been ruled unfit for play. No way was it fit for football.

BM: It all blew up five days later. Everybody had kept quiet about it because, unbeknown to me, Eamonn Andrews was planning to hit me with the *This Is Your Life* book, and they waited until after the show before the newspapers started headlining what had happened at Blackpool.

JG: I thought Ron Greenwood let you down big time. I didn't care about myself because I was planning to get out of the game at the end of the season. But he just threw you to the wolves. We were both suspended and even Alf Ramsey dropped you for a match. If you'd played it would have meant you beating Billy Wright's record of captaining England 90 times, instead of equalling it. The biggest mistake we made, Mooro, was losing that Cup-tie at Blackpool. If we'd won or got a replay nothing would have come of it. Greenwood could have punished us privately, but decided to let the press have a field day. He used us as scapegoats.

BM: D'you think he was getting his own back for what happened on the plane?

JG: Oh, you mean when that rascal Freddie Harrison spiked his drinks.

BM: We were in the upstairs bar of a Jumbo jet on the way to New York for a friendly match against Pelé's Santos. You and I were knocking back pints when Ron joined us and asked for a Coke. Freddie, my business partner, decided to lace the Coke with Bacardi, a juvenile thing to do but we giggled behind Ron's back.

JG: During the next hour or so Ron must have had five or six Cokes, all of them doctored by the mischievous Freddie. Ron finally realised what was going on and, to his credit, he laughed it off. The alcohol made his tongue much looser than he would have liked and he confessed he was thinking of resigning.

BM: Yes, that was embarrassing. And when he went back to his seat he dropped off into a heavy, drink-sedated sleep. Peter Eustace, who was not exactly Ron's greatest fan since being dropped from the team, had the rest of us in fits of laughter as he leaned over the snoring Greenwood, miming as if telling him exactly what he thought of him. Ron would have had a fit if he'd woken up.

JG: He never mentioned the resigning business again, but the Blackpool farce certainly gave him the chance to get his own back.

The story behind a picture: This photograph of Greavsie and Mooro – scanned from my 50-year-old Daily Express *scrapbook – was taken at Hendon Hall the morning after Jimmy had collected his gashed shin in the third match of the finals against France.* Daily Express *cameraman Norman 'Speedy' Quicke, Jimmy's best mate, said before clicking: "For gawd's sake look fed up, Jim. I want to get this in the paper." So Jimmy obliged. I was standing alongside Norman as a witness to Jimmy's exaggerated gloom. It was all done to please a pal, so that he could satisfy his picture editor. Now people coming across the photograph in the archives wrongly caption it as 'the moment Jimmy Greaves learned that he was out of the World Cup team.' That did not happen until nine days later, and the morning of the final, July 30 1966.*

BM: Let's be fair, Jim, for all his faults Ron was a gentleman who gave a lot to the game. He was as good a tactician as I ever met in the game, and he taught me a lot when I was a kid with the England Under-23s and then when he took over from Ted Fenton as manager at Upton Park.

JG: Yeah, Ron was out of the Walter Winterbottom school. A scholar and a gentleman. He couldn't understand how you and I could be less than serious about the game when we were off the pitch. It's history that I hit the bottle, but you could always out-drink me without showing any effect. We used to say you had hollow legs.

BM: I've always enjoyed a good drink, James, as you know. I couldn't believe it when you publicly admitted you were an alcoholic. All of us admire the way you've beaten your problem.

JG: Enough of rabbiting about me. This interview is supposed to be about you. With a gun to your head, who would have been your first choice for a World team from all the players you played with or against?

BM: That's easy, Jim. Pelé by a mile. He had everything – perfect balance, could shoot with either foot, had tremendous vision, was as brave as they come and had the agility of a gymnast. When we appeared together with Sylvester Stallone in the film *Escape to Victory* ...

JG: You were more wooden than the goalposts, Mooro.

BM: Thanks, Jimbo. I didn't expect an Oscar. Anyway, Pelé scored with a fantastic bicycle kick. What the public didn't know is that they shot that scene thirty times, and then used the first take! There's no question that Pelé was the greatest goalscorer of them all, with you the best of the Brits.

JG: If I was picking a World team defence, Mooro, I'll say this to your face because it's what I say behind your back ... you'd be my first choice.

BM: Stop it, Jim. You're making me blush.

JG: Could never understand why you didn't get a shot at a top manager's job. Nobody in the game had a better pedigree than you.

BM: Well I went for the top one, the England post. Sent a handwritten letter to the FA and didn't even get a reply. Then Elton John gave me the impression I'd got the Watford job and the next I knew he'd given it to Graham Taylor without a dickie bird to me. That disappointed me, Jim. Not so much that I didn't get either job but the way it was handled. Very disrespectful.

JG: Disrespectful? I can think of more fitting descriptions for the way the FA treated you, Mooro, but they would have to print it on asbestos.

BM: Well you know better than anybody, Jim, what it's like to be kicked by the FA.

This is me with Greavsie just a couple of weeks before his savage stroke in 2015. He is very happy to forget all about the 1966 World Cup final

JG: As everyone knows, Alf was not exactly my favourite person but we got on better than most people think He did what he thought was right and it came off for him. I had a lot more time for him than most of the blazered brigade.

BM: Alf won the World Cup, Jim. That ends all arguments.

I wanted to update the interview for a book we were writing about the greats of the game, and for both Jimmy and me there was no greater defender than Mooro. Greavsie and I had arranged to meet Bobby at the Capital Gold studio in January 1993, but we got a call from their switchboard, sending his apologies and asking us to postpone our meeting until a later date.

The interview never took place. Within a month lovely old Mooro had succumbed to his cancer.

One of England's greatest ever footballers – 'Sir' Bobby Moore – had gone, and suddenly everybody cared.

But where were they all when he needed them?

As I write, Bobby has left us, and Jimmy is confined to a wheelchair following his savage stroke. It's a cruel old game.

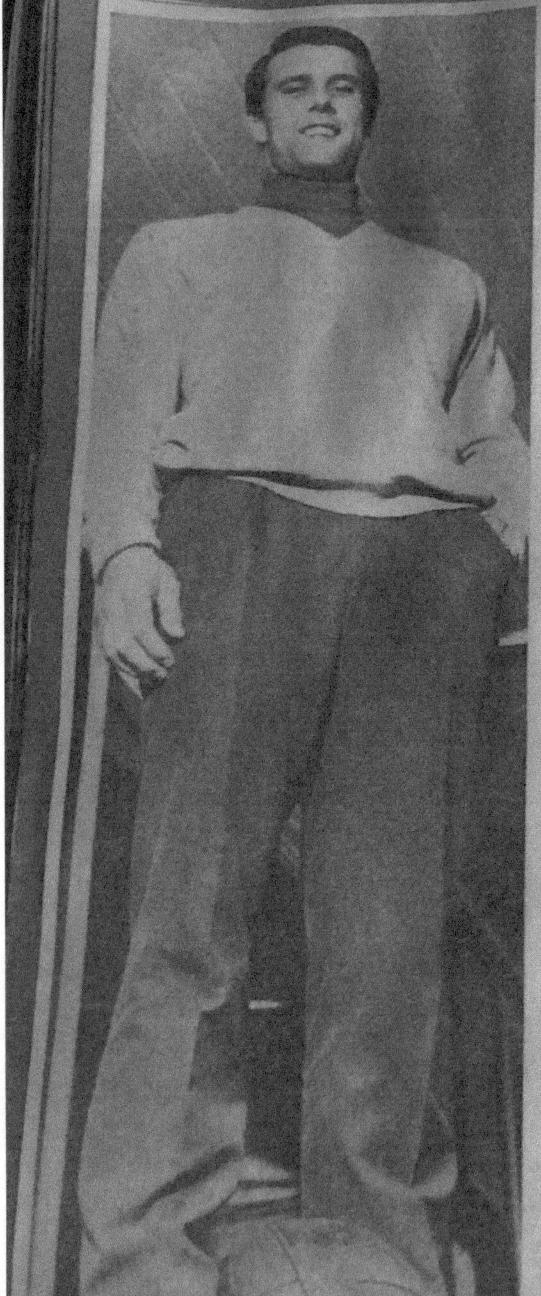

I feel ten feet tall. I go into every game feeling I have something to live up to

—GEOFF HURST (LEFT)

talking to

NORMAN GILLER

SIXTY-SIX days ago Geoff Hurst scored three goals that won the World Cup for England.

Last night Hurst described how this act of aggression against West Germany at Wembley on Saturday, July 30, has converted him into a world-class player :—

'I have been feeling 10ft. tall ever since that great day.

It has given me a new appetite for the game. I go into every match feeling that I have something to live up to.

People expect things from me now. I try not to let them or myself down.

Determined

I feared that this might all put extra pressures on me and that I would not be able to live up to the reputation I had made for myself in just one game.

But it has worked the other way. Instead of being under pressure I feel encouraged. I am a more determined player because of the World Cup.

I have confidence in myself now whereas there was a time when I wasn't sure if inside forward was the place for me.

I was a wing half five years ago. I remember having a shocking game in the reserves and our manager Ron Greenwood telling me I might be better off at inside left.

I began to wonder then if there was any future for me at West Ham.

Encouraged

But thanks to Ron's encouragement and advice the conversion worked out very well for me.

I have not thought ahead to the World Cup in Mexico. A lot can happen in four years.

My mind is on the present and doing as well as I possibly can for West Ham. After all, success for West Ham means success for me.

I owe nearly everything to my club. It's my right to do what I can in return.

The World Cup was the greatest thing that ever happened to me. I am sure the memory will spur me on to new success.'

It's astonishing that 50 years have flashed by since the 1966 World Cup final changed Geoff Hurst's life, thanks to three goals that gave him a unique place in football history. I was the first reporter to interview him at home after his hat-trick for England against West Germany, and he told me he felt 10-feet tall. I immediately got our *Daily Express* photographer Bob Stiggins to take this facing-page picture, featured in my 1966 cuttings book.

Suddenly Geoff Hurst and Martin Peters were thrust into the spotlight along with their well-established clubmate and captain, Bobby Moore. I have been around famous sportsmen for more than half a century, and I have never known anybody settle so comfortably to celebrity status than quietly confident Hurst, who took his instant world fame in his long stride.

Geoff – Sir Geoff – has always kept his feet firmly on the ground since his unforgettable match, except when heading the ball for West Ham, Stoke City and then West Brom. His final England caps count was 49 and he scored 24 international goals. He had a bash at management with Telford, then as assistant to Danny Blanchflower at Chelsea and briefly in charge at the Bridge, without touching the heights he had as a player. After two years coaching in Kuwait and flirtations with the sportswear industry, he walked away from an active interest in football and started an insurance business.

For fifty years he has travelled the world on the back of his fabled hat-trick, and is always one of the first names on the guest invitation list for any World Cup-associated events. He has always been a dignified ambassador for his sport and his country, but finds his football history can be wearing.

Sir Geoff can't go into new company without somebody asking about that second of his goals at Wembley, and whether it did or did not cross the goal-line. "What surprises me," he said, "is that they always ask it as if they were the first person ever to think of the question. If I had a pound for every time I'd been asked, I would be a zillionaire."

He and his lovely Lady Judith have been married for more than 50 years, and

This is the one man team

. . . Martin Peter's United

NORMAN GILLER

Martin Peters, the one-man team, Daily Express 1966

they had three daughters, the eldest of whom died of a brain tumour, a tragedy that the Hursts handled quietly, and with great dignity.

Just to give you an idea of what sort of man Geoff is: on the Monday after his hat-trick he spent the morning mowing his lawn, which had grown to jungle proportions in the eight weeks he had been away with England. Later, without a word to anybody, he took his mower to the nearby home of his good friend, *Daily Mail* football writer Brian James, and mowed his lawns front and back. Brian was out of action with a dodgy back and had no idea he was getting a free trim from a VIP gardener. Can't resist adding that Geoff has never believed in letting the grass grow under his feet.

Remarkably, neither he nor team-mate Martin Peters had played a single international before 1966, yet it's difficult to imagine the England World Cup win without the contribution of the Moore-Hurst-Peters West Ham trio.

Martin, Mr Elegance, was saddled with the description by Sir Alf of being ten years ahead of his time. Perhaps I didn't help matters by writing a feature in the autumn of 1966 that underlined that Martin was a one-man team. He played in every shirt for West Ham, including in emergency in goal, and it was ace *Daily Express* cameraman Bob Stiggins who patiently came up with the facing-page pre-Photoshop compilation of the versatile Hammer. It took over an hour to get all the photos, and Martin did not ask for a penny. Yes, another planet.

It was 1968 when Ramsey came up with the '10 years ahead of his time' label which became a burden for Peters. He admits struggling to come to terms with it before realising that Alf meant it as the supreme compliment.

There have been few players to compare with him for stealth and an ability to find spaces that nobody else had spotted until it was too late. His ball control was exceptional and his positioning at the near post revolutionary.

Feeling overshadowed by the more feted Moore and Hurst, Martin was convinced his career would benefit from a move, and for more than a year he was pressing for a transfer before managers Ron Greenwood and Bill Nicholson shocked the football world with a sensational deal on transfer deadline day 1970. It

'We won the Cup' – West Ham trio Martin, Bobby and Geoff

was football's first £200,000 transaction, a swap deal that took Peters to Tottenham in return for goal king Jimmy Greaves, who was valued as a £54,000 make-weight.

The first Greavsie knew of it was when he got a midday call at his Shenfield, Essex, home from Bill Nicholson, who told him: "Get yourself down to Upton Park. Ron Greenwood is waiting to talk terms with you."

A mile down the road Martin was getting a similar call from Ron Greenwood, telling him to get himself to White Hart Lane.

The move suited both Martin and Jimmy at the time, although it turned sour for Greavsie when he fell out with Greenwood over his handling of the infamous Blackpool Affair in the winter of 1971.

Peters had to overcome a lot of resentment from the supporters at Tottenham, because he was replacing the legend that was Greavsie, arguably the most popular player in Tottenham's history. Jimmy was even Martin's idol ever since he had watched Greavsie help his Dagenham school team beat Martin's school team 13-0. Peters was a spectator on the touchline. Jimmy scored 11 of the goals!

But Martin gradually won over the Tottenham fans with his performances as a gentle executioner, and he captured their respect but never their adulation. He later became an admired captain of Norwich City before moving on to Sheffield United, where he had a brief, bitter taste of management. United were relegated at the end of his first season in charge, and he resigned.

The quiet, reserved Peters was never cut out for the hazardous job of managing, and he quickly retreated from football to follow his old West Ham and England team-mate Geoff Hurst into the world of insurance. Football was such a strong call for him that he briefly made a playing comeback "for fun and fitness" with Gorleston in the Norwich and District Thursday League.

He and the loving Kathy have been married beyond their Golden Wedding, and as the 50th anniversary of July 30 1966 approached were concerned by Martin's fading memory as he succumbed to the ex-footballer's curse of Alzheimer's.

On the night of celebration after the banquet, they turned down Geoff Hurst's invitation to join them at Danny La Rue's nightclub.

"We preferred to be just with each other and went to our hotel room," Martin told me. "We didn't drink our champagne. I made us a pot of tea and we sat together on the bed just staring at my World Cup medal. Simple yet memorable. What happened to me that year was almost impossible to believe."

Sadly, between me interviewing Martin in 2015 and the publication of this book he has become the latest victim of the ex-footballer's curse of dementia.

He now struggles to recall the day that changed the lives of Bobby, Geoff and himself for ever. The contribution of Moore-Hurst-Peters gave Upton Park fans huge bragging rights – for ever after they claimed that West Ham had won the World Cup.

Back in 1966 there were five people heavily involved in the World Cup who lived within just a square mile of each other (or six, if you include me!). Bobby Moore, Geoff Hurst, Martin Peters, Jimmy Greaves and I were all near neighbours in Essex, as was Ken Aston, the head of the Fifa Referees' Committee. He was a primary school headmaster from Ilford, and standing a straight-backed 6ft 3in and with Dr Spock ears he must have been a daunting sight to his young pupils.

A lieutenant-colonel in the British Indian Army during the war, he served as a judge on the Changi War Crimes Tribunal and then returned to England to carry on what was a hobby as a referee, an authoritarian, yet who won the respect of the players because of his determination to show discretion rather than being an unthinking puppet of the rules.

I often gave Ken a lift to matches and he tried (and failed) to educate me about the laws of the game on which he was a walking record book. In fact he helped write and update a lot of them. Surprisingly for a hugely patriotic Englishman, he was always of the opinion that the controversial second Geoff Hurst goal in the 1966 World Cup final should have been disallowed. He kept this view to himself until standing down from his Fifa role after the 1974 World Cup.

His favourite party trick was to get a football and a sheet of plain A4-sized paper. He would put the ball down on the floor and tuck the sheet of paper under one side, not touching the ball, but within the full circumference of it. The paper was a make-believe goal-line.

"Now," he'd say. "Goal or no goal?"

"Goal," I'd say, playing his straight man.

"Wrong," he would reply. "The complete circumference of the ball has to be over the line. That was not the case with Geoff's second goal. No camera angle I've seen since has persuaded me that was a goal. On instinct, I know that I would have waved play on, and awarded a corner because a German defender had kicked the rebound behind the goal."

He confided: "The Soviet linesman has told me he didn't think it was a goal either after having seen replays on the cinema screen and television."

Ken Aston puts a protective hand on referee Rudolf Kreitlein's shoulder as he comes off the pitch with a police bodyguard at the end of the sensational England-Argentina quarter-final battle

Whenever I was in Ken's company I felt as if I were one of his pupils. Force of habit made him talk at you, and I used to wonder if I should raise a hand to get a word in. He was opinionated and egotistical, but that comes with the territory of being a good referee, otherwise you will be eaten alive by the arrogant players like Argentina's Antonio Rattin, who infamously got his marching orders against England in the explosive quarter-final at Wembley.

I have since met Tony several times, and you could not encounter a more charming companion, but that day in the World Cup he went too far with trying to dictate to the referee. Ken Aston was the man who came hurrying to the touchline to sort out the mayhem after German referee Rudolf Kreitlein had sent him off.

"There can only be one referee of a match," Ken told me, "and that cannot be a player. Rattin was trying to referee the game and was questioning every decision. Had I been the referee I would have taken him to the touchline and found an interpreter, and explained very clearly if he did not stop interfering he would be given his marching orders. Alf Ramsey was ill advised to publicly call the Argentines animals, but there was a lot of spitting going on when I was on the touchline trying to bring some sanity to the proceedings, so I could understand Alf's sentiments. Englishmen do not spit at people and find it despicable."

This was the worst scene in a World Cup match since the 1962 finals and Ken Aston was also bang in the middle of that explosive episode, when Italy and host country Chile got involved in a brawling battle that led to naked hatred between the South American and European football associations.

The hangover was still there when the 1966 finals kicked off, and helps to explain why Argentina came into the tournament with a suspicion that the Europeans were weighing everything against them before a ball was kicked.

The Chile-Italy battle in Santiago – which led to the countries breaking off diplomatic relations – was Aston's last World Cup match, and his farewell as a referee came in the 1963 FA Cup final when Manchester United beat Leicester City. He moved upstairs to become highly regarded chairman of the Fifa Referees Committee and the world's chief refereeing instructor.

Ken, who passed on in 2001 aged 86, left the legacy of the card discipline procedure. He told me:

> "The idea came to me after the Argentina game when I had to go on to the pitch to get Rattin off. The newspapers wrote that both of the Charltons had been booked. Neither player could recall having their names taken and Ramsey rang up the Fifa office for clarification because no one had seen the bookings. As I drove off in my little MGB down Kensington High Street, the traffic lights turned red. I thought, 'Yellow, take it easy, red, stop, you're off'. That's where the idea came from. I went home and discussed it with my wife, Hilda. I was scratching my head wondering how I could signal yellow and red to the players when Hilda came out of her sewing room with two cards, one red, one yellow and pushed them into my top pocket. So Hilda deserves a share of the credit."

His final word: "The game should be a two-act play with 22 players on stage and the referee as the director. There is no script, no plot, you don't know the ending, but the idea is to provide enjoyment, first to the players, then to the spectators and finally to yourself. That's the same whether it's Wembley or Hackney Marshes. A referee should be allowed to be inconsistent, a foul which merits a little chat one match might lead to a booking the next. It depends on the circumstances of the game. Referees must not have the power of discretion taken away from them."

Tofik Bakhramov, the linesman who became known around the world for signalling that Geoff Hurst's second goal in the final had crossed the line, became a hero in his homeland of Azerbaijan, and following his death at the age of 68 in 1993 the national stadium was named in his honour.

Despite what Ken Aston had told me, Bakhramov wrote in his autobiography *A Thousand and One Games*, that he believed the ball had bounced back not from the crossbar, but from the roof of the net. There is no film or photographic evidence to support this view. Sir Geoff Hurst was a guest of honour at the unveiling of a statue in Bakhramov's memory at the Azerbaijan stadium in 2006.

It could have been a statue to a goal.

8
THE EYEWITNESSES

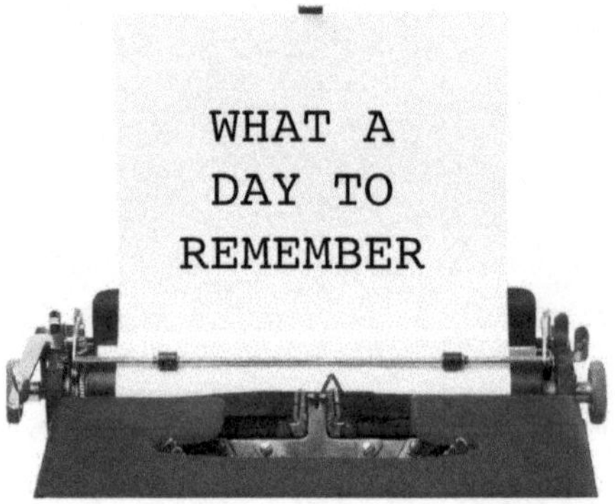

I STARTED out writing this record of July 30 1966 on my own but gradually gathered an army of football lovers who wanted to share their memories of a special day in our sporting history.

Many of the people who were eyewitnesses of the dramatic final at Wembley have passed on to the great football stand in the sky, but they left behind tales of the unexpected with relatives and friends, who have kindly shared them for posterity.

On the following pages I feature a cross section of the memories that were sent to me from all around the world, many from the actual observers, and even more from people passing on stories they were told or have picked up during conversations with fellow followers of the Beautiful Game.

My thanks to all those who contacted me with their contributions. I am publishing as many as I can, but apologise to those I have had to disappoint. If I had printed all your stories there would have been no room for me (there are those who consider that would have enhanced the book).

Here we go down the 1966 World Cup memory lane ...

PC TOM AND THE SIGNED PROGRAMME

Paul Gutteridge

King's Lynn, Norfolk

My Granddad Tom Venning was a local boy, having been born in North Wembley/ Sudbury in 1923, and after the war he joined the Metropolitan Police Force in 1951. At the time of the World Cup finals he was a member of traffic patrol based at Wembley Garage, with fifteen' years experience as a policeman in the area. He was accustomed to being used for different short term jobs having already been called on to be one of the motorcycle outriders and part of the protective detail for the Russian representatives when they attended Churchill's funeral the previous year.

For the World cup matches held at Wembley, the Metropolitan Police decided they wanted a small group of coppers with local knowledge during the tournament, people who would know exactly where they were within the area, and within the stadium, and would be able to call on their local knowledge should it be needed during the event. Therefore PC T.W.D. Venning, X646, known to his friends and colleagues as Bill, was made up to acting Sergeant (as identified by the fact his Sergeant's stripes were on an arm band, rather than being sewn onto his uniform) for the duration. Then, having been positioned in various key places during the other Wembley games, he ended up being promoted to the officer in charge of the players' tunnel on Final day.

In all the footage of the teams coming out for the kick-off, my Granddad can be seen stepping out onto the pitch before the players (I like to think of it as leading both teams out!). This is best seen in the World Cup final footage used in the 1969 movie *Till Death Us Do Part,* which showed some great colour footage!

As he was in a position to have access to everyone, he got a programme fully signed, including by every player from both teams, all of the match officials, and the coaching staff etc. He obtained these precious signatures by simply knocking on the dressing-room doors and asking everyone in the room to sign.

This programme probably had more autographs on it than any other which were signed that day, making it a unique piece of football memorabilia.

My Granddad was not a massive football fan, he would rather watch Wasps play rugby at Sudbury, and he used to be a spectator at the speedway when it was still held at Wembley, and he also marshalled at Silverstone on a regular basis. Granddad is also a lifelong cricket fan, but he had no passion for the beautiful game, and gave the football programme to his daughter, my mother.

My mum had just turned 17 years old, and was passionate about music but had no love of, or interest in football. She had about twenty pen pals dotted all over the world, from as far away as Uganda, Canada, Pakistan and Japan, with whom she exchanged letters on a regular basis, It was a bit like having Facebook friends from all over the globe these days, but without the annoying games and the constant offer of Ray Bans and Diet Pills at a bargain price!

Mum also had a few West German pen pals, one of whom was an avid football fan, and, as he was upset at his team's loss in the Final to England, she posted the precious programme to him in the hopes that it would help to cheer him up! As you can imagine, Mum has had a lot of years of comments from her four sons, myself included, who would all give their eye teeth to have that programme in their collections!

I was 22 in 1966 when I went to the World Cup final at Wembley from Truro. I only had two weeks' leave from work and the tournament covered three weeks. Nevertheless I saw all the games from the end of the first week up to the Final.

I kept all the tickets, programme and special edition papers as well as many other souvenirs. On Final day itself I purchased one of the original special programmes and have Geoff Hurst's autograph on the programme and ticket stub.

After the game we went into central London celebrating around Trafalgar Square (with a few thousand other people!). The atmosphere was unbelievable.

We stayed in Muswell Hill and believe it or not the England team coach used to be parked in a nearby side street! Presumably, the driver took it home after matches.

Geoff Hurst came to Truro a few years later doing public relations work for Renault when I was able to ask him to sign the ticket and the World Cup programme.

I also have Bobby Moore's autograph on a team photo.

On the morning of the final, we ventured into central London after breakfast to savour the atmosphere. There were German supporters everywhere, so we decided to get to Wembley early. We were lucky enough to purchase the first edition special programme that sold out before the kick-off.

We still could not believe that England had reached the World Cup Final. The only believable thing was the British weather, frequent showers.

What great memories, and sadly the chances of ever winning it again seem more remote than ever but you never know. I'm so pleased to be able to say I was there.

ONE OF THE YOUNGEST AT THE FINAL

Clyde Lester

Finchley

July 30 1966 was an experience of a lifetime, and I can say that even though I was just seven, surely one of the youngest at Wembley that historic day. I went to the final with my Grandfather Ben and my Dad, Tony. My Dad parked his Mini the night before near the ground and my Mum dropped us at Wembley on the day. The euphoria was overwhelming. The passion and pride made it an unforgettable experience.

In contrast, I went to England's drab, goalless opening World Cup match against Uruguay, too. It was an anticlimax as a game but the occasion was immense. Wembley was at its best. Unfortunately it now lacks atmosphere due to the corporate hospitality rather than having true fans.

Dad and I are both passionate Spurs fans and season ticket holders. But even if we won the Premier League (my lifelong dream) it can't match being there on the day we won the World Cup. Even 50 years on whenever I hear stories of '66 and say I was actually there everyone is amazed. Who was to know at the time it would be our finest hour and unlikely to be repeated.

I lived in Hendon at the time and used to cycle to Hendon Hall Hotel. The players would come out and talk to us and sign autographs. It was all remarkably casual. They frequently strolled up to Brent Street for tea. Can you imagine the prima donna players 'strolling' today! So many memories and the stupidest one is I was given a World Cup Willie toffee tin. My Mum told me not to eat them before dinner. Within minutes (before dinner) I went downstairs with blood pouring from my finger and had to confess I had raided the toffees and cut my finger on the tin. Dinner was postponed while I was taken to casualty for emergency stitching. A World Cup Wally!

I was then Viv Levenson and 18 years old when on July 30 1966 – along with the rest of the country – I was filled with the hope and expectation that our great England football team could lift the World Cup. I had been reading every newspaper article I could throughout the World Cup games and I knew that the England team were staying at the Hendon Hall Hotel.

As I lived in nearby Kingsbury I was hoping I could have gone to the hotel to wave the team coach off and to wish them good luck on that momentous day. It was not to be as it had been planned that I would be staying with my aunt and uncle in Shepperton, Middlesex, that weekend.

However, I was determined to wish them luck so I rang directory enquires for the number of the Hendon Hall Hotel. My favourite player was Geoff Hurst, so I cheekily decided I would take the chance that I could speak to him.

The number dialled out, the telephonist answered and I said, in my most mature voice, ' Can I speak to Geoff Hurst, please?' To my astonishment I was put straight through to Geoff!

I gulped a few times and apologised profusely for bothering him, and garbled that I just wanted to say good luck.

He was very kind and said it was no problem and thanked me very much for calling.

The last words we spoke were, 'Me: Good luck, you can win this, score lots of goals!'

Geoff, 'I will Viv, just for you!'

As each goal went into the net it was like a dream, with me shouting, 'Geoff said he'd score for me!'

To this day I'm convinced my good luck call helped get that hat-trick … well, maybe with a little help from the great Geoff Hurst!

I became a West Ham fan during that tournament and I am to this day.

Wonderful memories. I will never forget that day. A few years later I had a job at Wembley Stadium on the refreshment stalls and a friend worked in the dressing-rooms. He arranged for me to meet Geoff Hurst and Bobby Moore. What a day, shaking the hand of Bobby Moore, such a lovely man, and getting a hug from Geoff Hurst, who called me his lucky mascot.

At the time of the 1966 World Cup finals I was a football-mad 12-year-old Manchester United supporter. My father, then a top-flight sports writer with the *News of the World*, inexplicably decided we should move from our comfortable home, 20-minutes' drive from Old Trafford, to a small town 40 miles away called Thornton Cleveleys. Dad chose to purchase a newsagency in this little village, which was certainly not a centre of high commerce in Lancashire.

The rationale for the unexpected newsagency venture was never shared with our mum, Rose, or the seven children. We can only assume that Dad thought that he would enjoy getting up at 4.30 a.m. every morning, work 14-hour days and deliver newspapers in the wind, rain and snow. This business venture would not be provident for me on World Cup Final day July 30 1966

Football was in my father's blood. His Dad was the England international inside-forward David Jack, after whom I am named and who famously scored the first goal at Wembley for Bolton Wanderers in the historic FA Cup final of 1923.

Despite the business purchase, Dad continued to work as a freelance football writer in conjunction with selling newspapers and packs of Woodbine cigarettes, and he was on duty in the press box at Wembley Stadium on that special day in July 1966 … and others would be left to manage the demands of the Thornton Cleveleys newsagency.

I attended one match in the tournament, a group game at Old Trafford. Eusebio da Silva Ferreira, the greatest player to have come out of the African continent, scored for Portugal in a 3-0 victory over Bulgaria. That Lancashire-based group witnessed one of the best ever World Cup matches when Hungary beat Brazil 3-1 to knock out the favourites.

Now living Down Under, I still clearly remember watching on black and white television the Hungarian's second goal – a stunning volley by Janos Farkas after Florain Albert and Ferenc Bene combined beautifully. This will go down as one of World Cup's greatest ever goals, and this 12-year-old was completely hooked.

My World Cup memories include a slight North Korean player named Pak Doo Ik scoring the only goal of the game at Middlesbrough to send the Italians packing. Italy, boasting the legendary names Mazzola, Rivera and Facchetti, were outplayed by the marauding North Koreans who could have scored three that day. The English press, at that time not big fans of Italian football, were only too happy to report on the tomato pelting The Azzurri faced upon their return to Italy.

The West Germans and the Argentinians cruised through their groups, the Germans inspired by Franz Beckenbauer, yet to be crowned Der Kaiser. When the Argentine captain Antonio Rattin was sent off (somewhat harshly I can say 50 years later) in the quarter-final against England at Wembley, relations between the two nations sunk to depths only surpassed by the Falklands War, many years later. England manager Alf Ramsey branded the Argentine players "animals" and Ramsey physically intervened to stop players exchanging shirts at full time.

I was glued in front of the TV set totally wrapped up in the final when Wolfgang Weber slid home the agonising 90th minute equaliser, forcing the World Cup Final to extra-time.

Our six paper boys were obviously equally captivated by the game, and not one of them showed up to deliver the Saturday afternoon papers. Our mother Rose said to big sister Theresa and I, "The papers must go out – off you go".

Despite my pleas, I missed that historic half hour of football, arguably the most dramatic 30 minutes ever played in World Cup history.

I was on my Raleigh push-bike, delivering newspapers like a paper boy possessed, but did not get home in time for the extraordinary dramas.

Of course, I did eventually get to see that magical thirty minutes of extra-time and have relived the tournament many times, courtesy of the wonderful film documentary, *Goal*.

As a music lover, I consider myself blessed to have been brought up in England in the swinging sixties, but also as a football fan. I could have wished for nothing better than to witness the country of my birth, England, win the World Cup in my homeland. But duty called, and those papers had to be delivered. The memory of missing extra-time still burns 50 years on.

MILKING ENGLAND'S SUCCESS

Phil Hodgskiss
Rugeley, Staffs

As farmers in Staffordshire, my father and I had to plan our day around milking the cows. We had won our tickets for the final in a Villa Park raffle, and there was the slight problem that I had arranged to go to the wedding of my girlfriend Jean's best mate. I quickly decided that the priority was the football, which caused a lot of pouting, but after 49 years of marriage I think she has forgiven me.

The 6.30 morning session was easy enough, and the cows were due their second milking at 6.30 that evening. We worked it out that with Dad putting his foot down in his Morris Oxford we could just about get back in time. But nobody told Wolfgang Weber, who put us right behind the clock when his last-minute goal forced extra-time.

We couldn't leave without watching the last 30 minutes, which was probably the most dramatic football ever seen at Wembley. That extra-time was longer for my Dad and I than most people. While cheering on England we were sparing some thought for the cows back at the farm.

Throughout the game we could not hear each other talk because of the bashing of a drum by a cheerful Brazilian alongside us, and the constant cheering of the spectators. I've never known anything like it. The atmosphere was truly breathtaking.

We saw wonderful England skipper Bobby Moore collect the trophy from the Queen and then dashed back to the farm. The cows were moody because they were so heavy with milk, but my Dad and I would not have swapped the experience for anything.

What sticks in my mind all these years later is the sportsmanship of the German supporters. They were shaking hands with all English fans and were generous enough to say the better team had won.

My Dad and I were positioned on the halfway line with a good view of both goalmouths, and I can say with total certainty that Geoff's second goal was miles over the line.

If you think I am going to admit to making that up you will have to wait until the cows come home!

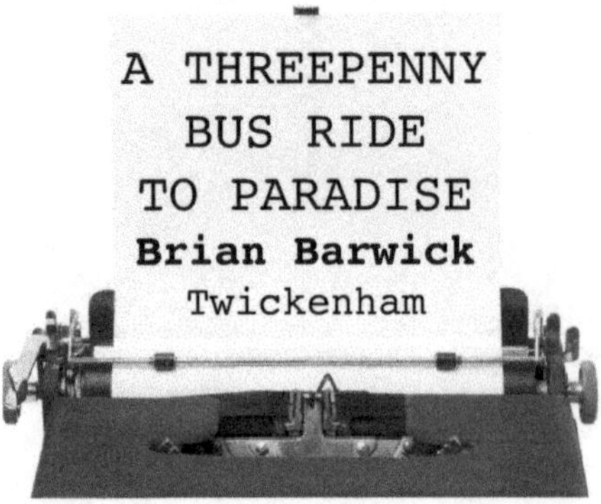

A THREEPENNY BUS RIDE TO PARADISE

Brian Barwick

Twickenham

Back in January 2005 in my first week as the incoming CEO of the FA I settled into my new surroundings by making one significant alteration to the office I was sitting in. On a bare white wall I hung a huge copy of that iconic photograph of England captain Bobby Moore, World Cup aloft, astride the shoulders of his team-mates on the famous day at Wembley back in 1966.

For me it represented the finest moment in English football history and I wanted it to be seen every time somebody came through my office door.

Over the past fifty years I've had the privilege of attending many World Cups across the globe in various professional capacities but back in July 1966, it was as a 12-year-old schoolboy that I took a threepenny bus ride along Queens Drive in Liverpool to see my first-ever World Cup match.

And what a match it was - holders Brazil versus in-form Portugal, Pelé versus Eusebio at a fever-pitch Goodison Park.

Pelé was kicked out of the game and Eusebio scored twice as Portugal sent the holders packing.

Portugal would go on to lose to England in a terrific semi-final at Wembley which set up the World Cup Final itself – England v West Germany on July 30.

In the Barwick household everybody was up bright and early to bag a good place to watch the TV. Oh, other than my dad, a police officer, who was up even earlier - to go to work!

By the time he returned from his shift, the game was underway and we were one down.

"We're one behind, Dad," I said, bringing him up to date as he settled into the *second-best* seat in the lounge (!)

The rest is history, mum and dad, my brother David and I followed every twist and turn of the match, including West Germany's last-gasp equaliser.

We were also chuffed to have one of our 'own' players in the side. As Liverpudlians it was great to see 'Sir' Roger Hunt in the line-up. Indeed eight different clubs were represented in Sir Alf Ramsey's chosen eleven. I think it is one of the elements that made the occasion that bit more special.

Of course, when Geoff Hurst rattled in his third, and England's fourth goal, we all went mad.

An hour later me and my mates were out in the Liverpool streets playing football and re-enacting the afternoon's great moments – although it was difficult to find anybody who wanted to play the part of England's opponents!

During the tournament, I had typed out a short report of every match I'd watched on television on my 'Petite' typewriter ... and sure enough later that night I wrote my own take of the big day.

Gosh, I wish I'd kept them.

A fortnight later, I was back at a rainy Goodison Park to see the 1966 FA Charity Shield between League champions Liverpool and FA Cup winners Everton.

Ee-aye-adio, they were peak days on Merseyside

The match was a big occasion in its own right, but made extra special when leading the two teams out on a pre-match lap of honour were England World Cup heroes Ray Wilson and Roger Hunt, holding aloft the star of the show itself – the World Cup. The crowd went absolutely barmy.

Over the past 50 years through a career in journalism, broadcasting and sports administration, I've met all of the famous eleven men who starred for England that day and, whilst at the FA, played a small part in making sure the 'other' eleven, who didn't start at Wembley, got World Cup-winning medals as well. I was chuffed with that.

But nothing will match the memories, that three weeks of watching that great tournament unfold on black and white TV, have a brief taste of it myself as Brazil and Portugal did battle, then sit back (in the best chair in the lounge!) and watch England WIN the World Cup Final!

Indeed as I type this I have a signed copy of that famous photograph of Bobby Moore and his team-mates staring right back at me.

It was a very special day.

Norman Giller Note:

Brian Barwick was Football Association Chief Executive from 2005 to 2008, and is a life-long England football fan, despite since switching to another form of the game. In an earlier life he was a powerhouse behind the scenes in television, first with BBC sport and then as a dynamic Controller of ITV Sport. He currently serves as the Chairman of the Rugby Football League (RFL) and Super League Europe Ltd, and is a Board member of the Rugby League International Federation (RLIF). He is also Chairman of football's National League and a member of The Football Association Council. But in 1966 he was just a wide-eyed footie fan won over by Alf Ramsey's Wingless Wonders.

CRUISING TO THE WORLD CUP

Bob Whitehead
Verwood, Dorset

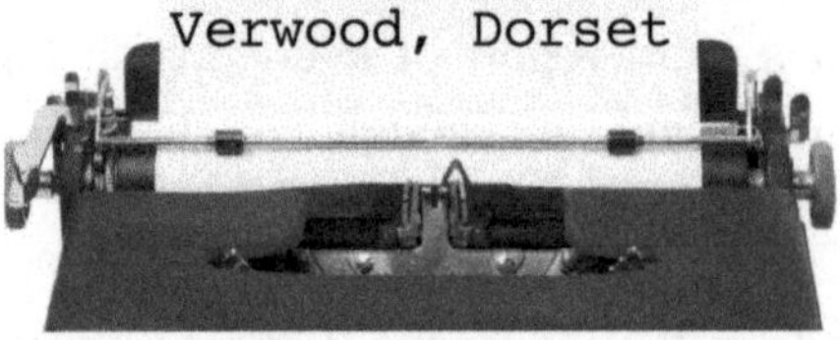

I was a printer on Cunard's *Franconia* when England played the final at Wembley, and we were going up the St Lawrence River on our way to Quebec. The captain decided to have the BBC overseas radio broadcast of the game relayed over the public address system so that no one would miss the excitement of the day. This was unheard of in those days, as usually passenger comfort was of the utmost importance and this included having peace and quiet, particularly going up the tranquil St Lawrence.

But realising the importance of the occasion to all on board including the outward emigrating passengers the game was relayed over the system to all.

All four members of the printing staff, me included, still had to work while the game was on. As the final progressed the excitement reached fever pitch, and at the end of the game when England had won, there was wild jubilation throughout the ship and our cup literally runneth over.

Our next day's issue of the "Ocean Times", which was printed daily whilst at sea, contained all the details of the historic win, which crew and passengers devoured eagerly.

LIKE WINNING THE FOOTBALL LOTTERY

Colin Bower
New Milton

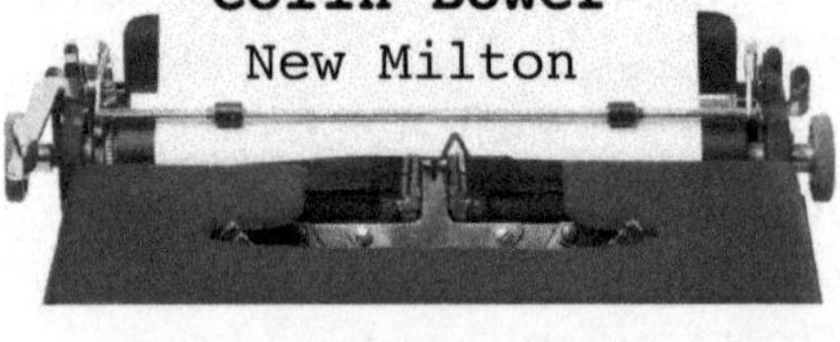

One of the marvellous things about the World Cup was the season ticket idea. In return for a pre-tournament payment of just £2, I bought my football fanatic father a season ticket for the five Wembley matches and the one game at White City Stadium leading up to the final. This bargain included the classic semi-final between England and Portugal, in which England really did look the part of world champions as they mastered Eusebio's brilliant Portugal team.

Dad's ticket then went into the draw for a Final 10-bob standing ticket and he won! At work, we raffled two Final tickets and I drew one of them. So Dad and I had both won tickets to see the match of a lifetime. It was as if we had both won the football lottery.

I was living in Nottingham at the time and I travelled down to watch England beat West Germany. I was behind the "they think it's all over" goal and my lasting memory is of Nobby doing his little jig while holding the trophy aloft.

Also standing out in my memory these 50 years on is the extraordinary work rate of Alan Ball and Roger Hunt, the composure of the supreme Bobby Moore, and the sight of big Jack Charlton putting a consoling arm around a forlorn-looking Jimmy Greaves after the final whistle.

I was fortunate to be at the final and two memories at the end of the match stand out for me:

As soon as the final whistle blew madness took over. Everyone was hugging everyone and I, in a state of euphoria, grabbed the nearest person and he did likewise. It is probably the first and only time a Spurs supporter, me, and a Liverpool supporter (he was wearing his scarf) were locked in a loving embrace and then jumping up and down together!

It is the nearest I have been to totally losing all control. Everyone was the same. Simply put we just didn't know what to do with our excitement!

It truly was a game and an occasion and a victory that united everybody throughout the nation.

As Bobby Moore prepared to take the Cup from the Queen I heard this one voice that appeared to be separate from the cauldron of noise.

'Oh Bobby, oh Bobby,' it whimpered in a lilting Irish brogue.

I turned to see this ruddy-faced Irishman, tears streaming down his face and trembling with emotion.

It was that kind of day!

MEMORIES FROM ACROSS THE POND

Hazel Cope

Pittsburgh

I wish my memories of The Great Match were clearer, but to be honest I didn't realise at the time what an amazing honour it was to be in Wembley Stadium to see England win the 1966 World Cup. I was not a born-and-bred football fan, but had married into the tribe. It was a mixed marriage in many ways – me from London, Alan from Yorkshire.

Watching *Match Of The Day* was a precious Saturday ritual for his family, and their proudest moment (pre 1966) was 1912 when their home team, Barnsley, won the FA Cup. Years later, Alan's Dad's almost-last breaths at age 86 were spent reciting the names of all the players in that immortal team.

He grew up watching them, and two years after t'Cup win he was shipped off to Gallipoli. It was five years before he saw Barnsley play again. However, we know from his diaries of the war years that he played many a game of football, especially between skirmishes in Egypt.

After his return to Barnsley he moonlighted as parking attendant at Oakwell Stadium, although he never owned a car. Alan would be in the Boys' Enclosure then, watching the Tykes.

Even though I lived near enough to a football club (Hendon) to hear the cheers from the stadium, I'd only ever been there once. The friend I was with and I chatted happily throughout the game, occasionally focusing on it to choose our favourite players, by which we meant the best lookers.

But in 1966, by the time England reached the quarter-finals the whole nation was agog with excitement. My mother and I visited a couple of dear old aunties that weekend. To our amazement they asked, no, told us, very sweetly, that after tea we would all watch The Match.

They'd rented a television (their first) for the games and were as fanatical as everyone else. We all rejoiced at England's win and had an extra slice of Aunty Daisy's Victoria sponge-cake to celebrate.

My husband Alan was absolutely thrilled when an Italian colleague, disgusted at Italy's group stage defeat by North Korea (!) offered to give us his tickets to the Final.

Of course, we snapped them up and our passion for England to win was even higher. We watched the semi-final on our own little black and white telly, and my husband claims that when England scored I tossed our baby son, David, in the air. (I definitely don't remember that, but anyway, I must have caught him).

Maybe it was that short flight which cemented the football fanaticism in David. He's played the game all his life, coached since teenage years and was voted the best high school boys coach in Colorado. Now his daughter carries the soccer flag. Emily is an awesome athlete who's won a Soccer scholarship to a Division 1 college (we live in the US now, it's Soccer to us).

We're proud of having helped establish Soccer clubs and being deeply involved in the early years of the game's growth here in Pittsburgh, Pennsylvania. Particularly gratifying is the popularity of the women's game.

I wish I'd had the chance to play, but I never heard of any girls playing when I was young, beyond kicking with the boys in the park occasionally, coats for goalposts sort of thing. We played field hockey at school – a much more violent game.

When the US Women World Cup Winners team played an exhibition game v. Costa Rica this summer at our Pittsburgh Steelers stadium, it was the highest attended soccer game ever in Pittsburgh. Over 44,000 joyous fans.

Enough boasting. Back to The Match. It was mostly standing room in stadiums then, and as the game went back and forth people jumped up and down so you really couldn't see much anyway, and the crowd noise was continuously deafening.

But I did see The Goal, the one that's been argued about ever since. We were high up, above the German end. The ball hit the underside of the bar and OF COURSE it bounced back down *inside* the goal. Definitely. I saw it. End of argument.

And then Geoff Hurst kicked in another (his third) to cement the win and we all went nuts. We'd WON!

That whole England team was full of distinct characters: the tall and short Charlton brothers, gentlemanly Captain Bobby Moore, handsome Hurst and so aptly named Nobby Stiles. It was wonderful to see their joy, and perhaps one day I'll be reciting their names on my deathbed.

It's hard to believe that two of the heroes, skipper Bobby and 'the baby' of the team Alan Ball, are no longer with us, but what an hour they lived!

Years later we took Emily and her Dad to England. Top of their bucket list of destinations was Wembley Stadium. The first question our guide asked was "What do you think that is?" and he pointed at a long white piece of wood hanging above us from the wall.

Three of the family unanimously shouted "The cross bar from the Final!" and almost fell down in worship. I watched them in awe, realising that was the highlight of their journey among a thousand years of English history.

1066 or 1966? Their answer was clear.

A KISS FOR GORDON BANKS

Joan Armstrong
Durham

For me, the most memorable moment came hours after I had watched the match on television. We lived in Balham then and I felt I had to be part of it. My late husband and I got on the tube and went to cheer the team as they arrived at the Royal Garden Hotel. There was a police cordon holding us back, but we broke through and I was pushed forward and found myself by the side of the coach as the players came off.

I managed to kiss Gordon Banks on the cheek and shouted, "Thank you, thank you, thank you" like a broken record. He gave me a great big grin and shouted: "Fantastic. Thank you for your support. We've never seen anything like it."

A police constable pushed between us, and then we stayed there for ages until the players came out on to the balcony with the World Cup. We cheered every one of them as they took turns holding it up, and then we went dancing down the road with complete strangers, all of us united in celebration. Going back home on the tube train everybody was singing and wearing huge grins. Few of us had been to the game but we all felt part of it.

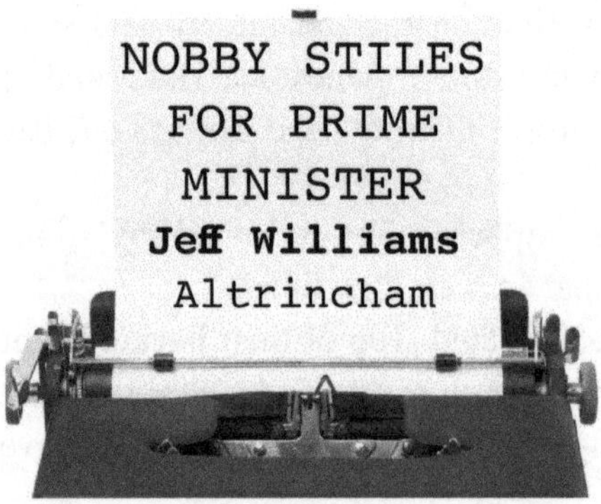

NOBBY STILES FOR PRIME MINISTER

Jeff Williams
Altrincham

Sadly, my Manchester-born Dad – George Williams – suffers from dementia and so he cannot provide this memory himself, but he always used to tell us how he went to Wembley for the semi-final and final holding a huge placard that he had made which read: 'Nobby Stiles for Prime Minister.'

He said that the British economy was in such a state at the time that even Nobby could have done a better job at No 10 than Harold Wilson.

I was born the year after the World Cup victory, and have grown up with tales of how Nobby was the most popular member of the team, even though his main job seemed to be to kick the opposition.

He remains a legend at Old Trafford, where all the old boys say that today's defenders are big softies compared to Nobby, who was only little but left his mark on the game in more ways than one!

My Dad always said it was a different game then – a man's game, he called it, when physical contact was not only allowed but encouraged. Now if a player breathes on an opponent he risks a yellow card.

Let's give the game back to the people. These days it costs an arm and a leg to go to a ground for a Premier League match to watch a load of overseas players. I can't see how England are ever going to win the World Cup again when our players can't get into the major club teams.

I think I'll copy my Dad and make a banner to wave at grounds:

'David Beckham for Prime Minister.' He'd sort it out!

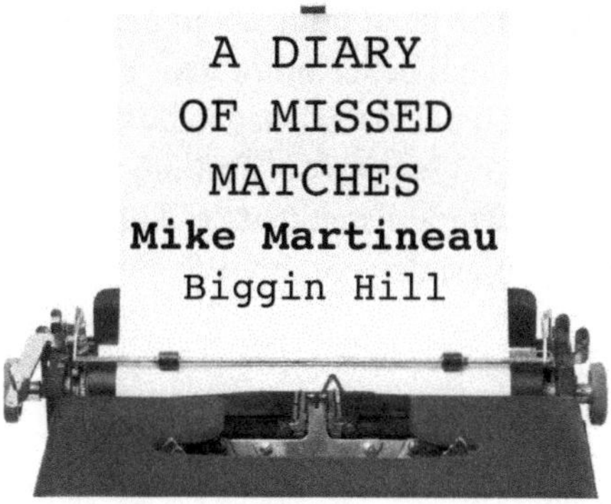

As somebody addicted to sports, I received a painful lesson in diary management in 1966. Where was I when the World Cup finals started? In Spain with my future first wife and friends, so I missed all the group games. My girlfriend and I decided to get engaged in Spain and came home and arranged a celebration with both sets of parents. And which evening did we choose? The night of the semi-final against Portugal! We sat in a half empty theatre watching Keith Michell and Glynis Johns in *The King's Mare*. We then went to a restaurant in Soho and were told the result by the waiters, who thought it odd that a football fanatic hadn't managed to watch the game.

As a guy who still reckons that Jimmy Greaves was at his best for Chelsea. I was enormously sad that he never played in the final, which I watched on my future in-laws' TV. It made such an impact that many refer to it as THE World Cup final, as if it is the only one ever played!

A FAIR WAY TO CELEBRATE

Peter Hicks

Brighton

I have some very fond and clear memories of that fantastic day in 1966. Our family and neighbours all crowded round the tiny black and white television set, and my sister and I prayed it wouldn't break down! I remember feeling terribly despondent when the Germans scored first, and I will never forget Geoff Hurst's second goal and that sweet, sweet shot for his third.

It was the evening I remember best! There was a fair in Brentwood, Essex, (and fairs were a big deal to a 13-year old) and it seemed the whole town turned up. The atmosphere was wonderful, smiles, pride, the friendly crowds, sheer joy and everyone celebrating a fantastic achievement. The great thing about the 1960s was the feeling that things were getting better and what better proof than England winning the World Cup! I wanted that night to last forever, but we had to be up early to catch the Dover ferry to France. We were going on our hols in Brittany. At the hotel, I told any young French boys and girls who would listen that "L'Angleterre a gagne la coup du monde". It was one of the happiest days of my life.

DRUNK FOR ONLY TIME IN MY LIFE

George Smith

Aberdeen

England won the World Cup on my 20th birthday, and for the one and only time in my life I got drunk as I joined my Dad in a dual celebration of my birthday and the Wembley victory. What I remember as well as the joy of watching Geoff Hurst's hat-trick on TV was the terrible hangover I had the next morning. I swore never to drink again, and I have been virtually tee-total ever since. I now live in Scotland where, as often as possible, I take great delight in dropping England's 1966 World Cup triumph into conversations I have with the locals. It is all banter, of course, but there are plenty of Scots who considered it a black day for football.

WHAT A TREAT FOR TEN BOB

Jim Gardner

Epsom

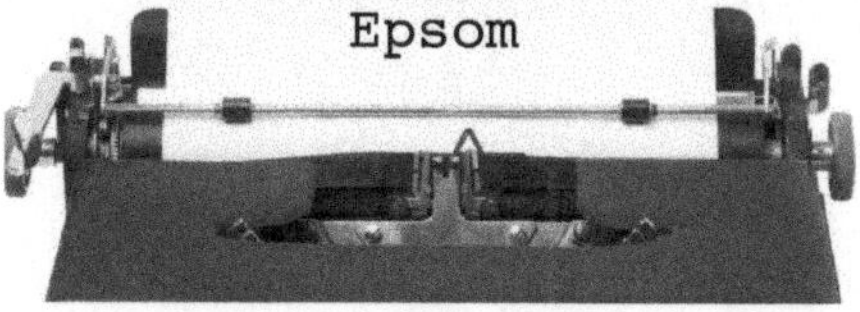

Nobody believes me when I tell them that I saw the final for ten bob! Yes, ten shillings or, in today's money 50p. Okay, I didn't get a seat, but I was standing at the end of the ground where Ray Wilson's mistake gave Germany their first goal and Hurst finished all arguments with the 'they think it's all over' goal. Not bad for 50p. My son goes to watch every Chelsea home match and pays £50. I know who got the best bargain!

The thing I remember most about the day, even more than the result, was the spirit of the crowd. It was like one big party, not a hooligan to be seen and everybody there to enjoy the occasion. The German supporters were wonderfully sporting in defeat.

I will never forget the sight of little Nobby Stiles dancing around with his socks down to his ankles. Has there ever been a more warming celebration after any match at Wembley? What a great sight. And all for ten bob.

SCOTLAND CLAIM THE WORLD CUP

Dave Baxter

Darlington

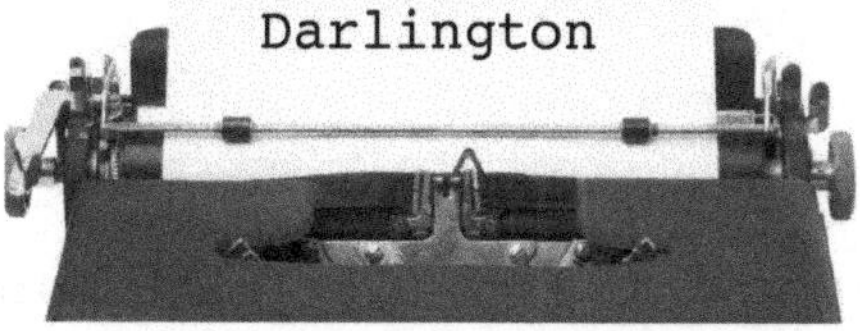

I grew up in a divided household, Mum was English and Dad Scottish. I always supported England and when it was a match against Scotland my Dad and I would almost come to blows with our opinions. But on that World Cup final day, Dad – now sadly gone – got right behind England and danced round the room with me when Geoff Hurst's second goal was allowed. Of course it crossed the line! Mind you, Dad danced even more happily when the Scots became the first team to beat the world champions at Wembley in 1967 and claimed the World Cup! More family arguments.

I went to Wembley on the morning of the match hoping to buy a spare ticket, but was unlucky and finished sitting outside the Stadium listening to the roar of the crowd and to the BBC commentary on somebody's transistor radio. I think there must have been as many outside Wembley as inside the ground. There were lots of Germans who had come over without tickets, and they were really sporting and joined in the applause for England when the final whistle blew.

From Wembley me and my mates, there were four of us all in our late teens, got on the tube train to Trafalgar Square and skipped in the fountains. We joined a conga of hundreds of people and danced around the square. An old-timer said it was the greatest night he'd known since we'd won the war. And that was against Germany, too!

My late dad's next door neighbour won a ticket for the final in a newspaper competition, and he couldn't go because he had a family wedding. He sold the top-of-the-range £3 15s ticket to Dad for £2 and he felt privileged to be at the greatest match in English football history.

He sat next to a New Yorker from the United States embassy in Grosvenor Square, who'd been given a ticket, and was watching his first ever 'soccer' match. He got so involved that when the final whistle blew he cuddled my Dad and said it was greater than the World Series!

They became pen pals, a friendship that lasted until Dad passed on last year.

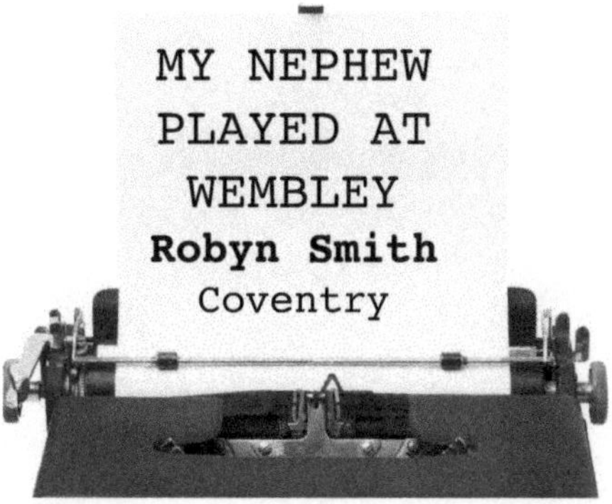

There was a special reason for me going to Wembley for the final, because my nephew was playing! Well, not exactly in the match, but before and during the interval. He was a trombonist in the marvellous Royal Marines band.

He later emigrated but before he went Down Under he presented me with a wonderful reminder of that great day – a World Cup programme signed by England captain Bobby Moore, which I treasure to this day.

Bobby took the trouble to thank the leader of the Marines band for their part in the day. That's the sort of thoughtful and caring captain he was, and it showed on the football field where he never ever put a foot wrong.

If anybody deserved to collect that World Cup, it was Bobby Moore. To this day I get angry when I think how the football establishment ignored him. He should have been an ambassador for the Football Association and, like his West Ham team-mate Geoff Hurst, a knight. Arise, Sir Bobby!

July 30 1966 was my brother Alexander's 21st birthday and I managed to give him the best possible present – a ticket to the Final at Wembley. I worked as a temp at the office of the Keith Prowse agency that had the franchise for the World Cup tickets, and I put my order in on the first day they became available. Because I got staff rates, I seem to remember the block of season tickets cost me £3!

Sadly my brother is no longer with us, but he always said that it was the best day of his life. So July 30 always has a very, very special place in my heart.

My own particular memory from that momentous day at Wembley late in July 1966 has a starting point two weeks earlier on the morning of England's second group match with Mexico. I was sat on the front steps of a nearby neighbour's house in Wood Green, North London, which modern day Google Maps tells me is only 10.1 miles from Wembley Stadium – so I was almost in the back garden so to speak! At that time, and in common with many thirteen-year-old boys from the era preceding the advent of computer games and the like, I had an active interest in constructing model airplanes from good old Airfix kits. In particular, anything from World War Two.

It so happened that my neighbour was a retired US Army Air Force officer who was based in England during WW2 and ended up with a 'GI Bride' and later decided to spend his retirement years in dear old 'Blighty'. For some reason I got speaking to him about my modelling activity. His eyes lit up, since he too did much the same thing as a hobby. He then mentioned that he had finished one model which he wanted to show me and disappeared back into the house for a minute or two. He then emerged with a most beautifully completed model of a Boeing B-29 USAAF Bomber – better known as a 'Superfortress'. Wow – I was dumbstruck at this beautiful piece of work. Cutting a long story short, he told me later that I could have it as a keepsake and so I duly took it home and placed it on its stand and sat it on top of a chest of drawers in my bedroom.

That evening, of course, England won 2-0 and so started a winning run that culminated in us arriving at this point on July 30 1966, leaving me totally convinced that my lovely Superfortress was not just a fantastic model, but one huge lucky charm!

So it was a bit of a shock then that after 10 minutes Helmut Haller opened the scoring for the West Germans, especially since I was still at an age where I couldn't believe that my lucky charm would ever let England down!! And then suddenly a brainwave struck … and something that my silly adolescent head hadn't previously taken into consideration: England, of course, had had to change their kit from the normal white shirt to the now legendary red one. They've changed! So I reasoned that by the same token I needed to change the direction that the Superfortress was facing! I duly dashed upstairs and turned the aircraft around

180 degrees to take this revelation into account. Well, and as if by magic, I arrived back into our front room at the very moment that Bobby Moore planted a free-kick straight on to head of Geoff Hurst and England were level at 1-1!! My late father just sat and roared laughing at me, but I didn't care, Dad, because I had just single-handedly proved that my lucky charm was still in good working order!

If you were alive and were of the age to reason, then July 30 1966 was one of those days that you could almost chart everything that you either did; where you were; or what may have happened to you that day, and I certainly have a list of them. However, it is the episode with the Superfortress that will always stand out since it primarily reminds me now of just how really simple that you view things in life at that innocent age.

My late grandfather, Charles Howe, was one of those "some people are on the pitch" referred to in Kenneth Wolstenholme's famous World Cup commentary. He used to tell us how he and half a dozen other supporters outran the stewards, thinking that the final whistle had blown.

They danced among the players after Geoff Hurst's shot had gone into the net. In several of the newsreels my granddad can be seen carrying a Union Jack and waving it in the face of Uwe Seeler.

Eventually he was frog-marched off the pitch by a burly policeman who said he could be arrested for disturbing the peace if he didn't get back on the terraces sharpish. Granddad waited for the policeman to go after somebody else and then darted back on to the pitch and cuddled his hero George Cohen, who played for the Fulham team that Dad supported.

George told him: "We couldn't have done it without the support. The crowd has been fantastic right the way through the finals."

Granddad was always telling the story in the local pub, and the Landlord used to shout – instead of 'Last Orders' – 'Some think the drinking's all over, it IS now.'

At granddad's funeral we played a recording of When the Saints (Reds). He was football daft and called July 30 1966 the proudest day of his life.

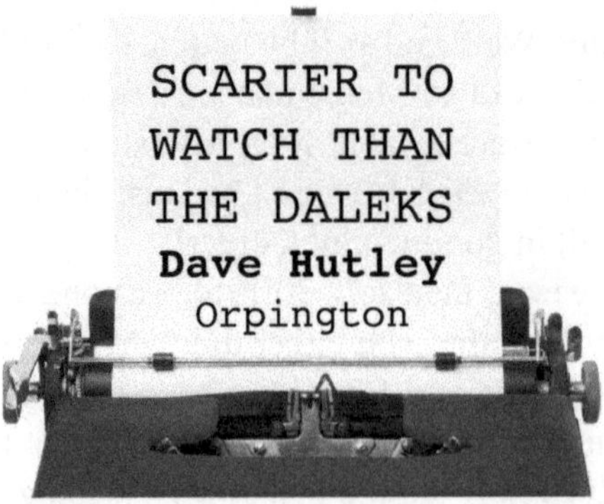

SCARIER TO WATCH THAN THE DALEKS

Dave Hutley

Orpington

I was 9-years-old and football mad like my 13-year-old brother and my dad, and for my mum I think it was a case of "if you can't beat 'em, join 'em", so she was a convert as well. However, in what I think was a distinct lack of forward planning on my dad's part, we were due to go on holiday on July 30 to our regular location of Westgate on the Kent coast. But earlier that year my dad had bought our first car, so for the first time ever, we were driving down rather than going by train – great excitement!

Obviously the decision was taken that we'd watch the game at home and then go straight off on our holiday, so the car was packed up and we were ready to go as the 90th minute approached. When Germany were awarded their free-kick, it was all too much for me and I hid behind the curtains, a place normally reserved for watching (or hiding from) *Dr Who* whenever the Daleks appeared. This was scarier. Of course we all know what happened next, the trip to Westgate was delayed still further but the wait was worth it and eventually we were on our way.

However, that wasn't the end of the day's dramas. As we headed down the A2 in our new-to-us Ford Escort we all noticed a burning smell and I uttered the infamous words, destined to become immortalised in our family history, "Don't worry, it's not us". Just as the final word left my lips, the car started to fill up with smoke from under the dashboard.

Dad immediately pulled over to the hard shoulder and we all clambered out. He tentatively lifted the bonnet and was greeted by a plume of smoke, though fortunately no flames. He made his way along the hard shoulder to find the nearest emergency phone while the three of us stood a safe distance from the car. After an hour or so the AA patrol man showed up and diagnosed a leaking radiator. He filled it up with water, but even as he was doing so it started to spill out like a fountain through the holes in the radiator. All he could suggest was that we drive a few miles at a time and then keep topping up with water, which is what we did. We eventually limped into Westgate past midnight.

Hardly the best of starts to the holiday. One thing's for sure – I never dared to make any guesses about the possible source of burning smells when in the car ever again. I was able to say: "But at least we've won the World Cup!"

THE BALL AND THAT LINESMAN

Frank Bowers

Carlisle

An old drinking pal of my Dad's was a Fleet Street photographer who sat alongside the net in which Geoff Hurst scored the controversial second goal of his hat-trick. He said he had the best view and that the ball hit the line and spun back. No way, he said, that the whole ball crossed the goal-line. So how on earth could a linesman thirty yards away and at an angle have been so certain that it did cross the line?

No wonder the Germans still protest to this day, and the South Americans remain convinced that the whole thing was fixed. I wanted England to win as much as the next man, but not by cheating. It all left a bad taste.

Those that say Hurst ended all arguments with his fourth goal forget that the Germans would not all have been parked in the English half chasing an equaliser if that second goal had been disallowed.

I know this is an unpopular view and it has got me into lots of angry debates, but I think honesty and integrity should be above all else in sport, otherwise what's the point in playing?

WEDDING DAY TELEGRAM

Jim Tattersall

Cyprus, ex-Hull

I was not the most popular bloke among my mates when I chose July 30 for my wedding day, but it was planned long in advance of the final. We had a side room at the hotel where guests could watch the match on TV, and it became crowded throughout extra-time. My best man in his wedding speech pretended I'd got a telegram from Alf Ramsey that read: "WISH YOU WERE HERE STOP. HOPE YOU SCORE TONIGHT, Alf and the Boys." Uh, we were divorced six years later when my wife ran off with the best man! I don't half miss him.

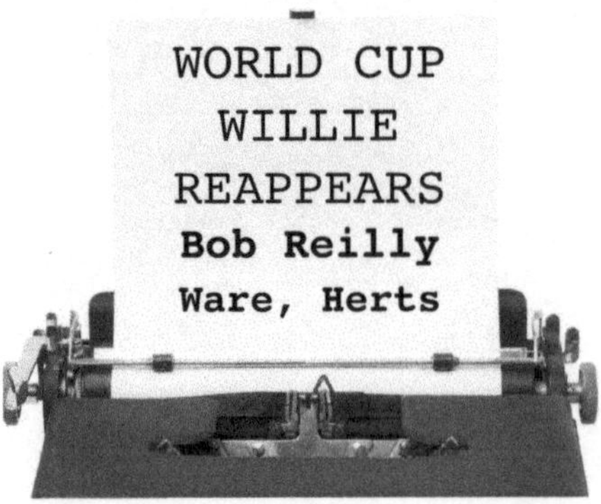

WORLD CUP WILLIE REAPPEARS

Bob Reilly
Ware, Herts

I was 21 at the time of the 1966 World Cup final, and spent most of my money on the latest clothes fashions and records, and thought I was Jack the lad, being a London boy and a mod. I considered anyone who lived outside of London beneath us.

I spent the two weeks around the World Cup final on holiday in Sandown, Isle of Wight.(foreign holidays were almost unheard of at the time) enjoying the sea, sun and sand as you do. I watched the match on black and white television in the lounge of the guest house where I was staying along with the other guests, and the owners and staff also piled into the room.

I particularly remember one guy who was a West Ham fan boasting the Hammers had won the World Cup. As a Spurs supporter, my only disappointment was that our Jimmmy Greaves was not playing.

Greavsie – along with Bobby Moore and Bobby Charlton – were considered our only world-class stars at the time. The rest of the team became legends for their achievement.

We did not realise at the time that history had been made. Now we all look back with pride. We tend to forget that it rained heavily that day because all our memories are bathed in sunshine.

I have only hazy recall of what I did after the match because along with many across the country I got quite intoxicated.

But something happened as we came into this 50th anniversary year that brought the memories flooding back. While clearing my late mum's bedroom prior to redecorating I had cause to open a chest where she kept her supply of bed linen and towels etc.

I was surprised and moved to find that right at the bottom was my World Cup Willie tee-shirt.

It had probably been there since 1966 and Mum had kept it as a memento. Like me, she was a lifelong Spurs fan and loved football in general.

Needless to say it would not fit me any more as I am three stone heavier than I was in 1966, but the sight of World Cup Willie suddenly reminded me of an historic day in our sporting history.

A ONCE IN A LIFETIME VICTORY

Tom Johnstone
Salford

I was born early in that summer of 1966, and apparently my father held me up in front of the television set while the Queen was presenting the World Cup to Bobby Moore and said: "My son, take a good look. You may never see this again in your lifetime."

Here we are fifty years later, and I am still waiting!

My late Dad, a fanatical Manchester United fan, was convinced we were going to win in the year David Beckham was at his peak, but apart from when we reached the semi-finals in 1990 in Italy there has been little danger of another England win in my lifetime.

Dad was right!

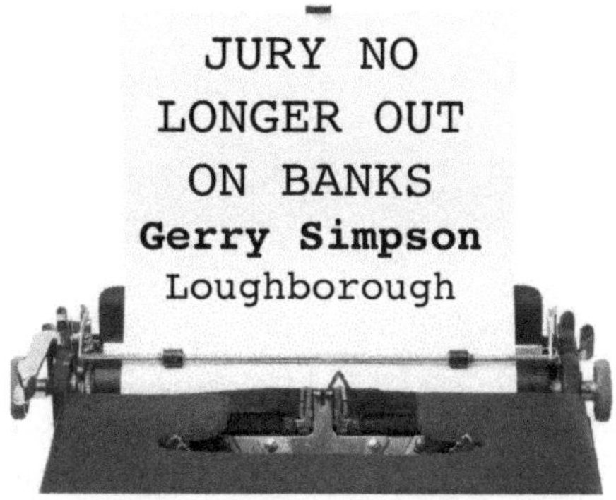

JURY NO LONGER OUT ON BANKS

Gerry Simpson
Loughborough

I was on jury service in Nottingham the week of the World Cup final and we were sent out to consider our verdict on the Friday before the final. We did not do it consciously, but we quickly came to a unanimous not guilty verdict, and so were in time to get home to watch the final!

I was particularly interested in watching my idol Gordon Banks, the greatest goalkeeper of all time. People seem to forget that if he had not made a brilliant fingertip save from (I think) Overath in the second-half West Germany might have emerged as the winners. We all remember the Hurst hat-trick, but let's not forget the saves by Banks.

A GREAVSIE SIGNED PROGRAMME!

Andy Hindmarsh
Winnipeg

My grandfather emigrated to Canada the year after England won the World Cup and for the rest of his life until his passing in 2012 he used to recite the winning team like a daily mantra. He never lost his love for soccer and continued to follow the game avidly on the television and radio from way out in the heart of Canada. When Bobby Moore and Jimmy Greaves came out here to play in Toronto in the 1970s he tracked them down and got them to sign his World Cup programme. I should not think there are too many 1966 World Cup final programmes signed by Mr Greaves!

THE GAME THAT LEFT US HOARSE

George Biddle
Southampton

I was fortunate enough to have a ticket to all the London matches,which strangely included one at the old White City stadium. On final day, along with a friend, we parked in a quiet side road, just a short stroll from the stadium. No parking charges! Walking up Wembley Way, I remember a lot of people holding handfuls of cash in the hope of buying a ticket, but nobody appeared to be selling.

The atmosphere before the game was one of anxiety rather than expectation. My abiding memory is of Bobby Charlton majestically sweeping through the midfield throughout the whole tournament. Most of us were not capable of being raucous when leaving the stadium after England's victory. We were all completely hoarse!

AN ALL-NIGHT VICTORY CELEBRATION

David Pope
London E.11

I have only a nine-year-old's memory of the final and recall my friend and I banging on the floor in excitement as we watched it on television. Somebody who has even hazier memories was a guy who was an official for my trade union. He was 19 at the time and went to the game. He told me that he got paralytic afterwards and crashed out on Shepherd's Bush Green (he's a QPR fan). He woke up next morning at 9am and rang home. His anxious mother asked where he'd been all night. He told her, and she said, 'What? On your own?' He replied, 'No, there's about 200 others here!' The victory was celebrated like no other.

A SHOE-IN FOR BOBBY CHARLTON

Bruce Lloyd
Wolverhampton

On the day of the final my mother came home from morning shopping to say she had just been in a local shoe shop with Bobby Charlton. We then lived in Hendon, near the hotel where the team was staying. Of course, we thought Mum had been mistaken, but after the game we heard Bobby say in an interview that he and Ray Wilson had gone shopping for shoes just a few hours before the match. Can you imagine that today! The players would be surrounded by security guards and they would send somebody else out to do their shopping.

Things were so different then, and have not changed for the better. Footballers today are too detached from the fans. My brother and I used to walk to Hendon Hall and talk to the players, who were only too willing to stand and chat. Who gets near their heroes these days?

CRASHING INTO A FINAL SEAT

George Regan

Nottingham

Unfortunately my father is not around any longer to tell the story himself, but this is what happened to him on the day England won the World Cup. He was a 19-year-old student, and on the day of the final cycled the six miles from his Finchley home to Wembley Stadium just to get a taste of the atmosphere. He planned to be home again in time to watch the game on television.

At traffic lights just a few hundred yards from the stadium he signalled to turn right but the driver of a car travelling behind him failed to stop and knocked Dad off his bike.

Thank goodness, Dad was not hurt, just badly shaken. His bicycle was a write-off, with the rear wheel a buckled mess that had to be replaced.

The driver of the car that hit his bike did the decent thing and stopped, and got out to make sure Dad was all right.

It turned out that he was a chauffeur driving officials from the Portuguese embassy to Wembley Stadium to watch the the final that was due to kick off an hour later.

The chauffeur got all Dad's address details, and he was sent a cheque for £50 that easily covered the cost of his bike. In fact, Dad, said, it would have bought three bikes.

And it gets better. One of the embassy officials fished into his pocket and came up with a spare ticket for the final!

Dad telephoned home to explain what had happened, and his father agreed to pick him up once the game was over He watched the incredible match from a seat just behind the Royal Box, and got a close-up view of captain Bobby Moore receiving the Jules Rimet trophy from the Queen.

It was one of Dad's favourite pub stories, telling it even to drinking buddies in the bars of Adelaide to where we emigrated in the 1970s. His most precious possession was the 1966 World Cup programme.

Dad passed on in 2011, and I am now back in England and looking forward to the Golden anniversary on July 30.

It's a story that I will hand down to my grandchildren.

WHO CARES ABOUT DEVALUATION!

Vic Savage
Taunton

On the day of the final, the train I was travelling on from Barnstaple in Devon got stuck outside Waterloo because of a signal failure. I was supposed to be meeting friends to watch the final on TV at a house in London. I finished up listening to it on a Philips transistor radio with a crowd of fellow passengers cheering England on. When Geoff Hurst scored the fourth goal to complete his hat-trick we danced around the station concourse as if we were at the stadium. The match brought the nation together at a time when it looked as if the country was going to go broke under the Wilson government. They devalued the pound and we couldn't have cared less!

CHARLTONS STOP THE TRAFFIC

Paul Vaughan
Newcastle

My memory of the World Cup is welcoming home the Charlton brothers, Jack and Bobby, to Ashington after the final. I was living there when England won the World Cup, and the entire North East stopped to cheer our lads on.

I knew their younger brothers Gordon and Tommy. Gordon was in the merchant navy and Tommy worked down the pit. Neither of them got to watch the final at Wembley, but their parents Cissie and Bob went down to London for it.

Thousands turned out to see the two lads driven through the streets in an open-top vintage Rolls Royce led by a brass band. It was one of the most exciting and proudest days our little town had ever known. They stopped the traffic.

WE ALL HAD FAITH IN ALF RAMSEY

Richard Preston
Trowbridge

On the occasion of the World Cup in 1966, my family and I had spent the previous week on holiday in Skegness. In order to watch the games we had to get a pass into the Miners' holiday camp, where as thirteen-year-olds my cousin and I watched the games on the lounge TV along with about sixty others.

For the final we were back in Leicester, so I watched on a rented, relatively small-screen black and white TV, with my mum and dad.

The biggest talking point was the absence of Jimmy Greaves from the team selection. He was without doubt the best footballer of the 1960s.

I realise now that back then throughout the finals I personally had total belief in everything Alf Ramsey said. He had told me England would win and I believed him, so I had faith in his team selection.

My first job was to handwrite the two teams into my tournament programme, which I still have as a reminder of that great day.

The game started and it almost seemed like minutes that England were 1-0 down, however I remember the commentator reassuring me that the first team to score in numerous World Cups had gone on to lose. So I did not lose hope.

Being from Leicester I was extremely interested to see how Gordon Banks played, and he made several quality saves throughout the game and the whole tournament.

When the Bobby Moore to Geoff Hurst combination led to a goal the house erupted. As England got on top, it became 2-1 as Peters scored.

As the end of the game approached the commentator prematurely talked about England winning and I remember my mother shouting at the screen for him to shut up. Of course the Germans scored in the last minute, but even then we all agreed that England would win, showing our faith in Alf again.

The over-the-line goal, my family ignored everyone other than the 'Russian' linesman', and we cheered loudly when he gave the goal.

As the game ended with that fourth goal my outstanding memory is of all the teenagers in our area going on to the street to re-enact the game. Wonderful 50-year-old memories of the summertime of life.

WHY MY HEART WAS WITH GERMANY

Burk Gravis

Edmonton

Born in Germany but living in London since 1953, my memories of that period were that I watched the entire World Cup on the TV as I could not get tickets. The irony is that for the Final I was actually back in Germany, in my home town Ludenscheid. On the ferry from Dover to Ostend we watched the Argentina game on the ship's TV, with great horror at the tactics of the South Americans.

On the day of the final, all my German relatives and friends were convinced I was supporting England, which was way off the mark.

When the referee and his nodding Soviet linesman awarded the third England goal I was given total grief as if I was to blame for the decision. Then, the fourth goal just aggravated the moment.

To this day they are all still positive I was "der Englander," even though I have travelled to Germany for many internationals supporting them.

I live in London with my English family, but I have to be honest and say my football heart remains with Deutschland ... as it did back in 1966.

WELCOME ALFRED ROBERT GEOFFREY

Joyce Phillips

Bristol

My late brother was born on July 30 1966 and Dad wanted to name him after the entire England team. After a lot of argument they settled on him being called Alfred Robert Geoffrey. My Mum went into labour at midday and Alfred was born just after the final whistle. Dad watched the match on a TV in the hospital in the days when husbands did not attend births. I don't think they could have dragged him away from the telly!

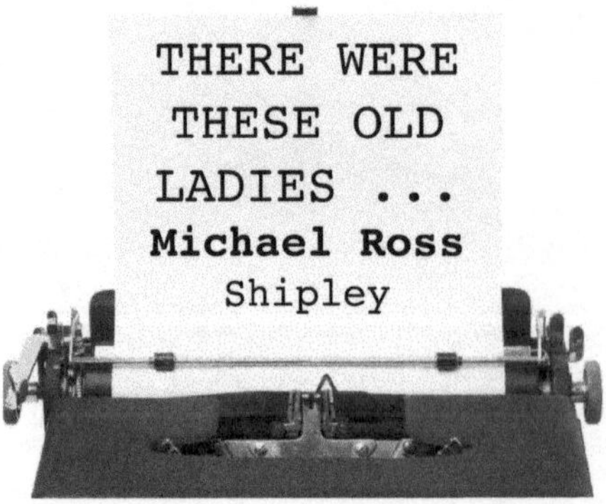

Not sure in this politically-correct age whether I should share this 50-year-old memory, but I will anyway! Some four hours prior to kick-off, I was on the tube going from Harrow to Finchley Road. Two elderly ladies were sitting opposite, and as the train arrived at Wembley Park they looked at the twin towers. One lady remarked to her companion: "It's the final today, dear." The other lady nodded, "I know." There was a momentary pause and the second lady then added: "It would be a great shame to get thus far only to lose to the Hun." The first lady nodded vigorously in agreement.

I remember thinking to myself that if those two old dears – with language going back to World War I and who clearly had no interest whatever in football – wanted England to win, there was no possibility of our being defeated. I still chuckle at the memory all these years later.

My granddad left me his 1966 World Cup programme in his will. It has the autographs of Bobby Moore, Alf Ramsey, Geoff Hurst and Matin Peters. I have been offered a lot of money for it by collectors, but I am keeping it to leave to my grandchildren.

Granddad was at the match and got the programme signed ten years later at a reunion of the World Cup winning team. He said July 30 1966 was the proudest day of his life.

FROM FIRST KISS TO LAST KICK

Ray Hardwick
West Molesey

My first memory of 1966 as a 14-year-old schoolboy was my first passionate kiss with a girl called Linda. She was gorgeous! But I didn't know how to 'progress' from the kiss, and lost out to a guy at school who did. But that was all forgotten when the World Cup came around. Football, football, football was all that mattered that year.

I followed everything about the World Cup in the papers, and on our black and white TV. I cut out the pictures of all the players and teams, and stuck them in a scrapbook.

My bedroom wall was plastered with pictures of the England team. There was no wallpaper left to be seen. All those players looking at me from the wall were, and still are, my heroes.

I enjoyed every game. I particularly remember the Argentinian captain Rattin slapping Bobby Moore's face, trying to provoke Bobby into retaliating, but our skipper just turned away and laughed. What a man, and what a fantastic example to youngsters.

Anyway, the final. My Mum used to work in a shop on Saturdays, and I remember her saying that on that day she didn't serve a single customer. Everybody who was not at Wembley was gathered around their TV sets or those of neighbours.

So it was just Dad and me watching the final. I remember nearly everything about the game, but if I think my memory is going, I occasionally dig out the World Cup film *Goal* just to refresh me about that dramatic match.

The crushing moment, of course, was when Germany equalised in the last minute of normal time to make it 2-2. My Dad swore, 'Bloody Germans', as if it was in the Second World War.

I went rushing up to my bedroom to pray as hard as I could to all my heroes on my wall that we would win in the end. What a relief when Geoff Hurst's third goal hit the back of the net. And what a summer we teenage boys had in the school holidays, playing football from dawn to dusk and pretending to be our heroes. I have never been more proud to be English since those wonderful World Cup weeks. Even better than kissing girls.

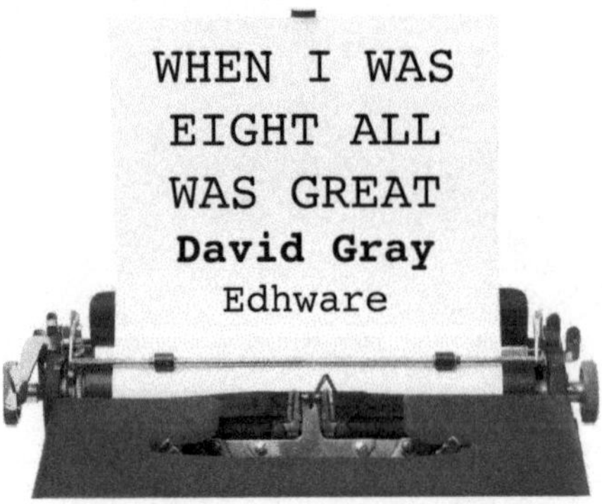

As a football-mad eight-year-old I lived near Queensbury Station, just two underground stops from Wembley Park, and my football education was being nurtured by watching my local team, Edgware Town, with the occasional visits to Chelsea, and Wembley Stadium to see the Amateur Cup Finals of 1965 and 1966.

I remember the anticipation to the World Cup so well even though it was nothing like the mass pre-tournament hype nowadays. I collected stickers of the players and had them stuck all over my bicycle and couldn't wait for it to begin. It didn't matter who they were or what country they came from, the stickers went on the bike!

My elder brother, Pete, had a ticket for the opening match, England versus Uruguay, but he was so disgusted with the negative play of the South Americans he decided that he wasn't going to go to any more games (bit of an error, that).

As the tournament grew I watched whatever game was put on TV. Apart from England's matches, I can remember Pelé being chopped out of contention, Hungary scoring a fantastic running volley, Italy crashing out to North Korea, and Eusebio's one man show bringing Portugal back from the dead against North Korea. Eusebio really was taken to the heart of the nation, his sportsmanship and great goals seemed to capture the imagination. Playing '3 and in' down the park if you weren't an England player you were either Eusebio or Pak Doo Ik!

On July 16, whilst England were playing a group match, my future wife, Michele, was being born less than a mile away from me, at Kingsbury Hospital. Obviously I didn't know her at the time but she still asks whether I would have gone to see her or watched the football, given the choice.

Sorry love, no contest!

Bobby Charlton's goal against Mexico has been seen thousands of times on TV, but it remains in my top ten goals of all time. What a magnificent strike. Then, getting past France with Nobby Stiles causing havoc, and on to the quarter-final against Argentina. A hot day, Rattin being sent off is a vivid memory as it was so rare in those days as players normally had to commit murder to get their marching orders. Hurst's great header and George Cohen prevented by Sir Alf from swapping shirts.

The semi-final versus Portugal was a classic match, it was the game everyone wanted as the final instead of either the workmanlike Germans or Russians who were in the other semi. Two more strikes by Bobby Charlton, a late penalty by Eusebio when Jack Charlton handled close to the line (he would have been sent off nowadays) and eventually a 2-1 win.

And so to the final. A showery and sunny day, with a tiny column in the paper telling us England would be playing in RED. I watched the match with my Dad and brother whilst Mum and sister went to Wembley ... to go shopping! 0-1 down, equalising, then the joy of going 2-1 up ... this is it, we are going to win the Cup. With seconds to go Jack Charlton is penalised for a foul and the Germans only go and score.

Extra-time! I thought the 'Russian' linesman with his white belt had said no goal at first. Then when Geoff Hurst scored his third and it was all over we all leapt about our living room in joy. I went straight out into the back garden to try and re-enact the goals, England were the World Champions, surely the first of many such honours. I am still waiting.

When I went to my Uncle's funeral up in Yorkshire about 20 years ago I could not believe my eyes when I saw Ray Wilson as the undertaker leading the coffin into the crematorium. The last time I'd seen him in the flesh was helping England win the World Cup in 1966.

As a former (very average) full-back myself, I had idolised both George Cohen and Ray Wilson. Now here was one of my heroes just a few yards away, and I tried to work out what would be the etiquette for asking somebody for an autograph at a funeral. I considered what my late football-mad Uncle would have done and I know he would have gone for it.

So after the service I worked up the nerve to ask Ray for his autograph, but he said in a firm but in no way arrogant way: "Sorry, not today, not when I'm working. Get in touch with me here." He gave me one of his cards and got on with his business. He had gently put me in my place, and I respected him even more.

He was a great footballer and then a caring funeral director putting his duty first. They don't make them like him any more. He sent me a signed photo.

HOOKED BY THE WEMBLEY PROGRAMME

Peter Haine

Stotfold, Beds

My ten-year-old schoolboy obsession with Tottenham Hotspur meant that I only became interested in the national team if one of our players was selected to wear the three lions. So when Dad announced that he had applied for tickets for the World Cup, I wasn't too excited. Even when he said that he'd a ticket for every game at Wembley, I didn't realise what that might lead to back in a time when there was very little football shown live on TV.

When Dad left home for Wembley to watch the opening match against Uruguay on July 11, I sat at home watching the television as the Queen declared the championship open. As usual, Dad returned with a programme. But it was different, as it was for the whole tournament rather than just for the Uruguay game. And it had space for filling in the teams and results for each game, as well as a couple of pages for notes. It was the start of me being completely hooked.

I still have the programme, and here is just one of my entries handwritten with loving care and attention, more so than with my schoolbooks:

> "The next surprise came from again, Everton, the place of football delight, where Portugal won a battle of wits. The Brazillians fielded a young team against the magnificent Portugal. Eusebio threatened the Brazillian goalkeeper with cunning corners, swerving free-kicks, and long goal kicks. Simoes got the first, with a mistake from the Brazillians. Eusebio scored his second and got Portugal's third goal just before the whistle. Brazil scored through Rildo."

Looking through the programme, I recall watching every England game (trying to see Dad in the crowd to no avail), and later hearing his excitement rise as England progressed.

On the big final day, I took up my usual position in front of the TV to watch the build-up whilst Dad went to the ground. I remember cheering in the street when we won, and waiting for Dad to come home. I waited a long time … he left Wembley and headed for the West End. I didn't get a chance to chat to him until Sunday afternoon when his hangover had worn off!

FERRY TO A FOOTBALLING FAIRYTALE

Colin Denham

Isle of Wight

My mate Pip Stears and I caught the early-morning ferry from the Isle of Wight on July 30 1966 and then travelled from Southampton to Waterloo by train and next on the underground to Wembley Park. I was 19, Pip 20 and for us it was a great adventure We have the ticket stubs to prove we went through Entrance 58, Turnstile 8, to stand for 10 shillings in the West Enclosure.

We were behind the goal where Geoff Hurst scored the fourth 'it's all over' goal. It's quite likely we were the only two from the Island to actually be there for the dramatic match.

Playing extra-time meant that by the time we got out of the stadium and down to the last ferry it was pretty late, but we were not bothered because England had won the World Cup.

And we were there to see it as day trippers!

As lifelong fans of Southampton we have met Terry Paine, who was in the England squad, and we were proud to share our memories with him.

THE HAILSTORM THAT HIT WEMBLEY

Jean Wright

Hatfield

My late grandfather was one of the Wembley groundsmen, and he said that six hours before the final there was a torrential hailstorm and the pitch was almost flooded, and the entire staff had to pitchfork it. Do you know if this is true?

I can only find references to heavy rain but not to a hailstorm.

Norman Giller: Yes, there was a hailstorm that saturated the pitch. Head groundsman George Stanton and his team worked wonders getting it match fit.

A FINAL LETTER TO MY SON

Rosina La Bas
Southampton

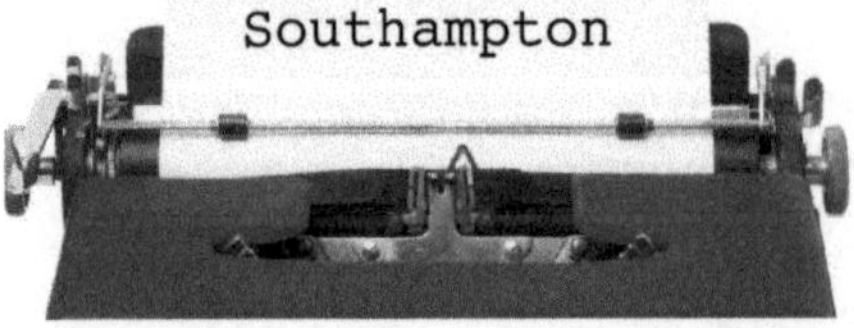

My 8-year-old son Kevin was on a summer holiday in Devon and desperately sorry to be away for the final with no TV, so as I watched the match for him I wrote a letter which I still have. It describes in note form the game exactly as it happened:

Dear Kevin, The team is the same as for the semi final, the Queen has arrived and the teams are in the tunnel waiting to come out. The crowd is going mad and shouting ENGLAND. No score after 10 minutes. Peters has had two good tries and now Haller has scored for Germany after 12 minutes.

Hurrah. Geoff Hurst has equalised with a header after 18 minutes with a pass from Moore who had a free kick after a foul.

Peters has his name taken for a foul. The referee seems to be all for Germany. Every time they foul England they get the free kick and the crowd boo the ref.

Banks just made a brilliant save, and if it wasn't for him Germany would be well in the lead because England's defence is not very good. Banks just made another good save.

Half time and the score is still 1-1. They're off again and it's pouring with rain, Jack Charlton is having ref trouble and so is Nobby, but the Germans get away with it. Peters just had another couple of misses. Banks just made his first good save in this half. Peters missed again. The crowd are singing what a rotten referee.

The German goalkeeper is down injured for the second time. Bobby Charlton just had a very near miss. Hunt made a lovely pass to Hurst, but he just missed it. Charlton just had a good try blocked. Now a beautiful goal by Peters at last so they're winning 2-1 with 10 minutes to go. Gordon Banks ran right to the other end to join in the celebrations. Peters missed again. There's 5 minutes to go. Germany have another free kick after Jack Charlton fouled. It was 30 seconds from the end when England thought they had won. Oh dear, what a shame Kevin.

They are going to play another 15 minutes each way. They're all very tired. Hurst has scored after 10 minutes after hitting the bar. Now he has scored again 30 seconds from the end to make it a hat trick, so he must be about the greatest. So England have won 4-2.The crowd has gone wild, the teams are doing a lap of honour. Nobby is doing a little jig. Enjoy reading if you have the time, Love Mum.

RADIO TIMES IN SOUTH AFRICA

Mark Neville

Knebworth

I was just three when the World Cup was played, but have a story to tell. My family were then living in South Africa, where my father, Gordon, was coaching a Durban United team. He tells me that he remembers that at the time of the 1966 World Cup final his side were playing a match, and he had his eyes on the game and his ears tuned to a transistor radio that he had on the side of the pitch, listening to the BBC overseas live commentary from Wembley. They did not have television in South Africa in those days, and so everything revolved around the wireless.

Dad grew up in Wood Green as a member of a devoted Tottenham Hotspur family, and his three brothers back in the UK were all glued to the TV screen watching the match. All of them were very disappointed that their idol Jimmy Greaves did not get into the team, but Geoff Hurst's three goals proved that the ex-Tottenham defender Alf Ramsey knew what he was doing.

SCOUTING FOR VICTORY IN SNOWDONIA

Dick Patterson

Walsall

We were on a scout camping trip to Snowdonia from Coventry, and listened to the match on a radio that kept floating in and out of the commentary, and we were never quite sure of what the score was. Then suddenly we heard the commentator screaming 'And Hurst has scored goal number four ... England have won the World Cup.' We danced around in the foothills of Mount Snowdown as if we had actually been spectators. I was thirteen at the time, and thought there would be plenty of chances to see England win the World Cup and actually be there. Now I am nearly at pension age, and still no sign of another final!

ALL THIS FOR JUST FOUR QUID!

Geoff Mills
Camberley

Aged 22 and recently married, I attended all six England group matches (Wembley and White City). Along with my Dad and brother we bought our tickets well in advance for the princely sum of £4, which seems incredible compared to today's prices.

At the start of the tournament I thought West Germany would be the winners and was glad to be proved wrong.

After the tedious opening match against Uruguay I didn't hold out any hope for England, but they improved as it went on. I vividly remember Bobby Charlton's stunning goal against Mexico, the controversial Nobby Stiles tackle on Simon of France and Roger Hunt's two vital goals against France to clinch a place in the last eight.

Then the quarter-final, Rattin's sending off and Geoff Hurst's headed goal from a perfect pass from composed skipper Bobby Moore. I still think Argentina could have won if they had concentrated on playing football, as they were an impressive team with many talented individuals.

On to the semi-final and two Bobby Charlton goals beating Eusebio's penalty. England had reached the final.

On Final Day we arrived at Wembley before the turnstiles were open and I remember it was raining quite hard. We went to our usual spot in bay B18, which was above the players' tunnel.

My Dad, brother and I went through all the emotions like the rest of the nation and were distraught when Weber equalised to send it to extra-time.

In extra-time – apart from Geoff Hurst's goals – I will forever remember the way Alan Ball kept going. It is almost impossible to believe anyone could have so much energy. We were worn out just watching him!

When Bobby Moore collected the cup from Her Majesty it was an unforgettable moment, and the parading of it around the stadium added to my memories that still seem fresh 50 years on.

Our celebrations were very low key because we were simply too drained by the rollercoaster of a match.

This was without doubt the best £4 I ever spent.

WATCHING IT ALL IN GERMANY

Alan Brown

Hamburg

I was 14 years old and living in Augustdorf in Westphalia, Germany, where my Army sergeant Dad was stationed, and we watched the match on television with a German commentary.

When Geoff Hurst's second goal was given after the ball hit the underside of the bar all the British soldiers insisted it had crossed the line, while the Germans watching with us in the communal hall said it had clearly not!

That argument still rages today, and every year on the anniversary here in Germany they come up with slow-motion replays and photographs to prove that the ball did NOT cross the line. I tell my German family – I married a fraulein – and friends to look in the record books where it states that England won 4-2, with three goals to Geoff Hurst.

End of argument!

THE DAY THE AERIAL FELL OFF THE ROOF

Tom Dyson

Majorca

We rented our first television specifically so that we could watch the finals at our home in Dunstable, and my Dad's language turned the air blue when on the day of the final the outside aerial fell off the roof. We could not get a TV repairman out at such short notice, and we finished up listening to the match on radio.

As I recall, there was an excellent commentary by Brian Moore in the days before he became a legend on television.

But, with respect, we would rather have watched it on our gleaming new rented Pye TV! It just sat there staring back at us blankly. How frustrating.

It is funny really, but my memories of that momentous July afternoon are all in black and white. Black and white Union Jacks dominate the video of my mind – hardly a flag of St George in sight. We were one nation then – no talk of independence for Scotland or Wales. Even the tournament's mascot World Cup Willie wore a Union flag – "Dressed in red, white & blue, he's World Cup Willie".

Then there is the black and white apparel of thousands of the more mature supporters, many of them with haggard almost worn-out faces, a legacy of war, rationing and ongoing austerity. But this was 1966, and, according to *Time Magazine* we were all swinging.

On a personal level, I suppose you could say I was "swinging": swinging in my guise as a rock 'n' roll publicist, yet having to play the conservative in my other role as editor/owner of *The Amateur Footballer* magazine. The Friday night had been a rave at Soho's world-famous 'Marquee', and come the Saturday morning I was more than just a shade delicate as I made my way in the company of my closest school friend to Wembley Stadium on the tube from Finchley Road Station. I was 20, and I was immortal!

There was noise – a happy, expectant yet nervous buzz – on the train, and there was billowing smoke from the numerous cigarettes being lit, often seemingly in unison. One or two glasses had obviously been downed, but the behaviour was exemplary; I cannot even remember any anti-German taunts: remarkable really, considering the War had ended just over 20 years before.

Neither my mate nor I possessed a ticket, but we knew there would be touts aplenty in and around the environs of the stadium. And indeed there were, all seemingly thin and wizened with a roll-up cigarette stuck to their thin lips. We bought a couple for a fiver (about £83 in current values), and then a couple of programmes, 2/6 each (13p in today's money), and found our way to the terraces.

There was no segregation, so there we were with a group of young Germans to one side, who were extremely matey, and to the other some guys from Liverpool, whose attitude, shall we say, was just a tad more machismo.

Indeed, once the game kicked off, the Liverpudlians (dyed-in-the-wool

Evertonians), began to chant "Hunt is a c***", every time the hardworking Liverpool forward came into contact with the ball. One of the Germans took me to one side and, sotto voce, asked why they were insulting their own player in such a vitriolic manner. I tried to explain about the whole Everton/Liverpool thing, but he still remained nonplussed.

We were all ready to celebrate England winning the World Cup at 2-1, with seconds left on the clock, when the Germans, who seemed down-and-out, found a second wind and managed, I know not how, to conjure an equaliser. Extra-time, and yet another 'Lucky Strike' was lit – it tasted foul. Dry mouth, dry throat, heart beating – this was not good.

A Hurst shot thundered against the crossbar; "Was it a goal?" I screamed. No one, not even the officials, seemed to know. Then suddenly the diminutive linesman from the Soviet Union, Tofiq Bahramov – he was from Azerbaijan, but the Press labelled him Russian – signalled to referee Gottfried Dienst from Switzerland. Then, following a conference, which to the majority of the near-100,00 present, seemed of interminable length, Dienst, almost begrudgingly, gave the goal. The German players were not happy, and our German friends looked like they needed a Valium or three.

A pall of smoke covered us all like a shroud, emanating as it did from thousands of cigarettes, cigars and pipes. The Germans puffed on small, smelly cheroots, but within seconds of Geoff Hurst blasting the ball into the net for his hat-trick, one of them handed me a large cigar, as he clapped me on the back and congratulated me. You could say that for me – someone who was conceived in the final weeks of the War - my distrust of the German nation ceased with that young man's charming gesture.

By this time I had a mouth like a plumber's handkerchief, but who cared, England were World Champions

Norman Giller Note:

This beautifully observed account of the final was submitted by Gianna Tesser, widow of Greg, who sadly passed on in 2014 shortly after committing these memories to his computer. Greg was, to say the least, quite a character. He was a prominent rock 'n' roll publicist, who worked with a whole kaleidoscope of stars ranging from The Yardbirds to Georgie Fame and the Blue Flames. He was also well known on the football circuit as the enterprising agent for players like Peter Osgood, Rodney Marsh and Charlie Cooke, all the shy, retiring ones! As you can tell from his descriptive words, he was also a journalist and writer of style and substance. It is fitting to have his memory of 'the greatest day' July 30 1966 recorded here. RIP, Greg.

BREAKING NEWS INTERRUPTS THE FINAL

Paddy Briggs

Teddington

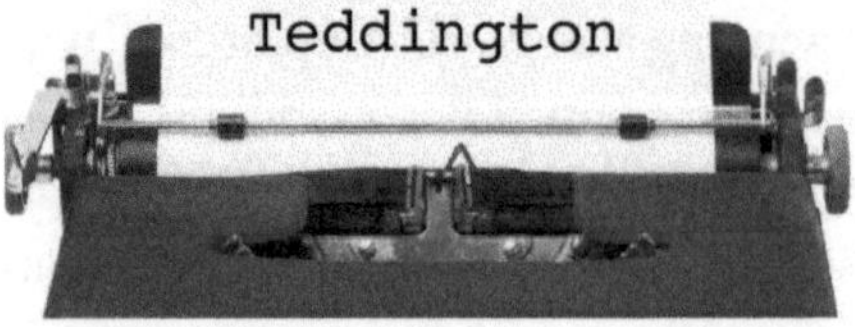

I was 19 and got tickets for the England Group games at Wembley, but couldn't get them for the knock-out stages. When England got to the Final my Dad announced that he was going courtesy of an early corporate hospitality offer!

My Mum decided to take the dog for a walk, and so I sat down to watch the final on my own. About 10 minutes before half-time the phone rang. Mum had fallen over on Bromley Common and broken an arm. Could I collect her and take her to Casualty at Bromley Hospital! Aaaargh.

I drove like a maniac, first to pick up Mum and the dog, then to deliver Mum to the hospital, which I did unceremoniously. "I won't be able to pick you up until after the game has finished" I told her. I was late picking Mum up of course after extra-time and the presentation ceremony. I think she forgave me. Dad came home and gave me the programme which I still have. Happy Days!

ON THE NIGHTCLUB STAGE

Bill Hawkins

Guilford

My late Mum was a waitress at Danny La Rue's nightclub, and was working the night of July 30 1966 when Geoff Hurst brought a group of England players and their wives to the club for the midnight show starring Danny and Ronnie Corbett.

She got a menu card signed by Geoff, Nobby Stiles and Alan Ball, and had it auctioned for charity a couple of years later. It would be worth a lot more today.

Mum said that Danny La Rue brought all the players up on stage and everybody in the nightclub stood and sang the England theme song of the day, When the Reds Go Marching In. I was just 10 at the time and remember going out as soon as the final whistle blew to play football with my mates in the street, and we all wanted to be Geoff Hurst!

FOOTNOTE: HURST AND FLYING EELS

Tony Bowyer

Colchester

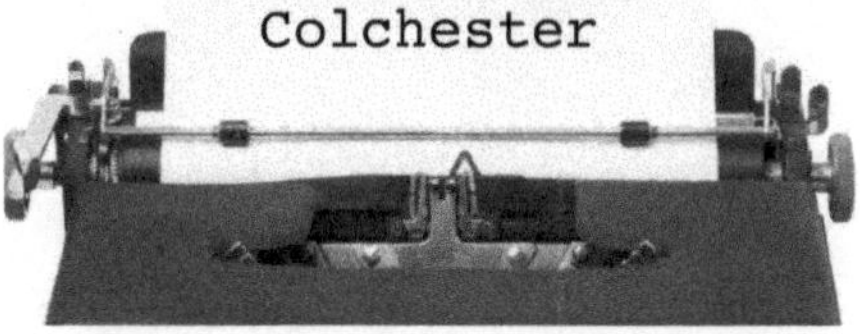

We were gathered with my Dad round the television – my elder brother Nicky, his best mate and me – when, with England winning the final 2-1 and just a few minutes to go, Dad suddenly announced we had to leave. He had arranged to collect Mum from the chiropodists at nearby Leigh-on-Sea, where she was having some corns removed. “Come on, boys,” Dad said, “England have got this won.”

Reluctantly, we went with him and when we got to the foot clinic Mum wasn’t ready. We waited outside near a jellied eel stall where we were astonished to find a small crowd listening to the game on radio. It was into extra-time! When Geoff Hurst’s third goal went in the man standing next to us was so excited he threw his carton of jellied eels into the air, and most of them landed on Dad’s head. It has remained a precious and hilarious memory for 50 years.

NOW LET’S HAVE ROVERS’ RETURN

Jeffery Booth

Blackburn

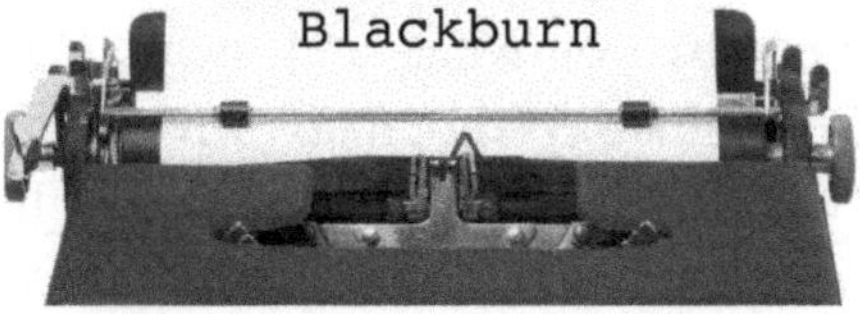

As the oldest, at 21, of seven brothers and sisters, I will never forget that day, July 30 1966, when we sat as a family crowded round the television, except Mum, who was in the kitchen keeping us stocked up with snacks and brew. As Blackburn Rovers fans we needed cheering up, because our team had just been relegated.

I recall getting so excited when Geoff Hurst equalised the Haller goal that I threw an apple in the air. Mum came in from the kitchen just as it hit the ceiling! She and our youngest brother, Roger, just three months old, were the only ones who did not get excited. But even Mum joined in the celebrations at the end as Hurst completed his hat-trick. I feel privileged to have watched it. Now we are waiting for England to win it again and for Blackburn to come back to the top.

An inspired move on the part of my father was to buy four tickets for every World Cup match to be played at Wembley in 1966, and he was lucky enough to see his beloved England play every game – whilst I remained locked up at boarding school for the duration of the group matches. Thanks to him, I did, however, see the quarter-final, semi-final, third place play-off and the Final itself. Two of our tickets were for seats towards the tunnel end of what I think was known as the North Stand (the upper section on the Royal Box side of the stadium), from where I had a great view of the infamous Rattin incident in the quarter-final which contributed towards Alf Ramsey labelling the Argentinian team as animals.

Then there was the wonderful semi-final versus Portugal, a game that would have graced the Final itself. A pity that it went on to be so overshadowed – especially given that it's been partly so by fifty years of debate about a doubtful goal, and, however inspired it was, a few seconds of commentary by Kenneth Wolstenholme.

But I digress, for, on Final day, my mother and sister were in our North Stand seats, and I was with my father in our two on what, as I recall, was known as the South Terrace (opposite the Royal Box) – not many rows back from, and, at that crucial moment in the 101st minute, literally looking right over the shoulder of, the 'Russian linesman'. And no, I'm afraid that I didn't think for one second that the ball crossed the line – but then I didn't care a jot about his ruling that it had because I was still incensed beyond belief over what I believed, and still believe, was the wrongful award of the free kick that led to the 89th minute West German equaliser. Jack Charlton did not 'climb' on Seeler, he just wanted the ball more.

But what a day it was, and what a year, in fact! My club Southampton promoted to the top flight of English football for the first time in the May, and then there we all were at Wembley to see England win the World Cup on July 30. And, to cap it all, especially for my father, that day was doubly amazing – it was his 50th birthday!

WEBER GOAL SPARKS A WALK OUT

Richard Crooks
Sheffield

Wolfgang Weber's last minute equaliser in normal time had caused the whole nation to hold its breath and watch in utter disbelief. Extra-time. Everybody settled once again by their television sets for their date with destiny ... everybody that is except for us in a little corner of Sheffield. The reaction to Wolfgang Weber's last minute equaliser had proved too much – the assessment at home was that we were far too over-excited for our own good. Decision taken by Dad to go for a calming-down walk into town before the impending start of extra-time; no reaction from Mother, who stood continuing with the ironing, watching the TV – our protestations and objections pushed aside

And so it was that Dad, me, aged ten, and my little brother walked into town, about a 20 minute walk, whilst the world watched the World Cup Final. It will come as no surprise to anyone that the streets of Sheffield were deserted, our walk unimpeded.

I remember looking briefly in the window of an electrical retailer, Wigfalls, on London Road, on the approach to the town centre – television sets in the window, all with black and white pictures; the sets transmitting the football but providing no indication of the score as the picture on the screen in 1966 was clear, and unblemished by anything as useful as the score between the two teams.

A walk into town and back again, arriving home at some time before 6 o'clock. The game finished. We had no idea what the score was. My mother was standing, completing the ironing. "What was the score ?" Her response was slow and deliberate. "They won of course" she said and smiled. From my view there was no of course about it.

I don't recollect my response to the news but I subsequently determined that should I meet a Mr Weber of Cologne who was in London on July 30 1966, and playing a game of football at Wembley that afternoon I would explain to him the gravity of his actions – I missed seeing England winning the World Cup because of his equalising goal in normal time!

A DAD AND DAUGHTER MOMENT

Sue Sirico

Virginia, USA

While now settled in the USA, I can still vividly recall jumping up and down and screaming on the sofa when Geoff Hurst scored that fourth goal to clinch England's victory over West Germany. I was just eight, but the memory has never left me.

Back then I was Susan Jackson and living in Binbrook in Lincolnshire, where my Dad was stationed with the RAF. I sat alongside him, completely captured by every kick of the ball.

It was a true dad and daughter moment.

Meantime Mum could not understand what all the fuss was about. She hated football and took refuge in the kitchen, while Dad and I shouted in excitement every time England mounted an attack.

When we won I ran out to share the news with anybody who was passing. As most of my friends were girls, to be honest they didn't care.

I was inspired to play soccer by England's victory, but went off it because my three younger brothers always insisted that because I was a girl I should go in goal, and they used to deliberately kick the ball at my nose!

But for me that final at Wembley was one of the highlights of my young life, and to this day every four years all stops for the World Cup when, just as back in 1966, I yell at the players and referee on the TV screen as if they can hear me.

My Hampshire-born Dad is 85, and throughout his life he has supported Portsmouth although now living in Cambridgeshire.

We still talk about that day in July 1966 when England won the World Cup and a dad and daughter shared something very special.

9
THE CAST: WHAT HAPPENED NEXT

FIFTY years on I trace what happened to each of Alf Ramsey's squad of 22 players who gathered at Hendon Hall for the World Cup challenge in 1966 following a warm-up tour of Scandinavia. Whatever next for the Boys of '66? Warning: It often makes for painful reading.

1. GORDON BANKS
Career span: 1958-1978 Clubs: Leicester, Stoke, Fort Lauderdale
England caps: 73
Leicester let Gordon go to Stoke in 1967 in the belief they had an even better goalkeeper in teenager Peter Shilton. His save against Pelé in the 1970 World Cup finals is considered one of the greatest ever. We wrote a book about it: *Banks v. Pelé, The Save that Shook the World.* Illness kept him out of the quarter-final against West Germany, and there was a theory he had been 'nobbled.' He lost the sight of an eye in a car smash in 1972, the year he was voted FWA goalkeeper of the Year. Gordon briefly continued his career in the USA where he was voted Most Valuable Goalkeeper. During his 73 international games he kept 35 clean sheets and lost just nine games. In 2016 he announced that the kidney cancer he thought he'd beaten had returned. He sold his World Cup medal for £125,750.

2. GEORGE COHEN
Career span: 1956-1969 Club: Fulham
England caps: 37
A knee injury finished George's career at the age of 29. He has spent months since his retirement from playing in hospital, fighting cancer and other physical problems. Property developer George and I compare our scars, both so far having survived bowel cancer. His nephew Ben Cohen was a member of England's 2003 Rugby Union World Cup winning team. He played 459 League games for Fulham, and a statue is going to be raised in his honour at Craven Cottage. George Best said: "He was the best full back I ever played against." His World Cup medal was put up for auction in 1998 and Fulham bought it for £80,000.

Gordon Banks, after the loss of his eye in the 1972 car smash

3. RAY WILSON

Career span: 1956-1969 Clubs: Huddersfield, Everton, Oldham, Bradford C.
England caps: 63

After his distinguished playing career, Ray kept a low profile away from football and became an undertaker in Huddersfield. Along with Roger Hunt, George Cohen, Nobby Stiles and Alan Ball he was belatedly awarded an MBE in 2000, far too late for the taste of many. He is warmly remembered at Goodison and at Huddersfield as one of the finest players ever to wear their club shirt. His World Cup medal was sold at auction in 2014 for £136,000, bought by Saracens Rugby Club chairman and famous sports memorabilia collector, Nigel Wray. On December 17 2014, Ray was the first of the July 30 winning team to hit 80. He now battles Alzheimer's.

4. NOBBY STILES

Career span: 1960-1975 Clubs: Manchester United, Middlesbrough, Preston
England caps: 28, goals 1

Everybody's favourite footballer despite his dedication to kicking opponents up in the air, Nobby wound down his playing career with Middlesbrough and then Preston, but his heart was always at Old Trafford, and he later returned to United as a youth team coach. He dabbled as a manager with Preston, Vancouver Whitecaps and West Brom, and he poured his money into an electrical contract firm that went bust. His health has collapsed in recent years, and half a century on from the 1966 triumph he suffers dementia and cancer. Manchester United bought his World Cup and European Cup medals for £200,000 when they were put up for auction in 2010. Nobby wanted his family to benefit from the proceeds.

5. JACK CHARLTON

Career span: 1952-1973 Club: Leeds United
England caps: 35, goals 6

One of the few of the Boys of '66 to make a success of management, Jack was in charge at Middlesbrough, Sheffield Wednesday and Newcastle before becoming a wonderfully entertaining, at times controversial and often successful manager of Ireland. After two eventful World Cup campaigns, he was rewarded with honorary Irish citizenship and there is a life-size statue of him at Cork Airport, showing him in his fishing gear and landing a salmon, which captured the pastime to which he has dedicated much of his life outside football. His 629 League and 762 total appearances remain Leeds United records. Jack has vowed never to sell his World Cup medal, but understands why many of his old colleagues have had to let their precious mementoes go. As he came into his eighties, he started to suffer the dementia curse of old footballers, and wept at the reception he received on a nostalgic return to Dublin "for a last look round."

6. BOBBY MOORE

Career span: 1958-1978 Clubs: West Ham. Fulham

England caps: 108, goals 2

It has been well chronicled how Bobby's death from cancer at the age of 51 in 1993 was greeted with national mourning, and the setting up of statues at Wembley and West Ham. A charity set up in his name by his widow Stephanie has raised more than £20-million for medical research. But the question I always ask is where was the Football Establishment when Bobby needed them? He scratched around playing in the United States, Hong Kong and Denmark when it cried out for the FA to employ him in, at least, an ambassadorial role. Bobby briefly managed at Oxford City and Southend United before going into the media world as a journalist and co-commentator. But only in death was he given the recognition he deserved.

7. ALAN BALL

Career span: 1962-1983 Clubs: Blackpool, Everton, Arsenal, Southampton, Bristol Rovers **England caps: 72, goals 8**

The 'baby' of the team was tragically the second of the Boys of '66 to depart when he died of a heart attack in 2007, while attempting to put out a fire in the garden of his Hampshire home. He was 61. Alan took his unquenchable love of football into management with Philadelphia Fury, Blackpool, Portsmouth, Stoke City, Exeter City, Southampton and Manchester City, without tasting the success he had experienced as one of the great midfield players of his generation. He had another tragedy in his life when his wife/childhood sweetheart Lesley died of cancer at 57, two years after his father had been killed in a car crash in Cyprus. Alan's World Cup medal and tournament cap were auctioned for £140,000 in 2005.

8. JIMMY GREAVES

Career span: 1957-1972 Clubs: Chelsea, AC Milan,Tottenham, West Ham

England caps: 57, goals 44

Of all Alf's squad, Jimmy has had the most eventful life since retiring at the all too early age of 31. Playing with non-League teams for fun, he became an alcoholic who was warned that drinking was killing him. Jimmy kicked the bottle and became a popular TV and media celebrity, particularly in a long-running double act with Ian St John on the *Saint and Greavsie* show. He found time to collaborate with me on 20 books. Awarded a World Cup medal in 2009, he later auctioned it for £44,000 – "because I needed the money!" In May 2015 he suffered a violent stroke and is now confined to a wheelchair. A benefit evening organised by his manager Terry Baker raised £35,000, and he was elected to the Tottenham Hall of Fame in his absence. His 357 'old' First Division goals is an unbeatable record because the division no longer exists.

Sir Bobby Charlton, fifty years on from the 1966 World Cup triumph

9. BOBBY CHARLTON

Career span: 1956-1976 Clubs: Manchester United, Preston, Waterford

England caps: 106, goals 49

Bobby's 106th and final England cap was in the 1970 World Cup quarter-final when Sir Alf made a mess of his substitutions and took England's most admired footballer off against West Germany. In 1968 Bobby had an even more emotional match when he helped Manchester United win the European Cup, with the history of the Munich air crash heavy in the air. After retirement he tried managing at Preston without any success, and then went into the travel business, and after his knighthood in 1994 became first a director of Wigan and then of the club closest to his heart, Man United. Sadly, for those of us who like happy endings, he rarely talks to his older brother, Jack, following a personal family feud. He remains English football's most famous and revered son. Sir Bobby has not been in the best of health in recent years, but still manages to be a regular spectator at his beloved Old Trafford.

10. GEOFF HURST

Career span: 1959-1976 Clubs: West Ham, Stoke, West Brom

England caps: 49, goals 24

Remembered for all time as the hat-trick hero and THAT goal in the 1966 World Cup final, Geoff played in Seattle and Ireland before trying management, first with Telford, then briefly and painfully with Chelsea before coaching for two years in Kuwait. He then left the football world behind to concentrate on building a successful insurance business. Knighted in 1998, he and his wife, Judith, privately handled the tragedy of losing their eldest daughter to a brain tumour. He travels the world representing his country and his sport with dignity, and is of course always linked to those three goals. Sir Geoff sold his World Cup medal to West Ham.

11. JOHN CONNELLY

Career span: 1956-1973 Clubs: Burnley, Man United, Blackburn, Bury

England caps: 20, goals 7

Having distinguished himself on a circuit of Lancashire clubs, John retired in 1973 and elected to make a break with football. He started a popular fish and chip shop in Brierfield called Connelly's Plaice rather than return to the joiner trade he had learned when leaving school. A quiet, modest man, John was a Justice of the Peace who often sat as a magistrate in the local courts and was respected throughout the community for his balanced and wise counsel. He passed on after a short illness at the age of 74 in 2012, the third of the Boys of 66 to go to the great football stadium in the sky, but lived long enough to collect a World Cup winners' medal in 2009. He is featured in Burnley's Wall of Legends at Turf Moor.

12. RON SPRINGETT

Career span: 1956-1973 Clubs: QPR, Sheffield Wednesday

England caps: 33

Ron returned to his original club Queen's Park Rangers in 1967 in a unique transfer, when the goalkeeper going the other way in a swap deal was his younger brother, Peter. He was one of the non-playing members of the squad presented with a World Cup medal in 2009 by Prime Minister Gordon Brown in a ceremony at Downing Street. After his retirement Ron, a humorous, likeable man, ran the Ron Springett Sports Shop close to the QPR ground before going back to his original job as an interior decorator. He became the fourth member of the squad to pass on in 2015, aged 80.

13. PETER BONETTI

Career span: 1960-1979 Clubs: Chelsea, Dundee United

England caps: 7

After playing 600 matches for Chelsea and a season with St Louis All Stars, Peter decided to drop out in style, moving to the Isle of Mull and becoming a postman. He came out of retirement as an emergency goalkeeper for Dundee United and got his taste back for the game that had been soured by his experience in Mexico, when he was the goalkeeper who took over from sick Gordon Banks and let in the three goals that put West Germany through to the semi-finals. He became the go-to goalkeeping coach for England, Newcastle United, Fulham, Manchester City and Chelsea. He played for Woking at 45, and even into his 70s he turned out in charity matches.

14. JIMMY ARMFIELD

Career span: 1954-1971 Club: Blackpool

England caps: 43

Jimmy was a fixture at Blackpool for 627 games and 10 years as captain before starting a managerial career with Bolton Wanderers in 1971. He led them to promotion as Third Division champions, and then took over from the controversial Brian Clough at Leeds United. There could not have been more contrasting characters. For Gentleman Jim the highlight was steering Leeds to the final of the European Cup in 1974-75 when they were runners-up to Bayern Munich in a final in Paris scarred by Leeds hooligans. A trained journalist, Jimmy decided to switch to the media world and was a highly respected reporter with the *Daily Express*, and later became a popular member of the Radio 5 Live team. In 2007 he revealed that he had been undergoing chemotherapy treatment for non-Hodgkin lymphoma. Church organist Jimmy is a freeman of Blackpool, and has the respect of everybody in football.

15. GERRY BYRNE

Career span: 1957-1969 Club: Liverpool

England caps: 2

Described by Bill Shankly as "the best professional I ever managed," Gerry was as Scouse as the Scotland Road pavement. He joked after receiving his World Cup medal from Gordon Brown in 2009: "There's one for the pub quizers. Who won a World Cup winners' medal after playing only two games in total for England?" Nicknamed 'The Crunch' because of his tackling power, Gerry's career was wrecked by a knee injury in the first match of the 1966-67 season. He became a member of the Anfield back-room coaching team, and then in his later years moved to a home in Wrexham where he became the fifth player of the squad of 1966 to pass on in November 2015, suffering from the ex-footballer's curse of Alzheimer's.

16. MARTIN PETERS

Career span: 1959-1981 Club: West Ham, Spurs, Norwich, Sheffield U.

England caps: 67, goals 20

Martin became British football's first £200,000 player when he moved to Tottenham in 1970, with Jimmy Greaves going to the Hammers as a £54,000 make-weight. Later, he became an acclaimed skipper at Norwich City. He may have been 10 years ahead of his time as a player, but when he tried modern management with Sheffield United he was not successful and walked away from the game to join Geoff Hurst in the insurance world. Always elegant and dignified on and off the pitch, Martin kept in touch with the game as a VIP greeter at Tottenham and West Ham, where he was briefly a director. There were concerns about Martin's health and fading memory approaching the 50th anniversary of the World Cup. Married to Kathy for more than 50 years, he cannot recall his vital part in the victory.

17. RON FLOWERS

Career span: 1952-1971 Clubs: Wolves, Northampton, Telford

England caps: 49, goals 10

The year after the World Cup triumph, Ron left Wolves to join Northampton Town where he had a spell as player-manager before taking the same role at non-League Wellington (later known as Telford United). He then returned to the Wolverhampton town where he is idolised to concentrate on his successful 'Ron Flowers Sports Shop' company. Following his retirement, Ron became a regular spectator at Doncaster Rovers in the town where he was born and at the club where his younger brother, John, and Uncle George Flowers had both been prominent players. On July 28 2014 Ron, the oldest member of the 1966 squad, became the first to celebrate an 80th birthday,

18. NORMAN HUNTER

Career span: 1962-1982 Clubs: Leeds United, Bristol City, Barnsley

England caps: 28, goals 2

After a long career marking people, the feared and fabled 'Bites Yer Legs' Hunter went into management with Barnsley, Rotherham and, briefly, his old club Leeds United after a stint as coach at West Bromwich Albion. He then became a much-in-demand after-dinner speaker, regaling audiences with his tales of physical encounters of the close kind in an era when the big boot ruled. Norman continued to have a keen interest in the game as a broadcaster on local Yorkshire radio. The two post-1966 World Cup memories he would like to erase are being sent on as a substitute in the 1970 quarter-final defeat by West Germany, and then missing the tackle that let Poland in for the goal that knocked England out of the 1974 qualification round at Wembley, a result that eventually cost Alf Ramsey his job. His 2004 autobiography was suitably titled, *Biting Talk.*

19. TERRY PAINE

Career span: 1957-1977 Clubs: Southampton, Hereford

England caps: 19, goals 7

After a club record 713 League appearances for Southampton, Terry became player-manager of Hereford while also serving as a Tory councillor in Hampshire. He had a spell as manager of non-League Cheltenham, combining that role with running a pub in the town centre. Then the never-idle Terry went off to a coaching job in South Africa, where he became a prominent football TV pundit and was also a member of the successful South African bidding team for the 2010 World Cup finals. He returned to the English game as coach at Coventry City, went again to South Africa and combined his broadcasting career with working as 'ambassador' for the Southampton club he served so well at the peak of his playing career. Terry was made honorary President of the Saints.

20. IAN CALLAGHAN

Career span: 1960-1982 Clubs: Liverpool, Swansea, Cork, Crewe Alexandra

England caps: 4

Cally remains a legend at Liverpool where he played a club record 856 League and cup games. He was 35 when he won his third and fourth England caps, by then an all-seeing midfield marshal rather than the jinking winger of his younger days. Cally could not let go the game he loved, and carried on playing with his old Anfield team-mate John Toshack at Swansea and on loan spells in the United States, Australia, Ireland and Norway before winding up at 39 with Crewe Alexandra. By then he had started a successful insurance business on Merseyside, and he is a regular visitor to Anfield, where he is President of the official Liverpool Fan Club.

Norman 'Bites Yer Legs' Hunter kisses his World Cup medal

21. ROGER HUNT

Career span: 1958-1972 Clubs: Liverpool, Bolton

England caps: 34, goals 18

Roger created a Liverpool scoring record of 245 goals that lasted until the emergence of Ian Rush two decades later. He then took his shooting boots to Bolton Wanderers and scored another 24 League goals before hanging them up and turning to a new life as a businessman. Roger joined the family road haulage business, and along with Gordon Banks became a member of the Pools Panel. It was a shock to those who thought they knew Roger when his long marriage ended in divorce, and he now lives with his new partner in Warrington.

22. GEORGE EASTHAM

Career span: 1958-1972 Clubs: Newcastle, Arsenal, Stoke City

England caps: 19, goals 2

Following skilled service with Arsenal, George moved to Stoke City immediately after the World Cup. At the back end of his career – and while dividing his time between England and South Africa – he scored the goal that won Stoke the 1972 League Cup final against Chelsea, their first ever major trophy. He had ten months in charge of Stoke before returning to South Africa, where he set up a thriving sportswear company. He played for Hellenic, like his father before him, and in his spare time coached a team of black township youth players. George always makes a point of visiting Arsenal and Stoke City on his journeys back to England .

THEY ALSO SERVED

Trainer **Harold Shepherdson** continued as Alf Ramsey's loyal right-hand man up until Sir Alf's dismissal in 1974, by which time he had become caretaker manager of the Middlesbrough club he had served since signing for them as a youth player in 1936. Harold passed on in 1995, aged 77. In 2009 his widow, Margaret, was at Downing Street to receive a World Cup medal from Prime Minister George Brown on her late husband's behalf.

Assistant trainer **Les Cocker** was also posthumously awarded a medal that was collected by his son, David, in 2009. Les, the England Under-23s trainer, worked at Leeds alongside Don Revie and went with him to Kuwait. On his return in 1979 he joined manager Billy Bremner as coach at Doncaster Rovers, and was just weeks into the job when he died following a heart attack, aged 55.

Wilf McGuinness joined the training team for the duration of the World Cup. He later had a brief spell as Manchester United manager in succession to Matt Busby. He managed in Greece, then at York and Bury before becoming a popular speaker on the after-dinner circuit.

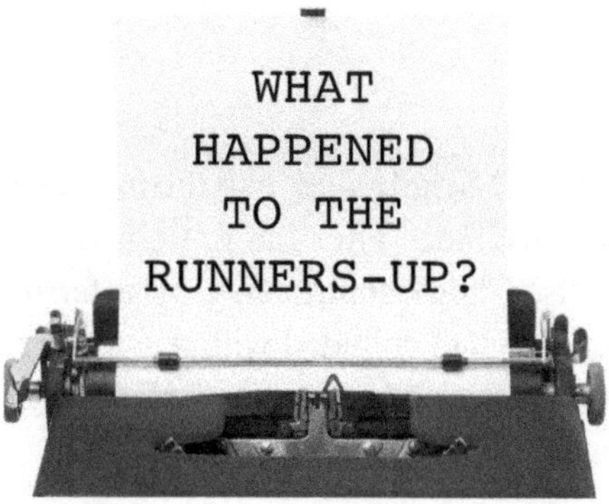

It took two to tango at Wembley, and West Germany were not just part of the dance but very nearly waltzed off with the crown. This is what happened to the runners-up after the 1966 ball was over ...

HANS TILKOWSKI

Major clubs: Westfalia Herne, Borussia Dortmund, Entracht Frankfurt

Caps: 39 (1957-67)

At the end of his playing career in 1970, Hans had spells managing Werder Bremen, 1860 Munich, Nuremberg, Saarbrücken and AEK Athens. He later devoted much of his spare time to raising funds for multiple sclerosis sufferers. His best-selling autobiography was called *Wembley-Tor* (Wembley-Goal) based around the Geoff Hurst goal that Hans insists did NOT cross the line. On July 12 2015, he became the first of West Germany's 66 team to reach 80.

HORST-DIETER HÖTTGES

Major clubs: Borussia Mönchengladbach, Werder Bremen

Caps: 66 (1965-74), goals 1

Hugely admired as one of Germany's greatest ever defenders, he became a cult hero because of the 'Iron Foot' nickname given to him by Gunter Netzer (the equivalent of our 'Bites Yer Legs' Hunter). He became a sportswear sales executive and kept his interest in football as a scout and part-time coach at TSV Achim, a club in a village near Bremen, where he settled down..

WOLFGANG WEBER

Major club: FC Köln

Caps: 53 (1964-74), goals 2

Then just 22, it was, of course, Weber's last-minute equaliser that took the final into extra time, one of his only two international goals. Retains a close rapport with Cologne, his home town club. Puts a lot back into sport as an enthusiastic supporter and adviser to the Special Olympics squad.

WILLI SCHULZ

Major clubs: Schalke, Hamburger SV

Caps: 66 (1959-70)

Known from the 1966 Finals as 'World Cup Willi," Schulz went into the insurance business in Hamburg while also selling slot machines after his retirement. He became a hard-hitting media pundit, and caused huge controversy by referring to the 1982 German team as 'gangsters' after they had colluded with Austria on a drawn World Cup match. A wealthy property developer, he remains a Hamburger SV 'advisory' director, and is idolised throughout Germany.

KARL-HEINZ SCHNELLINGER

Major clubs: FC Köln, AC Mantova, AS Roma, AC Milan

Caps: 103 (1965-77), goal 14

After his return to Germany from Italy, Karl-Heinz played briefly for Tennis Borussia Berlin, but he later elected to return to Milan, where he became a successful businessman. One of the finest left-backs ever to play the game, he remains admired in Milan, where in nine years he won eight Serie A titles and three European Cups.

FRANZ BECKENBAUER

Major clubs: Bayern Munich, New York Cosmos, Hamburger SV

Caps: 103 (1958-71) 103

Since retiring from his glittering career as a player (including collecting the World Cup as captain in 1974), the legend that is Beckenbauer has also enjoyed success in club management, winning domestic titles with Marseille and Bayern Munich and, of course, managing the 1990 World Cup winners. Bayern's omnipotent club president, he was the motivating force behind Germany's staging of the 2006 World Cup. He works for Sky Germany as a pundit and is an opinionated newspaper columnist. Franz continues a close friendship with Bobby Charlton.

.

HELMUT HALLER

Major clubs: Augsburg, Bologna, Juventus

Caps: 33, 13 goals (1958-70)

Haller, who famously left Wembley with the match ball, despite Hurst's hat-trick, played on until the age of 40, including five memorable years at Juventus. Charismatic, he had made a success of a fashion-shop business after a playing career in which he was noted for his dribbling skill and decisive finishing. Eyebrows reached crossbar height when in 2003 he married his third wife, a 21-year-old Cuban. Helmut suffered a heart attack in 2006 and eventually died in 2012 after complications caused by dementia and Parkinson's. He was 73.

WOLFGANG OVERATH

Major club: FC Köln

Caps: 81, 17 goals (1963-74)

Following his retirement, the master midfield organiser was elected President of the FC Köln club he had served so well as a player from 1962 to 1977. He gave up the Presidency in 2011 after a bitter boardroom split. Overath is one of only five players (along with Beckenbauer, Sepp Maier, Miroslav Klose and Italian Franco Baresi) to win World Cup medals for first, second and third places. He restricted his career-long rival Gunter Netzer to 37 caps.

UWE SEELER

Major club: Hamburger SV

Caps: 72, 43 goals (1954-70)

One of German football's favourite sons, Seeler played in the World Cup finals for the fourth time in 1970. He spent his entire club career with Hamburger and his service was rewarded when the club made him President in 1995. Uwe was forced to resign two years later following a financial scandal, though he was not implicated. In 2003 he was made a Freeman of the city of Hamburg, the first time the honour had gone to a sportsman. He was seriously injured in a car crash in 2010, but had made a remarkable recovery approaching his 80th birthday.

SIEGFRIED HELD

Major clubs: Kickers Offenbach, Borussia Dortmund, Bayer Uerdingen'

Caps: 41, 5 goals (1966-73)

Siggy has managed and coached a queue of clubs since he hung up his boots, including Schalke, Galatasaray, Dynamo Dresden, Leipzig, and national teams Iceland, Malta and Thailand. He later became supporters liaison co-ordinator with Borussia Dortmund, his club during the 1966 World Cup and where he is revered for his explosive exploits in the Bundesliga.

LOTHAR EMMERICH

Major clubs: Borussia Dortmund, K Beerschot, Klagenfurt, Würzburger

Caps: 5, 2 goals (1966)

The '66 final was 'Emma's' last international appearance for West Germany. He then did much of his goal hunting in Austria and Belgium, and later briefly worked as an electrician before returning to football as a coach with SV Spabrücken, Idar-Oberstein. Weinheim, and then Kirschweiler. He later teamed up with his old club and country side-kick Siggy Held as fans co-ordinator at Borussia Dortmund. In 2003 he became the first of West Germany's '66 team to pass on, beaten by lung cancer at the age of 61.

1974 and Helmut Schoen gets his hands on the Fifa World Cup trophy

From the moment Bobby Moore raised the World Cup in triumph after England's extra-time 4-2 victory at Wembley in 1966, it seemed almost inevitable that one day the intelligent and inventive German coach, Helmut Schoen, would eventually get his revenge. Four years later in Mexico he masterminded a World Cup quarter-final win over an England side arguably superior to the 1966 champions, and in 1974 he touched the Everest peak of his career when he guided West Germany to victory on home soil.

In 1996, this imposing, dignified and always courteous man became the second of two outstanding managers to fall victim to Alzheimer's disease within the month; Bob Paisley, of Liverpool, being the other. His rival Sir Alf Ramsey would soon follow the same sad route.

Like Sir Alf, Schoen's popularity among most of the players he coached bred loyalty and esteem. Berti Vogts, later coach to the German national team and a member of Schoen's most successful sides, said: "He was a man who only saw the good in players and people in general. For me he was the best and most successful trainer ever."

Schoen's extraordinary record is hard to match. He was appointed West Germany's coach in November 1964 and finished in June 1978. In that period the Germans were World Cup runners-up to England (1966), third in 1970, winners in 1974, European champions in 1972 and runners-up in 1976. His complete record: 87 wins, 31 draws and only 21 defeats. Wunderbar!

10
2016
THE REUNION
50 YEARS ON

THE place, the five-star Landmark Hotel in Marylebone, the date May 12 2016, the occasion: the 69th Football Writers' Association Footballer of the Year Dinner. Award winner Jamie Vardy was there to collect his trophy from FWA chairman Andy Dunn, and the Association thoughtfully decided to honour the newspaper journalists who had reported the England World Cup triumph 50 years earlier.

Fifteen of us who had survived the slings and arrows of outrageous fortune of the previous half century were invited, but with two – Brian James *(Daily Mail)* and Steve Curry *(United Newspapers)* – reluctantly pulling out at the last minute because of ill health. Those who made the reunion along with me were the over-80s Brian Glanville (*Sunday Times*), Ken Jones *(Daily Mirror)*, Hugh McIlvanney *(The Observer)*, David Miller *(Daily Telegraph),*Brian Scovell *(Daily Sketch)* David Meek *(Manchester Evening News*), and 70-somethings James Mossop *(Sunday Express)*, Alex Montgomery *(The Sun),* Nigel Clarke *(Daily Mirror*), Colin Malam and Bob Harris (*Birmingham Post*) and 68-year-old Michael Hart *(Evening Standard),* who had been the youngest in the Press Box.

We spent a lot of time respectfully reflecting on the major sportswriters who covered the final but had now gone to the great press box in the sky, including masters of the reporting art Geoffrey Green *(The Times*), Desmond Hackett *(Daily Express*), Donald Saunders *(Daily Telegraph),* Peter Wilson, Frank McGhee and Harry Miller *(Daily Mirror*), Laurie Pignon *(Daily Sketch*), J.L. (Jim) Manning, Ian Wooldridge and Roy Peskett *(Daily Mail),* Eric Todd and Albert Barham *(The Guardian)*, Bernard Joy *(Evening Standard)*, Vic Railton *(Evening News)*, Alan Hoby and Jim Connolly *(Sunday Express)*, Mike Langley *(Sunday People)*, Frank Butler and Reg Drury *(News of the World*), Peter Lorenzo, Frank Clough and Steve Richards *(The Sun*). I had better admit here that I am writing this list from memory, and apologise if anybody's name has slipped through the sieve of my mind.

The Press were all-powerful back in the 60s, before television, radio and later the social network took over as the main media furnace in which managers and players could get badly burned by the keyboard critics. Alf Ramsey took some terrible stick on the way to the finals and also during them, particularly after the opening match against Uruguay when England seemed short on ideas and invention.

Brian James, a gifted writer with the *Daily Mail*, was one of the few Fleet Street observers who stuck with his support of Ramsey and his prediction that England would win the World Cup in his report of the depressing goalless slog with Uruguay. He was rewarded with a warning from the Editor that he was making the *Mail* look foolish and that his job was on the line if England did not win the tournament. He was so elated when Geoff Hurst's third goal hit the net in the final that he jumped and punched the ceiling of the Wembley press box and had to have his bruised hand bandaged. Brian has since switched to writing about military history and has collected a BA and – at the age of 80 – an MA (hons). But he still considers the moment that his close friend Geoff completed the hat-trick the greatest experience of his career.

There was unanimous agreement during our reunion that Ramsey would have struggled to survive as a manager in today's football world, because he would have been so uncomfortable with the contractual demands for press conferences before and after matches.

He was like a man facing a firing squad when fielding questions, and particularly suspicious of the foreign press and seemed convinced they were trying to trip him up at every turn. For 'foreign' that would have included Scottish journalists. Throughout his career as player and manager he considered the Scots 'the auld enemy', and there was an infamous occasion when he arrived at Glasgow Airport on the eve of a Home International and was met by legendary Scottish football reporter Jim Rodger, a bull of a man who seemed as wide as he was tall. "Welcome to Scotland, Alf," said Jim, holding out the hand of friendship. Alf shot him that famed and feared cold-eyed glare. "You must be f***ing joking," he said, and shouldered his way past Jim without a backward glance.

Alf managed to pretend to ignore much of the dung that was dumped on him, but notoriously lost his temper twice with personal critics. He once took his jacket off in a hotel and offered to fight Eric Cooper, a Mancunian who continually mangled him in print as 'The Voice of the North' for the *Daily Express*. Alf had drunk more than his usual quota of his favourite gin and tonic tipple, and was ready to thump Cooper for his over-the-top assessments.

The other time that Alf let fly in front of startled witnesses was when he came face to face with Danny Blanchflower at a Football Writers' Dinner. Danny had been dishing it out against Ramsey's tactics on television and in his acerbic *Sunday Express* column, and Alf was still cold-stone sober when he confronted tee-total Danny at the reception before the Footballer of the Year Award ceremony, won that year by Danny's Northern Ireland countryman George Best.

Alf Ramsey is hardly the picture of warmth as he welcomes new signing Danny Blanchflower to Tottenham in 1954. Alf was about to depart to start a managing career at Ipswich, and Danny took over from him as Spurs skipper. They were to fall out with each other later in life.

"You're a bloody liar, the things you spout," Alf suddenly snarled, uncorking two years of suppressed anger. "What gives you the right to say what you like? You've never picked a team in your life. Managing from behind a typewriter is easy." There was an embarrassed silence before Danny said: "It's all about opinions Alf. Mine just happen to be different to yours."

They were sworn enemies for the rest of their lives, both passing on in the 1990s lost in a maze of dementia and unable to remember all the great things they had achieved in football. Danny later tried to show that he could manage with Chelsea, but was a disaster and returned to punditry with his ego crushed.

It was a young Scottish writer who captured the full meaning of England's World Cup victory at Wembley on July 30 1966. This was how Hugh McIlvanney, the master of all sportswriters, reported with a running report that he telephoned to the *Observer* at 5.20pm to catch the first edition:

> The greatest moment in the history of English football came at 5.15 this afternoon when Geoff Hurst shot the magnificent goal that made certain of the World Cup. It was Hurst's third goal, England's fourth, and, coming as it did in the final seconds of extra time, it shattered the last remnants of German resistance.
>
> Germany had equalized with the last kick in the regular 90 minutes, and they had gone within inches of repeating the blow in extra time when Seeler lunged in on a headed pass by Held. But Moore took the ball coolly out of defence and lifted it upfield to Hurst 10 yards inside the German half. The referee was already looking at his watch and three England supporters had prematurely invaded the pitch as Hurst took the ball on his chest. At first he seemed inclined to dawdle out time. Then abruptly he sprinted through on the inside-left position with German's Overath pressing him. As Tilkowski prepared to move out, Hurst swung his left foot and drove the ball breathtakingly into the top of the net.
>
> The scene that followed was unforgettable. Stiles and Cohen collapsed in a tearful embrace on the ground, young Ball turned wild cartwheels, and Bobby Charlton dropped to his knees, felled by emotion. Almost immediately it was over and the honour that had escaped England for so long had been won. Soon the players, who had forgotten the crippling weariness of a few minutes before, were hugging and laughing and crying with Alf Ramsey and the reserves, who must go through their lives with bitter-sweet memories of how it looked from the touchline.

Fifty years on, no British football reporter has been able to match it.

Among those missing from the reunion was the man who made headlines by not being selected for the final, the one and only Jimmy Greaves. He was lined up to add his input to this book until 'taken out of the game' by a violent stroke in May 2015. As I write he is battling for a decent quality of life, and having to adjust to a future in a wheelchair. He is, of course, fighting the good fight with all of his might.

Jimmy and I have collaborated on 20 books together, and at the summertime of his life there was nobody in football who could match his sharp humour (let alone his sharp finishing!).

He was still the old Jimmy when I told him I was writing this reconstruction of July 30 1966, and he had me roaring as usual when he said: "It's a day I'd prefer to forget, but just suppose it had been me banging in those three goals in the final. Geoff has since been a great ambassador for football, but let's face it, I would have been a disaster as a knight. In those days, the only tap I wanted on the shoulder was a beer tap."

Eleven years after the World Cup finals in England there was a five-a-side Queen's Jubilee tournament at Wembley Arena (the Empire Pool as it was called then) featuring veterans of '66. France were among the competing teams, and the social itinerary included a Thames pleasure boat trip from Westminster.

Looking across the deck, Nobby Stiles saw among the French players his old adversary Jacques Simon, the opponent he'd flattened with a tackle at Wembley that was so fierce some Fifa and Football Association officials demanded Alf Ramsey drop Stiles from his World Cup team. It was always Nobby's contention that what looked to many as a criminal assault had been accidental rather than intentional.

"I'd never had the chance to apologise," Nobby said. "Knowing he spoke English, I went over to him, and I started to explain that it was a badly timed rather than deliberately malicious tackle. I was just softening him up and he was smiling when Greavsie went and poked his nose in. He'd sussed what I was up to, and spoiled it all by creeping up to Simon and saying in a loud whisper, 'Don't listen to him. He kicked me all over the park for ten years, the dirty little bastard.'"

It was a typical Jimmy prank, and Simon and Stiles fell into each other's arms laughing. Greavsie, the man who missed the 1966 World Cup final, had scored again.

APPENDIX
FACTS
STATS AND
TRIVIA

● England were chosen as hosts of the 1966 World Cup in Rome on August 22 1960, just three days before the opening of the Rome Olympics. Many Fifa delegates were also serving with the IOC. There were three main contenders, and when Spain withdrew it was a straight fight between England and West Germany. It was England who won the bidding process by 34 votes to 27, with no extra-time needed. Shades of what was to come six years later.

● In 1964 sixteen African nations announced their boycott of the tournament in protest at a Fifa ruling that three second-round winners from the African zone should enter a playoff against the winners of the Asian zone for a place in the finals. The Africans argued that winning their zone was enough in itself to merit qualification, and they made a mass exit..

● Despite the withdrawal of the Africans, there was a record number of entries for the qualifying tournament, with 70 nations taking part. Following the bitter feud with the Africans, Fifa finally ruled that ten teams from Europe would qualify, along with four from South America, one from Asia and one from North and Central America.

● Portugal and North Korea qualified for the first time, while 1962 semi-finalists Yugoslavia and 1962 finalists Czechoslovakia were eliminated. England, of course, automatically qualified as host country, never having got past the quarter-final stage in four previous bids to win the World Cup.

● The format of the 1966 finals remained the same as in 1962: 16 qualified teams divided into four groups of four. Each group played a round robin format. Two points were awarded for a win and one point for a draw, with goal average separating teams equal on points. The top two teams in each group advanced to the knockout stage.

● The draw for the finals of the 1966 World Cup was staged on 6 January 1966 at the 5-star Royal Garden Hotel in Kensington, which had been rebuilt a year earlier and was a glass and stone structure that was iconic of the 1960s.The hotel was the Fifa and media HQ throughout the finals.

● It was the first World Cup draw ever televised, and the Fifa President – the imposing, 6ft 3in tall former English referee Sir Stanley Rous – was in the chair and ruled proceedings with the humourless officiousness of the schoolteacher he used to be. He often reprimanded the chattering delegates and media for talking while he was talking. Try to see newsreel of it. Much of it could have been scripted for *Monty Python*.

● England, West Germany, Brazil and Italy were the four seeded teams. These were the four groups and how they finished after the qualifying rounds:

GROUP 1

Jul 11	Wembley	England	v	Uruguay	0-0
Jul 13	Wembley	France	v	Mexico	1-1
Jul 15	White City	Uruguay	v	France	2-1
Jul 16	Wembley	England	v	Mexico	2-0
Jul 19	Wembley	Mexico	v	Uruguay	0-0
Jul 20	Wembley	France	v	England	0-2

	P	W	D	L	Gls	Pts
ENGLAND	3	2	1	0	4-0	5
URUGUAY	3	1	2	0	2-1	4
Mexico	3	0	2	1	1-3	2
France	3	0	1	2	2-5	1

GROUP 2

Jul 12	Hillsborough	West Germany	v	Switzerland	5-0
Jul 13	Villa Park	Argentina	v	Spain	2-1
Jul 15	Hillsborough	Spain	v	Switzerland	2-1
Jul 16	Villa Park	Argentina	v	West Germany	0-0
Jul 19	Hillsborough	Switzerland	v	Argentina	0-2
Jul 20	Villa Park	West Germany	v	Spain	2-1

	P	W	D	L	Gls	Pts
WEST GERMANY	3	2	1	0	71	5
ARGENTINA	3	2	1	0	41	5
Spain	3	1	0	2	45	2
Switzerland	3	0	0	3	19	0

GROUP 3

Jul 12	Goodison Park	Brazil	v	Bulgaria	2-0
Jul 13	Old Trafford	Portugal	v	Hungary	3-1
Jul 15	Goodison Park	Hungary	v	Brazil	3-1
Jul 16	Old Trafford	Portugal	v	Bulgaria	3-0
Jul 19	Goodison Park	Brazil	v	Portugal	1-3
Jul 20	Old Trafford	Bulgaria	v	Hungary	1-3

	P	W	D	L	Gls	Pts
PORTUGAL	3	3	0	0	92	6
HUNGARY	3	2	0	1	75	4
Brazil	3	1	0	2	46	2
Bulgaria	3	0	0	3	18	0

GROUP 4

Jul 12	Ayresome Park	Soviet Union	v	North Korea	3-0
Jul 13	Roker Park	Italy	v	Chile	2-0
Jul 15	Ayresome Park	Chile	v	North Korea	1-1
Jul 16	Roker Park	Soviet Union	v	Italy	1-0
Jul 19	Ayresome Park	North Korea	v	Italy	1-0
Jul 20	Roker Park	Chile	v	Soviet Union	1-2

	P	W	D	L	Gls	Pts
SOVIET UNION	3	3	0	0	61	6
NORTH KOREA	3	1	1	1	24	3
Italy	3	1	0	2	22	2
Chile	3	0	1	2	25	1

QUARTER-FINALS

Jul 23	Hillsborough	West Germany	v	Uruguay	4-0
Jul 23	Goodison Park	Portugal	v	North Korea	5-3
Jul 23	Roker Park	Soviet Union	v	Hungary	2-1
Jul 23	Wembley	England	v	Argentina	1-0

SEMI-FINALS

Jul 25	Goodison Park	West Germany	v	Soviet Union	2-1
Jul 26	Wembley	England	v	Portugal	2-1

3rd/4th PLACE PLAYOFF

Jul 28 Wembley Portugal v Soviet Union 2-1

WORLD CUP FINAL

Jul 30 Wembley England v West Germany 4-2

WORLD CUP 1966 FINAL STANDINGS

		P	W	D	L	Goals	Pts
1.England	Champions	6	5	1	0	11 3	11
2.West Germany	Runners-up	6	4	1	1	15 6	9
3.Portugal	Third	6	5	0	1	17 8	10
4.Soviet Union	Fourth	6	4	0	2	10 6	8
5.Argentina	Quarter-finals	4	2	1	1	4 2	5
6.Hungary	Quarter-finals	4	2	0	2	8 7	4
7.Uruguay	Quarter-finals	4	1	2	1	2 5	4
8.North Korea	Quarter-finals	4	1	1	2	5 9	3
9.Italy	Round 1	3	1	0	2	2 2	2
10.Spain	Round 1	3	1	0	2	4 5	2
11.Brazil	Round 1	3	1	0	2	4 6	2
12.Mexico	Round 1	3	0	2	1	1 3	2
13.Chile	Round 1	3	0	1	2	2 5	1
14.France	Round 1	3	0	1	2	2 5	1
15.Bulgaria	Round 1	3	0	0	3	1 8	0
16.Switzerland	Round 1	3	0	0	3	1 9	0

Group 1

TEAMS: England France Mexico Uruguay

11.07.66 Wembley Stadium. 87,000
ENGLAND 0 URUGUAY 0

ENG: Banks Cohen Wilson Stiles J.Charlton Moore (c) Ball Greaves R.Charlton Hunt Connelly
URU: Mazurkiewicz Troche (c) Manicera Ubiña Goncalves Caetano Cortes Viera Silva Rocha Pérez

13.07.66 Wembley Stadium. 69,000
FRANCE 1 MEXICO 1 (HT 0-1)

FRA: Aubour Djorkaeff Budzinski Artelesa (c) de Michéle Bosquier Herbin Bonnel Combin Gondet Hausser
MEX: Calderon Chaires Peña (c) Núñes Hernández Diaz Mercado Reyes Borja Fragoso Padilla
Scorers: Borja 40 for Mexico Hausser 62 for France

15.07.66 White City Stadium. 45,000
URUGUAY 2 FRANCE 1 (HT 2-1)

URU: Mazurkiewicz Troche (c) Manicera Ubiña Goncalvez Caetano Cortes Viera Sacia Rocha Perez
FRA: Aubour Djorkaeff Budzinski Artelesa (c) de Bourgoing Bosquier Simon Bonnel Herbet Gondet Hausser
Scorers: de Bourgoing 1pen for France Rocha 27 Cortés 32 for Uruguay

16.07.66 Wembley Stadium 92,000
ENGLAND 2 MEXICO 0 (HT 1-0)
ENG: Banks Cohen Wilson Stiles J.Charlton Moore (c) Paine Greaves R.Charlton Hunt Peters
MEX: Calderon Chaires Peña (c) del Muro Núñes Hernández Diaz Jauregui Reyes Borja Padilla Scorers: R. Charlton 38 Hunt 75

19.07.66 Wembley Stadium 61,000
URUGUAY 0 MEXICO 0
URU: Mazurkiewicz Troche (c) Manicera Ubiña Goncalvez Caetano Cortés Viera Sacia Rocha Pérez
MEX: Carbajal Chaires Peña (c) Mercado Núñes Hernández Diaz Cisneros Reyes Borja Padilla

20.07.66 Wembley Stadium 98,000
ENGLAND 2 FRANCE 0 (HT 1-0)
ENG: Banks Cohen Wilson Stiles J.Charlton Moore (c) Callaghan Greaves R.Charlton Hunt Peters
FRA: Aubour Djorkaeff Budzinski Artelesa (c) Herbin Bosquier Simon Bonnel Herbet Gondet Hausser Scorers: Hunt 29 76

Group 2

TEAMS: Argentina Spain West Germany Switzerland

12.07.66 Hillsborough 36,000
WEST GERMANY 5 SWITZERLAND 0 (HT 3-0)
GER: Tilkowski Höttges Schulz Weber Schnellinger Beckenbauer Haller Brülls Seeler (c) Overath Held
SWI: Elsener Grobety Schneiter (c) Tacchella Führer Bäni Dürr Odermatt Künzli Hosp Schindelholz
Scorers: Held 16 Haller 20 Beckenbauer 40 52 Haller 78pen

13.07.66 Villa Park 48,000
ARGENTINA 2, SPAIN 1 (HT 0-0)
ARG: Roma Perfumo Marzolini Ferreiro Rattin (c) Albrecht Solari Gonzalez Artime Onega Más
SPAIN: Iribar Sanchis Eladio Pirri Gallego Zoco Ufarte del Sol Peiro Suarez Gento (c) Scorers: Artime 65 79 for Argentina, Pirri 72 for Spain

15.07.66 Hillsborough 32,000
SPAIN 2, SWITZERLAND 1 (HT 0-1)

SPAIN: Iribar Sanchis Reija Pirri Gallego Zoco Amancio del Sol Peiro Suarez Gento (c)

SWI: Elsener Brodmann (c) Leimgruber Armbruster Führer Bäni Stierli Gottardi Kühn Hosp Quentin
Scorers: Quentin 29 for Switzerland Sanchis 58 Amancio 75 for Spain

16.07.66 Villa Park 51,000
ARGENTINA 0, WEST GERMANY 0

ARG: Roma Perfumo Marzolini Ferreiro Rattin (c) Albrecht Solari Gonzalez Artime Onega Más

GER: Tilkowski Höttges Schulz Weber Schnellinger Beckenbauer Haller Overath Seeler (c) Held Brülls
Sent off: Albrecht (67)

19.07.66 Hillsborough 31,000
ARGENTINA 2, SWITZERLAND 0 (HT 0-0)

ARG: Roma Perfumo Marzolini Ferreiro Rattin (c) Calics Solari Gonzalez Artime Onega Más

SWI: Eichmann Brodmann (c) Künzli Armbruster Führer Bäni Stierli Gottardi Kühn Hosp Quentin
Scorers: Artime 52 Onega 81

20.07.66 Villa Park 51,000
WEST GERMANY 2, SPAIN 1 (HT 1-1)

GER: Tilkowski Höttges Schulz Weber Schnellinger Beckenbauer Emmerich Krämer Seeler (c) Overath Held

SPAIN: Iribar Sanchis Reija Glaria Gallego Zoco (c) Amancio Adelardo Marcelino Fuste Lapetra
Scorers: Fuste 24 for Spain Emmerich 39 Seeler 63 for West Germany

Group 3

TEAMS: Brazil Bulgaria Hungary Portugal

12.07.66 Goodison Park 48,000
BRAZIL 2, BULGARIA 0 (HT 1-0)

BRA: Gilmar D.Santos Bellini (c) Altair Henrique Denilson Lima Garrincha Pelé Alcindo Jairzinho
BUL: Naidenov Shalamanov Vutzov Gaganelov (c) Penev Kitov Zhechev Yakimov Dermendyev Asparoukhov Kolev
Scorers: Pelé 14 Garrincha 63

13.07.66 Old Trafford 37,000
PORTUGAL 3, HUNGARY 1 (HT 1-0)

POR: Carvalho Morais Baptista Vicente Hilario Graca Coluna (c) Augusto Eusebio Torres Simóes
HUN: Szentmihalyi Mátrai Káposzta Sovari Mészöly Sipos (c) Bene Nagy Albert Farkas Rakosi
Scorers: Augusto 2 65 Torres 89 for Portugal Bene 59 for Hungary

16.07.66 Old Trafford 26,000
PORTUGAL 3 BULGARIA 0 (HT 2-0)

POR: J.Pereira Festa Germano Vicente Hilario Graca Coluna (c) Augusto Eusebio Torres Simóes
BUL: Naidenov Shalamanov Vutzov Gaganelov (c) Penev Zhekov Zhechev Yakimov Dermendyev Asparoukhov Kostov
Scorers Vutzov 7 og Eusebio 38 Torres 82

15.07.66 Goodison Park 52,000
HUNGARY 3, BRAZIL 1 (HT 1-1)

HUN: Gelei Mátrai Káposzta Szepesi Mészöly Sipos (c) Bene Mathesz Albert Farkas Rakosi
BRA: Gilmar D.Santos Bellini (c) Altair Henrique Gerson Lima Garrincha Tostão Alcindo Jairzinho
Scorers: Bene 2 Farkas 64 Mészöly 72 p for Hungary Tostão 14 for Brazil

19.07.66 Goodison Park 62,000
PORTUGAL 3, BRAZIL 1 (HT 2-0)

POR: J.Pereira Morais Baptista Vicente Hilario Graca Coluna (c) Augusto Eusebio Torres Simóes
BRA: Manga Fidelis Brito Orlando (c) Rildo Denilson Lima Jairzinho Silva Pelé Parana
Scorers: Simóes 15 Eusebio 36 85 for Portugal, Rildo 73 for Brazil

20.07.66 Old Trafford 22,000
HUNGARY 3, BULGARIA 1 (HT 2-1)

HUN: Gelei Mátrai Káposzta Szepesi Mészöly Sipos (c) Bene Mathesz Albert Farkas Rakosi
BUL: Simeonov Largov Vutzov Gaganelov (c) Penev Davidov Zhechev Yakimov Kotkov Asparoukhov Kolev
Scorers: Asparoukhov for Bulgaria.14
Davidov 42:Mészöly 45 Bene 54 for Hungary

Group 4

TEAMS: Chile Italy North Korea Soviet Union

12.07.66 Ayresome Park 22,000
SOVIET UNION 3, NORTH KOREA 0 (HT 2-0)
USSR: Kavasashvili Ponomarev Shesterniev (c) Khurtsilava Ostrovski Sabo Sichinava Chislenko Malafeev Banichevski Khusainov
KLD: Lee Chanmyung Park Lisup Shim Yungkyoo Lim Zoongsun Kang Bongchil Park Seungzin (c) Im Seunghwi Han Bongzin Park Dooik Kang Byongwoon Kim Youngil
Scorers: Malafeev 31 Banichevski 33 Malafeev 88

13.07.66 Roker Park 30,000
ITALY 2, CHILE 0 (HT 1-0)
ITA: Albertosi Burgnich Facchetti Rosato Salvadore (c) Lodetti Perani Bulgarelli Mazzola Rivera Barison
CHI: Olivares Eyzaguirre Cruz Figueroa Villanueva (c) Prieto Marcos Araya Tobar Fouilloux L.Sánchez
Scorers: Mazzola 9, Brison 86

15.07.66 Ayresome Park 16,000
CHILE 1, NORTH KOREA 1 (HT 1-0)

CHI: Olivares Valentini Cruz Figueroa Villanueva (c) Prieto Marcos Araya Landa Fouilloux L.Sánchez.

KLD: Lee Chanmyung Park Lisup Lee Dongwoom Lim Zoongsun Oh Yoonkyung Shin Youngkyo Park Seungzin (c) Im Seunghwi Han Bongzin Park Dooik Kim Seungil
Scorers: Marcos 26 pen for Chile, Park Seungzin 88 pen for North Korea

16.07.66 Roker Park 32,000
SOVIET UNION 1, ITALY 0 (HT 0-0)

USSR: Yashin Ponomarev Shesterniev (c) Khurtsilava Voronin Sabo Danilov Chislenko Malafeev Banichevski Khusainov

ITA: Albertosi Burgnich Facchetti Rosato Salvadore (c) Lodetti Leoncini Bulgarelli Mazzola Meroni Pascutti
Scorer: Chislenko 57

19.07.66 Ayresome Park 18,000
NORTH KOREA 1, ITALY 0 (HT 1-0)

KLD: Lee Chanmyung Ha Yungwon Shin Yungkyoo Lee Dongwoon Oh Yoonkyung Park Seungzin (c) Im Seunghwi Han Bongzin Park Dooik Kim Bonghwan Yang Seungkook
ITA: Albertosi Landini Facchetti Guarneri Janich Fogli Perani Bulgarelli (c) Mazzola Rivera Barison
Scorer: Park Dooik 41

20.07.66 Sunderland Roker Park 22,590
SOVIET UNION 2, CHILE 1 (HT 1-1)

USSR: Kavasashvili Getmanov Shesterniev Afonin Voronin Markarov Ostrovski Korneyev Metreveli Serebrianikov Porkuuan
Chile: Olivares Valentini Cruz Figueroa Villanueva Prieto Marcos Araya Landa Yavar L.Sánchez
Scorers: Porkuyan 29 85 for USSR Marcos 32 for Chile

Quarter-finals

23.07.66 Wembley Stadium
ENGLAND 1, ARGENTINA 0 (HT 0-0) 90,000
ENG: Banks Cohen Wilson Stiles J.Charlton Moore (c) Ball Hurst R.Charlton Hunt Peters
ARG: Roma Ferreiro Marzolini Rattin (c) Perfumo Albrecht Onega Solari Artime González Más
Scorer: Hurst 79 Sent off: Rattin (35)

23.07.66 Hillsborough 34,000
WEST GERMANY 4, URUGUAY 0 4:0 (1:0)

GER: Tilkowski Höttges Weber Schulz Schnellinger Beckenbauer Haller Overath Seeler Held Emmerich
URU: Mazurkiewicz Troche (c) Ubiña Goncalvez Manicera Caetano Salva Rocha Silva Cortés Pérez
Scorers: Haller 10 84 Beckenbauer 70 Seeler 75
Sent off: Troche (49) Silva (54)

23.07.66 Goodison Park 40,000
PORTUGAL 5, NORTH KOREA 3 (HT 2-3)

POR: J.Pereira Morais Baptista Vicente Hilario Graca Coluna (c) Augusto Eusebio Torres Simóes
KLD: Lee Chanmyung Lim Zoongsun Lee Dongwoon Shin Yungkyoo Ha Yungwon Oh Yoonkyung Park Seungzin (c) Im Seunghwi Han Bongzin Park Dooik Yang Seungkook
Scorers: Park Seungzin 1 Lee Dongwoon 22 Yang Seungkook 24 for North Korea Eusebio 27 42 pen 57 59 pen Augusto 79 for Portugal

23.07.66 Roker Park 27,000
SOVIET UNION 2, HUNGARY 1 (HT 1-0)

USSR: Yashin Ponomarev Shesterniev (c) Voronin Danilov Sabo Khusainov Chislenko Banichevski Malafeev Porkuyan
HUN: Gelei Matrai Kaposzta Meszöly (c) Sipos Szepesi Nagy Albert Rakosi Bene Farkas
Scorers Chislenko 5 Porkuyan 49 for USSR Bene 58 for Hungary

Semi-finals

25.07.66 Goodison Park 39,000
WEST GERMANY 2, SOVIET UNION 1 (HT 1-0)
GER: Tilkowski Lutz Weber Schulz Schnellinger Beckenbauer Haller Overath Seeler (c) Held Emmerich
USSR: Yashin Ponomarev Shesterniev (c) Voronin Danilov Sabo Khusainov Chislenko Banichevski Malafeev Porkujan
Scorers: Haller 44 Beckenbauer 68 for Germany Porkujan 88 for USSR
Sent off: Chislenko (44)

26.07.66 Wembley Stadium 95,000
ENGLAND 2, PORTUGAL 1 (HT 1-0)

ENG: Banks Cohen Wilson Stiles J.Charlton Moore (c) Ball R.Charlton Hurst Hunt Peters
POR: J.Pereira Festa Baptista Carlos Hilario Graca Coluna (c) Augusto Eusebio Torres Simóes
Scorers: R.Charlton 30 79 for England Eusebio 82 pen for Portugal

Third place match
28.07.66 Wembley Stadium 88,000
PORTUGAL 2, SOVIET UNION 1 (HT 1-1)
POR: J.Pereira Festa Baptista Carlos Hilario Graca Coluna (c) Augusto Eusebio Torres Simóes
USSR: Yashin (c) Ponomarev Khurtsilava Voronin Danilov Korneyev Sichinava Metreveli Banichevski Malafeev Serebrianikov
Scorers: Eusebio 12 pen Torres 88 for Portugal Malafeev 43 for USSR

The Final

30.07.66 Wembley 94,000
ENGLAND 4, WEST GERMANY 2 aet (HT 1-1, 90m 2-2)
ENG: Banks Cohen J. Charlton Moore (c) Wilson Stiles R. Charlton Peters Ball Hunt Hurst
GER: Tilkowski Höttges Schulz Weber Schnellinger Beckenbauer Overath Haller Seeler (c) Held Emmerich
Scorers: Hurst 18 101 120 Peters 78 for England
Haller 12 Weber 90 for West Germany

● TOTAL ATTENDANCE; 1,563,135

● TOTAL GOALS SCORED IN 32 MATCHES: 89 (2.8 per game)

● TOP DOZEN SCORERS

1. Eusebio (Portugal) 9 goals in 6 matches
2. Helmut Haller (West Germany) 6 goals in 5 matches
3. Valeriy Porkuyan (USSR) 4 goals in 3 matches
4. Geoff Hurst (England) 4 goals in 3 matches
5. Ferenc Bene (Hungary) 4 goals in 4 matches
6. Franz Beckenbauer (West Germany) 4 goals in 6 matches
7. Luis Artime (Argentina) 3 goals in 4 matches
8. Eduard Malofeyev (USSR) 3 goals in 5 matches
9. Jose Torres (Portugal) 3 goals in 6 matches
10. Jose Augusto (Portugal) 3 goals in 6 matches
11. Roger Hunt (England) 3 goals in 6 matches
12. Bobby Charlton (England) 3 goals in 6 matches

● MOST GOALS (TEAMS)

		Goals	Games	Pens	Average
1	Portugal	17	6	4	2.83
2	West Germany	15	6	1	2.5
3	England	11	6	0	1.83
4	Soviet Union	10	6	0	1.67

● The plan was for all of the games in England's group to be staged at Wembley. However, France v Uruguay was due to be played on a Friday, which clashed with the regular greyhound meeting at Wembley. So the match was switched to the ancient White City Stadium, home of the 1908 Olympics. Talk about football going to the dogs!

● PLAYER AWARDS

Golden Boot: Eusebio (Portugal)
Young Player: Franz Beckenbauer (West Germany)
Goalkeeper: Lev Yashin (Soviet Union)
Player of Players: Bobby Moore (England)

● SENT OFF
Hector Silva (Uruguay)
Antonio Rattin (Argentina)
Rafael Albrecht (Argentina)
Igor Chislenko (USSR)
Horacio Troche (Uruguay)

● ENGLAND PLAYERS BOOKED
Nobby Stiles for a tackle against France
Jack Charlton for a tackle against Argentina
Bobby Charlton for dissent against Argentina
Martin Peters for a tackle against West Germany

● Betting favourites before the tournament: Brazil (2-1), England (4-1), Italy (7-1), West Germany (10-1)

● The semi-final between England and Portugal was originally scheduled for Goodison Park, but was switched to Wembley for what Fifa described as "economic reasons." They said they wanted to reach as wide an audience as possible to bring in extra revenue. But the critics of Fifa and the FA said it was another case of host country England being shown favouritism.

● England's goalless draw in their opening match against Uruguay meant they were the first eventual World Cup champions not to win their first match in the tournament.

● Fifa's disciplinary committee cautioned Argentina for their violent play in the scoreless draw with West Germany, in which Rafael Albrecht was sent off for kicking Wolfgang Weber in the stomach.

● Portugal beat the Soviet Union 2–1 to take third place. Portugal's third place remains the best finish by a team making its World Cup debut since 1934. It was subsequently equalled by Croatia in the 1998 tournament.

● England's total of eleven goals scored in six games set a new record low for average goals per game scored by a World Cup winning team. The record stood until 1982, when it was surpassed by Italy's twelve goals in seven games; in 2010 this record was lowered again by Spain, winning the Cup with eight goals in seven games.

● England's total of three goals conceded also constituted a record low for average goals per game conceded by a World Cup winning team. That record stood until 1994, when it was surpassed by Brazil's three goals in seven games. Spain again lowered the record to two goals by conceding them during the group stage and then shutting out its four knockout stage opponents by 1–0 scores.

● The national anthems were sung before the final, but were not played in the earlier matches. This was because the organisers (Fifa and the FA) feared that North Korea's presence could cause problems with South Korea. The Foreign Office reluctantly agreed to allow them in provided no flags were flown. This meant that the £1,000 spent on flagpoles and giant flags at each of the grounds was wasted.

● North Korea would have made it into the semi-final if Eusebio had not taken over with a four-goal barrage after Portugal had gone 3-0 down. Pak Doo Ik became almost a household name in Britain and a football god at home after scoring the sensational match-winner to knock out mighty Italy in the group match to become the first Asian team to reach the quarter-finals.

● Eight venues were used for the 1966 World Cup. Wembley, built in 1922, was the youngest of the grounds. The most used venue was Wembley, which hosted nine matches, including all of England's six games, the final and the third place match. Goodison Park was used for five matches; Roker Park and Hillsborough both hosted four. Old Trafford, Villa Park and Ayresome Park staged three matches each, and London's White City one.

● These were the players who missed out from Alf Ramsey's original short list: Gordon West (Everton), Tony Waiters (Blackpool), Keith Newton (Blackburn), Chris Lawler (Liverpool); Paul Reaney (Leeds), Gordon Milne (Liverpool), Marvin Hinton (Chelsea), John Hollins (Chelsea), Tommy Smith (Liverpool), Terry Venables (Chelsea), Barry Bridges (Chelsea), Peter Thompson (Liverpool), Peter Osgood (Chelsea), Derek Temple (Everton), John Kaye (WBA), Fred Pickering (Everton), Joe Baker (Nottingham Forest), Gordon Harris (Burnley).

● The German team that played in the final against England is still the youngest ever to appear in a World Cup final.

● In the final at Wembley, of the 22 players 20 were equipped by Adidas. Gordon Banks and Ray Wilson were the boot rebels. They appeared in Puma boots after having worn Adidas in the early rounds. Rudolf Dassler, boss of Puma, brother and deadly rival of Adidas founder Adi Dassler, persuaded them the night before the final that Puma would give them better footing.

● For the British nations (apart from automatic qualifiers England), the 1966 World Cup was a forgettable experience. None of them managed to qualify for the tournament. Northern Ireland, with their new star George Best on parade, needed to beat Albania away in the last qualification game, but could only draw 1-1.

● Supporters north of the border were furious with Scottish managers Bill Shankly (Liverpool) and Matt Busby (Manchester United), who refused to release their Scottish players for a training get-together ahead of the decisive qualifying game against Italy. One of Scotland's best ever national teams, featuring players like Billy Bremner, Denis Law, John Greig, Alan Gilzean, Jim Baxter, Jimmy Johnstone and Pat Crerand, failed to qualify for the World Cup down south.

● The Jules Rimet Trophy was retired after Brazil won it outright with their third World Cup win in 1970. It was put on display in Rio in a cabinet with a bullet-proof glass front. In 1983, the wooden rear of the cabinet was forced open and the cup stolen again. The trophy has never been recovered, and is believed to have been melted down. Only one piece has been found, the original base which is kept in Fifa's Zurich headquarters. A replica was made and presented to the then Brazilian military president João Figueiredo in 1984. Another replica sits in the National Football Museum in Manchester.

● Roger Hunt, Bobby Charlton and Jack Charlton are the only players to still own their precious 1966 World Cup medals. The other eight players have sold theirs to collectors or to museums: George Cohen was the first to sell in 1998, and it was bought by Fulham for £80,000. The Gordon Banks medal was bought at auction in 2001 for £124,750. Ray Wilson's was sold for £80,000 in 2002. Alan Ball was the fourth to reluctantly let his medal go for £164,800 in 2004. West Ham paid £150,000 each for the medals won by Bobby Moore, Geoff Hurst and Martin Peters. Nobby Stiles got a record £188,200 when Manchester United bought his medal at auction in 2010.

An unofficial poll for the top 10 goals in the 1966 World Cup finals listed the following:

10. **Eduard Malofeyev** (USSR v North Korea, Ayresome Park)
Josef Sabo found Malofeyev deep in the Korean penalty area with a precise 20-yard chipped pass that he took on his chest and then volleyed past the goalkeeper.

9. **Eusebio** (Portugal 3, Brazil 1, Goodison Park)
Four of Eusebio's nine goals that made him top scorer came from the penalty spot. The pick of the bunch came following a headed lay-off from Jose Torres and he nearly broke the net from ten yards.

8. **Lothar Emmerich** (West Germany 2, Spain 1, Villa Park)
A rifled left foot shot on the half volley from the tightest of angles near the bye-line that found the far top corner of the net, with the Spanish goalkeeper catching thin air.

7. **Garrincha** (Brazil 2, Bulgaria 0, Goodison Park)
Highlight of a miserable tournament for '58 and '62 champions Brazil was a trademark swerving right foot free-kick from Garrincha that scorched over the wall from 20 yards. Unstoppable.

6. **Gérard Hausser** (France 1, Mexico 1, Wembley)
Three Mexican defenders were sent the wrong way as Hausser dribbled and dummied his way to the edge of the penalty area before scoring with a deadly accurate low right-foot shot.

5. **Franz Beckenbauer** (West Germany 5, Swiss 0, Hillsborough)
Collecting the ball in the centre-circle, the 20-year-old Beckenbauer kept his composure as he outpaced a pack of chasing Swiss defenders, drew the goalkeeper off his line and slotted home a slide-rule right foot shot.

4. **Luis Artime** (Argentina 2, Spain 1, Villa Park)
Luis Artime instantly brought a long pass under control with his right foot and swept the ball into the net with his left, with the Spanish defence in total disarray because of his speed of touch and thought.

3. **Bobby Charlton** (England 2, Mexico 0, Wembley)
It was the moment that England started to believe they could win the Cup. Bobby Charlton collected the ball in the centre-circle, raced forward with the ball at his feet, feinted to wrong-foot the Mexican defenders and then unleashed one of his right-foot rocket shots from 25 yards.

2. **Janos Farkas** (Hungary 3, Brazil 1, Goodison Park)
Ferenc Bene crossed from the right and the sprinting Janos Farkas met the ball on the volley and sent it crashing right footed into the Brazilian net from ten yards. Puskas would have been proud of it.

1. **Geoff Hurst** (England 4, West Germany 2, Wembley)
How could it be any other when you set the goal in the context of its meaning to English football. Hurst ran on to an inch-perfect pass from Bobby Moore, galloped forward under pressure from the chasing Wolfgang Overath and beat goalkeeper Hans Tilkowski with a ferocious left foot shot from 15 yards.

The goal completed the first hat-trick in a World Cup final with the last kick of the match and the last kick of the 1966 tournament.

I could not have made up a better finish to my journey back to July 30 1966

It's all over now.

Thank you for your company. Let's do it again one day. Hopefully we do not have to wait another 50 years. I might just not be here.

NORMAN GILLER

HEADLINES DEADLINES ALL MY LIFE

Introduced by
RICKY
TOMLINSON

My 100th book, available now post-free, cut-priced at
www.normangillerbooks.com
Please support this hungry writer. Thank you

"A remarkable book by a remarkable man"
Professor Roy Greenslade, The Guardian